WHO ARE THE GUILTY?

A STUDY OF EDUCATION AND CRIME

WHO ARE THE GUILTY?

A STUDY OF EDUCATION AND CRIME

David Abrahamsen, M.D.

COLUMBIA UNIVERSITY

GREENWOOD PRESS, PUBLISHERS
WESTPORT, CONNECTICUT

The Library of Congress has catalogued this publication as follows:

Library of Congress Cataloging in Publication Data

Abrahamsen, David, 1903–
  Who are the guilty?

  Bibliography: p.
  1. Criminal anthropology. 2. Crime and criminals––
United States. I. Title.
HV6035.A2 1972   364.2'0973   70-143306
ISBN 0-8371-5807-9

Grateful acknowledgment is made to Virgil Maskham, for permission to reprint the quatrain, "Outwitted," by Edwin Markham.

Originally published in 1952 by Rinehart & Co., Inc.,
New York

Reprinted with the permission of David Abrahamsen, M.D.

Reprinted in 1972 by Greenwood Press, Inc.,
51 Riverside Avenue, Westport, Conn. 06880

Library of Congress catalog card number 70-143306

ISBN 0-8371-5807-9

Printed in the United States of America

10 9 8 7 6 5 4 3

FOR *Frank Fremont-Smith, M.D.*

FOREWORD

I T IS difficult to say when I really started to write this book. To be sure, it was many years ago, at a time when I often wondered, sometimes with acute surprise, sometimes even with horror, about people's behavior. Some questions about their conduct were answered through my medical studies, others when I later studied educational psychology, neurology, psychiatry and anthropology.

In my studies of the emotionally disturbed or delinquent human being, I found him to be an intriguing entity. Frequently, however, this entity was only apparent; beneath his surface he seemed disjointed. At times he was so disturbed, hostile and defiant that he barely answered any questions. In my contacts with children and adolescents in schools and mental-hygiene clinics I was struck by their often plastic minds, while in my studies of adults in hospitals, courts or prisons I encountered rigid personalities. Behind all these cases was disturbed or antisocial behavior carried out by suffering, but nevertheless human beings.

It was in 1944 with the support of The Josiah Macy Jr. Foundation at the Psychiatric Institute, in the Department of Psychiatry, Columbia University, that I was able to obtain answers to some of the baffling problems in human behavior. Our purpose in this research was to ascertain the relationship between psychosomatic disturbances and emotional maladjustment with or without delinquency as they occurred in schools and homes, and to determine the emotional relationship between the school, family and the children. As we investigated children and adolescents and their families, it

appeared that the behavior of the child was to a large extent a reflection of the family in which he lived. The emotional climate of
the home in large measure determined what kind of a child that
home raised. Then, too, the delinquent had an emotional need to
commit his acts just as the ordinary person, though unconsciously,
may feel the need to become emotionally or physically ill. It was
also striking that many times the causes for antisocial acts were
due to the particular social climate in which the individual lived.
This social environment had brought about a faulty development
of the individual's social and moral standards.

All these findings, which were further confirmed in our research
carried out under the auspices of the Department of Mental Hygiene,
State of New York, confronted me with one major problem. Here
was not only a question of prolonged psychiatric treatment of
singularly disturbed emotional conditions expressed in delinquent
activities, but also a question of changing the emotional attitudes
responsible for men's criminal acts through educational measures
on a large scale.

This book therefore constitutes a broad mental-hygiene plan
based upon educational aspects and represents a synthesis of our
present knowledge about the relationship between the human
mind and delinquent activities. For that reason I am not here as
much concerned about our laws as about the emotional conditions
which bring the human being to commit the crimes which necessi-
tates such laws. Laws are necessary to protect society and individuals, but laws will only have meaning if we know the reasons why
people commit antisocial acts.

This is one more reason why education as a long-term measure
must be applied if we are going to counteract crime successfully.
Such understanding would give an indication of what is going on
inside the delinquents. Only then can we hope to help and eventually cure some of them and thereby rid society of one of its worst
evils, because it is evil not to be good.

Since this book is based upon my own experiences, it contains life
histories of living individuals. In order to protect these living persons, I have had to disguise identities by changing many details.
I regret to have been compelled to do so but the rights of individ-

uals constitute one of our most precious assets. However, I have tried to keep those details which I have felt have been basic to each personal history.

I would like to thank Dr. Nolan D. C. Lewis, Director of the Psychiatric Institute and professor of psychiatry at Columbia University, for his stimulating interest in my research. I want to express my gratitude to The Josiah Macy Jr. Foundation. I would also like to express my gratitude to my wife who in a large measure has made the book possible by assisting me throughout this large undertaking.

This book in general is intended for the student, parent and schoolteacher, for the psychiatrist, educator and lawyer, as well as for persons working in the field of emotional adjustment, in delinquency and allied sciences. It is my hope that it may become a primer about education and crime. I have written it in the attempt to make the reader see and hear so he can feel what is happening in this vast but little understood area of human behavior.

DAVID ABRAHAMSEN, M. D.

November, 1951
Columbia University

CONTENTS

WHO ARE THE GUILTY?

A STUDY OF EDUCATION AND CRIME

1

Who Are the Guilty?

M OST people believe that criminals are solely responsible for their guilt. Crime and criminals have existed since man was born, and society, from the earliest primitive cultures until our own, has been more intent on punishing the wrongdoer than in understanding why he broke its laws.

My work has, for years, led me into the study of the maladjustments of individuals, especially delinquents, and through them to the riddle of crime itself. I found that I was faced not only with the problem of handling those unfortunates who were truant or who had stolen or raped or even killed. I was also faced with a necessity for complete reorientation of our basic understanding of criminal behavior.

I reached the inescapable conclusion that society, with all its ramifications of family, school, community and government agencies, had to share the responsibility of guilt together with the particular individual involved. I had to believe that the offender becomes guilty because of the influence of his family, his education, and of society. This is not to say that there is no weakness in the person who commits the crime. But as we examined case after case we invariably asked ourselves: "Where were the parents, the school, the community, when this crime was committed?"

Emotional and delinquent problems, be they child's or adult's, do not just start out of nowhere. They have to have a nourishing soil in which to grow. This soil can be found within the family, within, society, or within the offender himself.

I have always believed that science needs to be interpreted in a social and humanistic way. That is what we shall have to keep in mind when we start to see the impact of crime and what it means to each one of us.

Every year about one million people walk in and out of prisons, jails, and reformatories, which means that one out of every 150 people in the United States is arrested each year. It is true that about 50 per cent of these are arrested more than once during the year, but the fact remains that the crime rate here is higher than in Italy, which has the highest rate in Europe, and more than ten times higher than in Scandinavia.

In 1950, according to the Federal Bureau of Investigation, 1,790,030 crimes took place, which means a crime every eighteen seconds. In an average day, 301 persons were feloniously killed or assaulted, 140 persons were robbed, 1,120 places were burglarized, and 468 cars were stolen. In addition, 2,681 other thefts occurred every day. If we then add the fact that about twenty million people gamble, which in most states is illegal, these figures give us an impression of how big a part crime plays in American life.

Moreover, it is on the increase. In 1950, every sort of crime, except robbery, increased. While the population of the United States between 1940 and 1950 grew 14.3 per cent, serious crimes grew 18 per cent. It is difficult to know how many billions of dollars this costs us each year. The greatest part of this astronomical cost, by far, is due to organized crime activities. The Federal Trade Commission estimated that one racket which dealt with the selling of worthless securities pocketed during ten years 25 billion dollars. When Capone was at the height of his career, his income was estimated to be about 30 million dollars a year. Let us consider for a moment how much a small-fry gambler earns on his slot machines. Let us say he owns 200 machines, each averaging a take of $50 a week; his total take is $10,000 a week. Of this the gambler himself gets half, $5,000 a week, and the rest goes for expenses. Five thousand a week is $260,000 a year, and that is from slot machines alone.

When we add to this incredible amount of money the unhappiness and tragedy crime brings in its wake for the criminal himself, his family, and his community, then it becomes clearer what crime means to society.

What are the reasons for so much crime in this wealthiest country on earth? And why has it taken so many diversified forms, ranging from the singular crime such as robbery, rape, kleptomania or murder, to the organized forms such as gambling, fire-setting with insurance fraud, betting, kidnaping, climaxing in gangsterism and racketeering? Not only is the criminal himself involved but, in organized crime, he involves others seemingly innocent, be they politicians, college boys, policemen or high officials.

We can ask whether the politicians, college boys and policemen are as honest as they are supposed to be. Or is their antisocial behavior rather an indication of a general breakdown of people's ethical and moral standards? Do the roots of this antisocial trend go deeper than that, into the community of the criminal's family, or to the very core of the ciminal himself, his personality?

The statistics given here are so appalling we are compelled to raise the question whether this country is, by nature, more lawless than other countries. We think of the vastness of this land and of its heterogeneous population, which bring about a variety of living conditions, customs and habits out of which can grow a general, often latent, friction and unrest. Where such tension exists, violent reactions with criminal intent rather than soft-spoken words may follow.

We also think of the enormous material resources not found anywhere else in the world, resulting in unusual opportunities but also creating a high degree of competition unmatched elsewhere. Much of this keen competition is instrumental in creating a "climate" of crime, particularly strong in large cities; in some individuals it produces ideas of "throat-cutting." Although that attitude does not necessarily lead to killing, the many crimes and minor infractions of the law reflect the tense and unsound atmosphere in which such people live.

The frequency of crime has also been attributed to the youthfulness of our country. The US can be compared with an adolescent, filled with power but also not yet free of childish emotions.

While we are busily ascribing so many evil things to the country, it is easy to forget that American materialism is, to a large extent, the very basis for our wealth, and our spiritual success. The Pericles

5

period of Athens and the Renaissance of Italy came, by and large, as a result of great material wealth, achieved under strenuous competitive conditions. In this respect we see that the same forces which tend to work for destructive purposes can also work for constructive aims.

Another accusation lodged against Americans is that they are "money conscious," that they are obsessed by money, that it is the measure of their achievement. Therefore the greed for money can be said to be partly responsible for widespread criminal activities.

I shall never forget my surprise when, during the first few months after I arrived in this country, I heard people interrogating each other so frankly about how much they were earning, in short "how much they were worth." To me, at that time a newcomer, it seemed so startling that I can quite understand how one might receive the impression that here ordinarily a man can be bought —which is, of course, not always true.

This money consciousness recalls some of the facts brought out in the Kefauver investigations: that as early as 1947 the New York State Police knew that gambling casinos were operating wide open at Saratoga, though it was not until late in 1949 that they did anything about them. On the contrary, evidence brought out that the State Police received money for "protecting" the transportation of funds from bank to casino, that Frank Costello and Joe Adonis had had financial interest in these casinos, and furthermore that other persons involved in underworld activities had much to say concerning the selection of state officials. We should include here also the corruption and favoritism, especially in local governments, which are frequently found to have a money basis. And last but not least, the basketball and football scandals in institutions of higher learning, where money seemed to play a conspicious part.

In any deal involving money we can question whether greed for money in general has been the real basic factor that has instigated unlawful acts. We can often add that a lust for power was also present in men guilty of such acts. But not even that has always been the basic driving force. I rather believe it was the search for success that drove them, and money and power were instruments in achieving it.

6

But this drive for success must in turn be based upon an emotional need in the individual, else we would not see it operating continuously and repeatedly. Everyone has a more or less deep-seated desire to better himself. In some people this can be accomplished by acquiring power, either in the form of money or influential position. Since these people feel insecure and their personalities lack the inner resourcefulness to overcome their anxieties, they have to bolster their Ego, their own self-reliance; and they can do so only by external means. If they, therefore, acquire power, it is not true; it is false, something to cover up the failure they feel within themselves. While a power-laden man appears on the surface to be the most confident man in the world, his power is only a veneer over his anxieties and frustrations. That is one of the reasons why he always has to have more money or more power so he can have more success.

Do not misunderstand me. To be the first one, the most successful one in a given field, is all to the good, but only if such success is based upon an individual's real endowment. Not all people possess the qualifications for success. Only a few are chosen to compete for the highest honors, and even they do not always reach the top. The rest are pushed aside, but many so treated refuse to accept such decision. Instead, with their ambitions strongly geared, they try again and again to better themselves. New frustrations arise in them with each new pushing around from their social milieu. They become resentful and hostile. And then they begin to discover "short cuts," to help themselves in various ways, including lawless ones.

While short-cutting to reach a goal is a constructive act with one person, for another it can become destructive.

Because of ambitions furthered through every channel and device, a particular individual may lose sight of himself. He may become so involved in his ambitions, in his drive for power, in his own world, that he loses the reasonable proportions between what is right and what is wrong. In this connection consider for a moment the atomic spies, many of whom apparently have had a set of values different from the ordinary citizen and therefore did not seem to know that what they were doing was wrong. Only when they

7

were detected did some of them suddenly "realize" their acts were wrong. Their moral standards, however, could have been brought about through a faulty identification with their own country, which again could have been the result of a lack of identification with their parents. In one case reported in the newspaper the spy rebelled violently against his father; in another, the spy was completely dominated by his older sister, who was a spy herself and who in turn seemed to have been dominated by her strong mother. Here again the father was weak. This distorted evaluation was brought out by strong emotional needs which had to be satisfied, and which developed into an unrealistic attitude.

It is this unreal attitude, whatever the mechanism, that we find developed in so many offenders; sometimes it goes so far that they become insane, or, to use a medical term, psychotic. In general this feature of unrealism is so indistinct that we are not able at first glance to recognize it. Yet it is there and makes itself more or less felt in every delinquent. The fact that practically all of them believe they will never be caught is a most revealing facet of this unreal attitude. They may not be caught by the police but they may be caught by their own consciences or they may be turned upon by their accomplices.

The main point is that in many instances we find a peculiar symbiosis between politics and crime, both being the result of a city and national development in which graft and competition for high political office play a fateful part.

All too frequently we read in the newspapers that such and such an official has been accused or convicted of some political corruption. He has taken graft, he has been mixed up in a racket, he has aided or been given aid by known underworld characters. On reading such a story most of us are inclined to say, "There are always some crooks in politics." But why? Why do we seem to take for granted that where there is politics there is also corruption?

True, all of us have been deeply shocked by the scandals in the tax bureau and other government agencies. But we forget that scandals prevailed in high places in the 1870's and 1880's, and again in the early 1920's. Because corruption has never been sufficiently interrupted, it has become so imbedded in American life that we are inclined to overlook it. It is contagious. Not only does it degrade the individual spiritually and lead to the disintegration of the whole personality, it also leads to the disintegration of a country. A superficial reading of history lets us believe the Roman Empire fell because of external causes; a closer reading reveals that it fell because of internal corruption.

Corruption is more dangerous than disease. The mind may die of it.

In order to understand the corrupt politician it is necessary to look behind the story in the newspaper and see the man himself. We must look for the personal motivation that drove this man, the social forces brought to bear on him, the standards—or lack of them —by which he lived, and which, taken all together, have led him to commit a criminal act. Let us go behind the scenes in one such case and see what we find there.

When I first met George he was serving a five-to-ten-year sentence for income-tax evasion and extortion. Although it could not be proved during his trial that he dealt in gambling and liquor, it was strongly suspected; also that he paid off the police who protected the gambling places in his district. It would be hard to estimate how large his income was, but suffice it to say it was more than the average man dreams of. George would have gone on making this huge sum had he not become involved in a flagrant graft case, which was in great measure due to his appalling lust for power. He wanted to become head man in a large district in the city; that was his nemesis because in order to do so he had to deal with unions from which not even his political friends could save him.

All George's criminal activities were a matter of record. Yet when I questioned him, he gave me an involved and evasive story about his dealings, conclusively denied everything, and ended by saying he had been framed. Seeing his innocent-looking face, one could easily have been misled. But, although sometimes a person may be framed, this was not the case here. The facts were irrefutable. Yet he maintained so righteous a front, so innocent a demeanor that his view was supported by his friends outside prison who carried on a vigorous correspondence with him and kept him supplied with frequent food packages.

Many might think that this was highly intelligent. Yet his IQ was only 86, which is lower than average. He had gone only as far as the fifth grade in school when he quit, apparently to go to work. His work record, however, was spotty, indicating that he had little endurance and felt much dissatisfaction. He was in reality anxiety-ridden and filled with insecurity, all of which could be explained by the fact he had grown up in poverty and developed the idea that he had to be a success. That success could only be achieved through money, regardless of the means.

How could a man with such a low intelligence and such infantile emotions make good? Society provided him with the means; and in his case they could only be illegal ones. Because of his shortcomings he could not compete in an honest world; instead he resorted to bookmaking, vice, liquor.

The first round was his. He had been a captain in his election district and through hard work had convinced the political leaders that he was the right man for them. When there was an election, he showed them he could get out the vote. When a voter in his district was sick, he saw to it the family received a relief check. Thus he acquired money and some power in his district; but because of his own emotional insecurity he demanded more material security and therefore was always looking for new opportunities which would give him more power. Through money he had become a political "social climber," and this is a predominant character trait in nearly all of those who combine politics with crime.

In his climbing George encountered other climbers of the same caliber though on a higher level of influence. The fact stands out that all gangsters or political racketeers form a hierarchy made up just as any other hierarchy in society. The more organized and well-knit such a formation is the more power it has; this is especially true of organized crime. In general we can say that organized crime is one expression of extortion and bribery to which certain members of society are compelled to submit. From a social point of view the exploitation may be legal or illegal, but not necessarily criminal. When a kidnaper uses threats to exploit a victim or a bank-robber menaces a bank teller, that is illegal. But how about the racketeer who gains control of restaurants, garages, cleaning and dyeing establishments or the trucking business? How about the politician who squeezes his constituents by giving out jobs according to his mood, which was what happened in George's case?

He had, as part of a hierarchy, become involved in a struggle for power, a cultural struggle, where extremely high money interests were at stake. In order to succeed, he had to compete with those who were already in the game. While previously he had committed unlawful acts on a small scale, not very noticeable, he now met a society which permitted illegal actions on a large scale. In that city there was a great demand for illegitimate services to be performed for people outside any racketeering, and George became part of an organization which claimed to perform those services for people who were themselves engaged in lawful activities. For that reason his actions, as in all racketeering, became on the surface a legitimate undertaking. It was even brought out that some law-abiding citizens welcomed this assistance. George's immediate associates therefore did not need to use much violence or coercion. But when competing racketeers started to invade his territory, he had to resort to force to keep his power. He became a victim of his own ambitions and frustrations and of the way society functioned—or more correctly, of the way society should not function. That this man became part of a crime syndicate was due not only to his own shortcomings, but also to the fault of a society which tacitly permitted the expansion and continuation of his antisocial activities. This silent permission simply nourished his childish and unrealistic feelings so he lost sight of what was right and what was wrong.

Is it any wonder that this man denied everything about his crime? According to his own code of living, developed through the years, he had come to feel the things he did were right; and those standards were right for the kind of society in which he lived. The fact is that every person is equipped with his own special inclinations and dispositions. It follows that there are certain individuals whose conscience—or technically speaking, Superego—is influenced by their immediate surroundings. If their environment is delinquent, it may color their conscience so that they accept criminal standards. That is just what we find in professional criminals, profit murderers, gangsters or others whose antisocial activities are readily accepted by their whole personality.

This brings out another point. People's standards differ according to the social layer in which they live. It is as natural for a boy brought up in a delinquent area to steal as it is for another boy raised in a good neighborhood not to steal. Both boys identify themselves with a subgroup of their culture because they themselves need support from that subgroup; they need to belong. When the first boy commits a crime, he is simply responding to the antisocial tendencies already present in that subgroup, and thereby dynamically expressing himself.

Criminals, like George, who deal with organized crime all their lives are therefore genuinely surprised when they are criticized, and sometimes tried and convicted, for crimes they have committed. The average citizen is also surprised and cannot believe the delinquent was unaware of the antisocial nature of his actions. The accused tries to defend himself by denying the criminal character of his behavior and insists that he is in reality a good citizen. When Frank Costello, for instance, was asked at the Kefauver investigations in 1951 what good he had done for his country, he answered, "I paid my taxes." It sounds self-consciously naïve and innocent, but I wonder whether he did not mean in all seriousness that the only good thing he knew he could do for this country was to pay his taxes. Probably throughout his life he had never learned anything but the antisocial side of life.

Thus we see that the American scene is dominated by different, frequently contradictory cultures, each with its particular customs and mores. One is an unethical or a-ethical trend; another is puritanic. When these conflict it is no surprise that, while this country is the wealthiest in the world, it has, at the same time, the highest rate of crime in the world. Our society can be said to be at fault in that our goals and our practices do not harmonize; therefore the machinery of our law enforcement is not up to its task. This is not a question of how one single individual from a certain cultural setting reacts to surroundings outside that situation, but how all those living as a group in the same culture adjust to an environment outside it. Although we cannot as easily distinguish between personality adjustment and group adjustment, it is the latter type we will have to deal with if we are to solve the problem of organized crime. This, as well as individual crime, will be a question of a long-range plan of education.

As to George's fate—when he was in his fifties he was released from prison, and what happened to him is exactly what anyone would expect.

We must acknowledge that society was, to a large extent, responsible for George's antisocial activities, and for that matter for all types of organized crime. While we can point out that this man received a headstart through his own personality defect, it is easily seen that he inherited, so to speak, the environment in which he was raised. This antisocial environment acted as a precipitating event (or as constant precipitating events) and kept alive his criminalistic tendencies. What is more important, he became exposed to the criminal environment without being consciously aware of it. Every human being is a psychobiological individual who, consciously or unconsciously, is tied up, intimately with his environment. Even if we say that his mind is behind every action he performs, including the antisocial ones, he and his environment still form a functioning unit.

Yet it is impossible to state where the individual begins and where the environment ends. When a man eats or breathes, who can say at what point the food or the air cease to be part of the surroundings and become part of the man? Determining this point is more difficult when it concerns the individual at the social level. We can never understand his reaction toward society if we do not consider him as a social unit. Each person is part of the environment of every other person, and since they are both dynamic elements which involve a constant interchange of influences, there is no distinct separating line between them. We are led to believe that society is not only the sum of the people who constitute it, but that it also contains each individual's relationship to other individuals and to the group as a whole.

I have delved into the dynamic functioning of the individual at such length to emphasize the fact that his reactions are a mirror of

13

his environment. Society puts its laws upon him, and since he usually does not want to be troubled, he behaves the way society, or its subgroup, orders him to. What he may think as an individual is not of much social importance. If he behaves according to society's standards, then he reaps the benefits at its disposal. He receives favors and esteem, he achieves a sense of belonging, all of which are values appreciated by all of us. Whatever the standards are, high or low, their importance to the individual is the same, as was the case with George. He believed he used his own head in estimating the situation around him, while in reality he merely followed the standards his own society had established. We then see that he adopted the greatest part of his antisocial code from that society.

This may not always be the case in antisocial behavior. Sometimes a predominant part of antisocial climate is played by the more immediate community, sometimes by the home, sometimes it lies in the personality of the offender himself.

Let us next examine a case where the community was involved.

Fred was a sensitive, shy, seventeen-year-old boy, who apparently because of extensive reading had fallen in love with books as well as with his teacher at the overcrowded high school he attended. So strong was his need for attention from this teacher that one day, when she seemed to ignore him, he became very upset and angry and left the class. He was back at school the next day but that afternoon it was discovered some money had disappeared from the lockers. The teacher announced the fact to the class, and asked whoever was guilty to admit the theft; no one answered. After class three boys, including Fred, lingered behind as if with a desire to speak to her privately. But she was too busy, she had too much to do, there was no time to talk with any of them. During the following weeks more money disappeared, and the school principal was compelled to interrogate the class. Again no one admitted the thefts. The next week Fred stayed home, apparently because of a cold. That week no thefts took place, except for some pencils, which was a common occurrence.

In the next few months Fred became silent and moody; whenever he spoke to anyone, which was seldom, he used obscene language. It surprised the teacher that he made out so poorly on his English test and, since there had been complaints about his obscenity, she tried to talk with him. The moment she mentioned his poor showing on the test, the boy became very upset, refused to talk, and left the room. The next day Fred's father, realizing the boy was upset, talked with his teacher. She told him about the stolen money. When he returned home he found some of it in Fred's room. The boy then admitted he had stolen it.

Later, when I talked with Fred, I pieced the story together. The external or precipitating event here was the teacher's rejection of a boy who for a long time had been rejected by his mother. Fred's mother was rather cold and did not understand that her son needed affection and attention. Unhappy and depressed at this deprivation, he tried to find this attention elsewhere, selecting the teacher for that purpose. But when he was also rejected there, this slight became the great event which turned him to stealing. His theft was a form of revenge, at least temporarily.

Fortunately Fred received psychiatric treatment; he graduated from high school and college and is now happily married. The main point is that if the teacher had had the understanding or the time to give Fred what he needed, he probably would have been able to stay out of trouble. If the community had not permitted overcrowding of its schools to the extent that teachers had no time for the individual needs of their students, much sorrow might have been avoided. Basically, of course, it was Fred's mother who was at fault; but the precipitating factor came through Fred's immediate community.

As we can see from this case, Fred was in conflict with himself. This conflict could not be seen or felt by anyone. The boy was not even aware of it himself. Only later, when he told me that he knew he should not steal and yet felt he had to because "there was no way out," did he understand the conflict. Only when he grew emotionally did he comprehend his search for attention.

This brings out the important point that Fred had both social and antisocial tendencies. That is what we find in all people except gangsters who, for reasons we shall later see, seem to possess only criminal traits. Since we all have constructive and destructive traits, we can readily see that the inclination to commit crime is found all over the earth and has, as a matter of fact, been present in all societies. Delinquent behavior is much more widespread and goes much deeper than the special circumstances attending it would indicate. This means neither more nor less than that there must be something within ourselves which contributes to a large extent to criminal activities. The antisocial tendencies we have seen through the ages—and still see—depend upon basic human traits and the reactions which we find in all people.

As long as antisocial tendencies are present in all of us, it follows that the large majority of criminals are not so very different from the average law-abiding citizen. They differ from each other in degree and not in type. All human beings follow the same psychological processes, although in varying degree, and it is impossible to conceive of a man who has a basic personality structure totally different from somebody else. We may conclude that criminals in their basic personality make-up are more *like* the average citizen then unlike him.

Does this sound startling? It is not more startling than our inability to solve the problem of crime. One reason for this inability is that we have up until today been more interested in getting the criminal punished according to law than in finding out what made him tick—or more correctly, what did not make him tick in his environment. Of course some attempts have been made to discover what made the criminal commit antisocial acts, but only recently. It was not until the last century that society started to be interested in the offender himself. And such an interest came only as a result of scientific discoveries in the general fields of chemistry, sociology, human and animal life. As science widened man's horizon and increased his insights into the workings of society, that knowledge stimulated new investigations of social forces and their influence upon the individual. When Quetelet around 1850 hit upon the idea that man's behavior in general was influenced by his environment, Morel in 1857 applied that hypothesis to the criminal and advanced the theory that he was the end result of mental, physical and moral influences.

The immediate effect of Morel's idea was lost because, in 1859,

Darwin published his "Origin of Species" where he stated, among other things, that man and animals possessed the same instinctual drives and that the psychological and physiological functions had been developed as an adjustment to environment. This made a tremendous impression, especially in the field of criminology where, as a rule, every new thought was viewed with suspicion. It was not until 1876 when Cesare Lombroso (1836—1909), an outstanding physician and anthropologist of the time, wrote a little pamphlet which he later expanded into the three-volume *L'Uomo Delinquente* (*Criminal Man*), that Darwin's biological theory was applied specifically to an offender.

Although today we disagree with Lombroso's ideas that the criminal was born that way, nevertheless Lombroso can be considered the founder of scientific criminology. In America a similar type of anthropological study has been used by Earnest A. Hooton in his book, *The American Criminal* (1939). Furthermore, Lombroso insisted that the criminal himself be examined, which was the same as implying that the criminal was the cause and the crime the result. Today such a statement seems self-explanatory. But it was only a few years ago, when I had published my first book, *Crime and the Human Mind* (1944), that people were startled by the fact that there is the same connection between the criminal and his act as there is between any man and his acts.

Mankind for centuries has speculated about behavior. Philosophers, poets and artists have all done their share to solve the riddle of human behavior in general, but the mind of the criminal was not given much attention. Yet Benjamin Rush ("America's first psychiatrist") as early as 1786 made the observation that delinquent behavior was accompanied by a certain state of mind, and another outstanding psychiatrist, Isaac Ray, differentiated between the criminal and the insane person. However, it was not until recently that efforts were made to find the basis for criminal behavior. William A. White, William Healy, Winfred Overholser, Karl A. Menninger, Sheldon Glueck, Gregory Zilboorg, Benjamin Karpman, Thorsten Sellin and many others are names which come to mind. Some of our research has resulted in unfounded or unproved conclusions because we have not yet been able to establish a scientific medium where criminals can be explored with all the means at our disposal.

We are still more concerned about investigating the crime—for the very practical reason that there are so many offenders there is hardly time for anything else. Still it is quite possible that a solution to the problem would be more readily found if we concentrated on exploring the criminal's personality make-up and his emotional and social relations rather than only the crime itself.

The fact is that crime in general does not depend only upon external circumstances as such. This may be true in certain cases, such as during a holdup when the victim screams so that the robber is frightened into shooting. In that case it is the event which drives him to kill. We must remember that a person who commits a crime produces within certain limits, most often unwittingly, situations or circumstances of which he himself becomes a victim. Thus, the human element is always present in delinquent acts, colored by the particular external circumstances and determined by the personality of the offender.

We have said that the home, like society at large and like the immediate community, can be a factor in delinquent behavior. Over and over we see the fateful influence of one family member upon another, even though both may be unconscious of it. The enormous influence parents exert over their children can hardly be stressed enough.

Take the tragic case of Alice. At the time she came to me she was twenty-two and looked thirty-three. She had stolen various expensive dresses and perfumes valued at several thousand dollars, all of which her father, a wage earner, had paid off on her promise to pay him back. Since she was earning but thirty dollars a week and could spare him only five dollars every pay day, it would be a long and painful process. Alice, however, was completely undisturbed by this. She was equally undisturbed by the fact she had given birth to an illegitimate child whose father was a Negro. She had given the baby away for adoption and had been paid a substantial sum—money which, incidentally, she had squandered in a few days. She was much more concerned as to whether she should marry the father of her child or one of several other suitors.

When Alice talked with me on her first visit I could almost feel the sparks flying from her. Her answers came like shots from a machine gun, so filled was she with scorn and hatred for all human beings. This hatred was directed at men in particular; she liked to hurt them, tantalize them, play with them. While carrying on one seemingly serious affair with the man who had been the father of her child, she had met several others with whom she was intimate. If a man complained about her faithlessness, she immediately denied any relations with anyone else and convinced him that she was really an innocent young girl working very hard to make both ends meet.

Her tastes were expensive, and she was at one and the same time involved with three young men of considerable means, all of whom showered lavish gifts upon her and all of whom wanted to marry her. She manipulated things in such a way that not only did all three know each other, but also she was able to play one against the other. When one day she told me she could not make up her mind, I found it necessary to question whether she really wanted to marry anyone. She blurted out instantly, "I hate them all," and got up and began to walk agitatedly around the office. She started to cry; between sobs I heard her say, "I am not a bad girl, I am not a bad girl."

I answered that it was not a question of being good or bad, but of what her future was to be if she did not get hold of herself. She only sobbed, "I don't want to live."

By that time she was overcome by strong guilt feelings, unconscious though they were, and was craving sympathy from me. In reality, what she had wanted all her life was sympathy and love from her father, which meant, in this case, that she wished she could receive that love without feeling guilty about her mother. The truth is that her father unwittingly was in love with his daughter. Until Alice was seventeen, he had ruled her life. He saw to it that she could not care for any of the young men who courted her. When she had a date, her father was jealous and tried by devious means to keep her close to himself. The first mistaken thing she did was to run away from home, which was a rebellion against being too attached to her father. But when she was brought back after a few days her feelings toward him awakened and unconsciously she felt guilty toward her mother. Wherever she was, at home or away, she felt something was wrong; hence her vagrant life. In the intervening years she had come to feel hatred for her father whom she really wanted to destroy, and this hatred she transferred to every man she met.

Alice's father was a selfish and emotionally insecure man who, in his turn, had been strongly attached to his mother. To see his daughter date someone meant she was unfaithful to him, a thing he unconsciously felt she should not be, since he himself had been faithful to his mother. Therefore he tried to keep Alice in place. She took revenge by disgracing him through stealing, and by having a child, just as though she had said to him, "Look, I can do without you." All these feelings were unconscious. Alice did not know the reasons for her acts any more than her father knew them for his.

Here we see what havoc the emotions can play upon the individual. People believe they think with their intelligence, but that is far from the truth. Our feelings are always intermingled in our decisions; our actions are led by our feelings, unconscious though they may be. In Alice's case, neither father nor daughter had the slightest idea of their true feelings. Therefore he was indignant and righteous at her behavior. Alice, on her part, was completely ignorant that her stealing and having an illegitimate child were a revenge and a punishment of her parent.

Although we have known for some time that our emotions play an important part in our decisions, it was Freud who showed us that our feelings are frequently repressed and suppressed so that we do not know the true motivations for our actions because our emotions are buried too deeply in us. It is only when solving mathematical problems that we may say we use our intelligence. And even here the working out of a particular problem may be stalled if the individual—depending upon his feelings about it—has a resistance to finding a solution. The average man may use intelligence to rate and test whatever situation he faces, but as a general proposition it may be said his emotions affect and interfere with the intellectual process. The same mechanism operates in his actions. His

20

deeds spring from motivations different than he supposes, most of them unconscious.

The criminal may be as unaware of the motivations for his crime as the ordinary citizen is of the reasons for actions which do not violate any laws. As a matter of fact, the criminal very rarely knows completely the reason for his conduct. Only when he has learned about himself (specifically, through psychoanalysis) will he become aware of his motivations. Therefore, to the casual observer there seems on the surface to be little or no connection between the criminal and his act.

Yet if we stop for a moment and think of our behavior in general—as we seldom do because we take everything for granted—we will find that our actions are always tied up with our personalities. Whatever we do expresses something in us. Our looks, the way we laugh or eat, the way we dress or walk, reflect the way we think and feel. So intimately are our actions knitted to our minds and bodies, and so automatic have some of these actions become to our conscious minds, that we are unaware that all our deeds are the results of adaptations effected by our personalities. The way this process takes place is not fully understood because to the average man most of it occurs unconsciously. But, conscious or unconscious, the attempt at adjustment is made; and whatever the result, the personality is an integrative part of it.

The criminal is unaware of the connection between his mind and his deeds, and he is unaware of the adaptation—or more correctly, the maladaptation—his personality make-up has undergone in order to adjust to the prevailing situation. The driving forces in any offender, as well as in any law-abiding citizen, are his emotional strivings and his goals. It is these emotions which make human behavior in general, and criminal behavior in particular, so much of a riddle. This is clearly shown in the following case.

Peter, at nineteen, was serving a long prison term, having been convicted as a third offender for grand larceny. When he was eleven he had learned to drive a car and found it so thrilling it was necessary for him always to have a car. Since he had no lawful means of getting one, he stole one. He was caught, brought to court, and given a suspended sentence. He had been hardly a week on proba-

21

tion before he stole another car, drove it around town and had a collision. He was again brought to court. Once more he received a suspended sentence. A well-meaning citizen gave Peter a job in his factory. One day Peter was asked to drive a customer to the station. Having safely delivered his passenger, Peter did not return to the factory but drove the car hundreds of miles into another state where he sold it. This time he was picked up by the police, returned to his home state and sent to a reformatory. After six months he was paroled for good behavior and found himself a job. But in a couple of months he became restless; he walked into a garage one day and got himself a car under false pretenses.

He drove into another state, where he had to abandon the car because he had no more gasoline. He took another, drove it only a few miles, parked it, and found himself still another, in which he proceeded to a large city. Here he sold it, walked around the block, picked up a new one which was parked in the street and drove away. In the course of four months, before the police finally caught up with him, Peter took about thirty cars. I say "took," because to Peter it was only taking a car, not stealing it. On the surface it would seem that the continuous car thefts were motivated by revenge. That came out also in one of the first interviews I had with him when he said, "I like to get even with people."

It was much later he realized this idea of revenge was only a surface motive. We may understand this better when we learn that Peter had been in an orphanage until he was ten. At that time he was brought to live with a distant relative on a farm. Peter never knew who his mother was; he asked about her constantly but never received an answer. Little by little he "forgot" about her except for once in a while, such as the time in prison when he had a dream which he told me about in an excited way. He saw a woman waving to him; then she started to walk farther and farther away from him and he tried to follow her. But he could not keep up and she disappeared.

Peter realized the woman was his mother who was waving goodbye to him. He said quietly, "I am trying to find my mother. I have always tried." After a long pause I asked, "Have you ever done anything to find her?" He looked up, turned to me, and I could see

22

a ray of light pass over his face. "Sure," he answered. "I couldn't find her fast enough so I used a car."

In that moment he understood with his feelings why he had stolen all those cars. At the same time, however—and this is more important—a car in itself had a meaning to him. In a symbolic way it represented his mother. Since he could not get her, he had to have a substitute, and a car was that substitute. Hence his thrill every time he drove a car; hence his continuous stealing.

To the average reader such an explanation may seem farfetched; yet clinical experience shows that a car often stands for a woman. In daily language we often call a car "she"; when we have the tank filled with gasoline we say, "Fill her up." To Peter the meaning of the car was a revelation which came only after a long period of psychiatric treatment. But it was a meaning that made sense to him, unconscious though it had been for so many years.

Peter's case shows how decisive and fateful personality factors are in criminal behavior as compared with influences outside the individual. Since there is a great deal of intermingling among the forces in society, community, family and the offender himself, we can see their relative influence. Each individual is a member of his society, his community, his family, and is part of himself. All human behavior, and for that reason criminal behavior, thus has four roots, each one influencing the others.

The causes of crime are relative; one factor is more prominent in one case than in another, but all are interrelated. When we have to deal with four different more or less unknown elements, each of which is more or less unknown in its working and in its effect, we should not be surprised that we have met with such extreme difficulty in trying to find the causes of criminal behavior. When we add that these factors and their effects take place in an offender who, practically speaking, knows nothing about himself, we will perhaps better understand what obstacles science has had and still has in ascertaining the basis of crime.

Only when we understand the reasons for criminal behavior can we correct it, and only when we realize why a criminal behaves as he does have we a chance of solving the riddle of crime. Here again it should be stressed that the mental mechanism of the antisocial person is very much the same as that of anyone else, for the difference is one of degree and not of type. Criminal behavior is part of human behavior, however repugnant such an idea may be to many. Remembering the great instability in the four elements which take part in forming the offender, and remembering that these same elements also make up the law-abiding citizen, it is easy to see why there exists so much confusion as to who is really guilty in creating the criminal in society.

As I read story after story from my files, I can still see those four human beings I have described. And I can see many, many more pass in review. They all leave me with one question: Who are the guilty?

2

Early Signs in Juvenile Delinquency

ANTISOCIAL and social traits originate from basic instincts in all of us. Yet most of us are able to conform to the rules of society. The person who is unable to do so finds himself, consciously or unconsciously, in the same emotional state of rebellion and unrest as manifests itself in early infancy and childhood. The child spits out his food, or he turns away his head from his mother's breast, not only because he may be overfed or underfed, or because he does not like to be fed at that particular moment, but also because of his emotional reaction to his mother. This reaction may be instinctive and show up when he is two years old in the form of opposition toward the command of his parents. If mother or father tells the child not to touch a cake, or not to climb the chair, the next thing they know the child is touching the cake or climbing the chair, all of which is an expression of his growing personality, or technically speaking, his growing Ego.

Such negativistic or increased resistive behavior is a characteristic—and usually temporary—stage of a child's development. While previously his parents were compelled to serve him because he was so small and helpless, he now, having reached his second year of life and being able to speak a little, understands that he has to submit to their demands. The ability to express himself verbally accelerates the development of his Ego, and the evolution of his speaking ability permits him to express his negativism. While the boy was

25

formerly omnipotent in his own world, now he has to defend his Ego against his intruding and bothersome parents. He still wants to be the master, but he has to give in, though only under protest. He does not want to give up the fight because this means that his Ego becomes devaluated. By the time he is four, he usually yields to his parents.

In some children, however, this negativistic attitude persists. It may take on the character of disobedience or rebellion against the dictates of parents, an attitude which later on may manifest itself against the laws of society. This basic rebellion results in development of certain symptoms, such as truancy, aggressiveness, or a generally spiteful attitude.

In addition to these basic feelings of rebellion, other signs related to fear develop. The child becomes exceedingly shy, turns away from strangers or screams on the least provocation. Beneath all this fear or rebellion are anxieties which keep the child in an emotional state of tension, bringing forth emotional reactions and formation of symptoms. These symptoms, in addition to truancy and spite, can be: excessive or aggressive bullying, temper tantrums, bedwetting, revenge attitudes like petty stealing, or feelings of hostility and resentment. Sometimes the child turns the aggressiveness against himself; he starts biting his nails, or he gets tense and moody, which may in turn bring out other symptoms, such as general fatigue, or psychosomatic symptoms like headaches, colds, indigestion and proneness to accidents.

Let me here state most emphatically that the early signs of delinquency may not be significant in themselves, but added together they gain in importance. Furthermore, at the present time we do not know of any symptoms in delinquency, with the possible exception of an antisocial character, which cannot also be a symptom of an emotional disorder. Signs indicating an antisocial pattern may also point to a deep-seated mental condition without criminalistic manifestations.

Of all these symptoms, truancy, in combination with other types of aggressions, is possibly the most important one in children insofar as later delinquency is concerned. It has been estimated recently that about 90,000 children are absent from New York City public schools every day, and that of these children about 2,000 are reported to the Bureau of Attendance for investigation every day; of them 600 are found to be illegally absent every day. They suffer from obvious emotional and psychosomatic problems which need immediate attention. When we examine the records of adult offenders, we find truancy as a common phenomenon in most of them.

By truancy, I do not mean the occasional absence from school once a year or so; that is rather "normal." I rather believe that the child who has played hookey once in his life is a happier child than the one who is too timid and afraid to stay away for once. In the same way as there are different causes for any symptom, so there are also varying causes for truancy. It may be due to rivalry between brothers and sisters, or to physical defects such as bad eyesight or hearing; it may be due to poor scholastic standing, or to fear and shyness of teacher or authority, all of which may be traced back to a child's early development. Last but not least it may be due to the parents' inconsistent handling of the child, alternating from severe discipline to too much leniency, all of which result in serious frustrations.

In general we may say that the causes of a child's delinquent behavior may be traced to his parents, particularly to his mother's emotional attitude toward his early instinctual manifestations, which may be partly caused by her own personality make-up or by other elements from his environment. In addition, his antisocial attitude is also accentuated by the particular way his Ego and Superego (conscience) develops.

Such delinquent behavior arises chiefly when the child's immediate environment is spiced with uncontrolled emotional outbursts among his family members. In short, the existence of family tension coupled with the mother's attitude toward her child's early instinctual reactions may be considered instrumental in the formation of an antisocial character. What is affected in the child is his personality. In a broad sense he fails to develop the ability to distinguish between reality and fantasy, or what we have called development toward the Reality Principle.

Into the making of this unreality goes a great deal of magic thinking and feelings of omnipotence, two phenomena we find in

27

many children and frequently in psychotic persons. The child may imagine that he can obtain things through some strange force, or he would like to be a person who could manage everything in the world regardless of weather, gravitation or anything else. Superman is an imaginary person formed in the mind of the child every day, reflecting his wishes and daydreams; even many an adult would like to have the power of a superman so he too could be omnipotent and carry out all his desires like a forceful man. This magic thinking we find in myths and legends throughout human history. It is a result of archaic thinking, derived from our instincts which always demand fulfillment. When our instinctual life overpowers us, the strong wishes dominate to such an extent that the individual loses his sense of reality and often cannot separate reality from unreality.

The following case may illustrate the different phases of the development of antisocial activities in a boy. Alex was sent to us because he had become a nuisance in his school. His mother told me at the first visit that she had had difficulties with him when he was three years old at which time he had started bedwetting; that stopped, however, when he entered school. When he was seven he used to come home extremely dirty; he was disobedient and refused to do his homework. He became cruel toward younger children, tortured dogs and cats for his enjoyment and began to stay away from school, giving all sorts of excuses. At times, when he provoked his mother and the other children in the neighborhood he was spanked. But nothing seemed to help. He refused to wash his hands before meals and was punished by being directed to the kitchen where he had to eat by himself. This he seemed to like. In spite of his poor attendance in school, he managed to keep up with the other children in his class. If it had not been for the fact that he could not get along with the other boys, he might even have continued in the same school. But since it had been discovered that he had stolen money from his classmates and told lies about them and was always considered a mischief and a serious troublemaker, he was transferred to another school. This had no effect on his behavior.

Alex was the older of two children of well-to-do parents. His father was a salesman. A rigid disciplinarian, he was often away from home for legitimate and illegitimate reasons, as for example going on drinking sprees with his friends. When he came back from these escapades, his wife was angry and upset and scolded him, all of which resulted in arguments and quarrels that continued far into the night. Alex was a frequent witness to these violent outbursts, but neither parent understood that the boy could react against these heated discussions.

Alex's mother belonged to an old, well-established family and had married her husband as a second choice. She was his intellectual and social superior and felt uneasy in the company of his coarse friends from whom she therefore withdrew, a matter which was a source for new arguments.

When Alex's younger sister was born, all his mother's attention centered around her, and Alex was left to himself. It was at this time that he started bedwetting. In the following years the father traveled extensively, and the children were left in their mother's care. One afternoon when he arrived at his home in a drunken condition, the mother took both her children and moved to her sister's house. Her husband, however, traced her, threatened to kill himself and did not give in until his wife promised to move back with him even though she refused to have sexual relations with him. As a precaution against him, she persuaded her sister to live with them and from then on the two women ruled the house. New quarrels started, which Alex witnessed, and this time it was the husband who left the house. His wife did not even try to keep him back, and that was the last Alex saw of his father.

Such was the home atmosphere where Alex lived and grew up. He resented his mother, hated his father, and was scornful of his little sister. The mother's relationship to her boy and her own personality make-up were of the greatest importance for Alex's emotional development. She had made up her mind to make Alex into the best boy in the world. He started to talk and walk when he was nine months old, and when he was about two and a half he was already toilet trained, a point of which she was very proud. The mother was therefore shocked when Alex started bedwetting at the age of three. Since she herself was domineering and opinionated, she did not listen to anyone but herself. When Alex often overate because of his voracious appetite, she was rather proud, and could not understand why he should not eat when he wanted to. On the other hand she did not permit him to play in the apartment, as he would untidy it. She suppressed all his outdoor activities because he always got "mixed up with the wrong boys."

It may have seemed that Alex's mother had complete control over him, but this was only on the surface. Actually, he was able to get away with whatever he wanted to, and he knew it quite well. His mother had endless discussions and quarrels with him, and it usually ended with him getting his way. On the one hand she wanted to make him into a shining example for others and on the other she limited activities which might have developed his potentialities. Her feelings toward Alex became ambivalent or opposite. On the one hand, for instance, she wanted him to be an athlete, on the other, she did not want him to be; then, according to her, he would become rough. As a matter of fact, in my talks with the mother she showed a great deal of hostility toward the boy, who had tied her down "during the best years of her life." One day she said to me, innocently, "If Alex only had been a little girl, everything would have been all right," not knowing that many of her son's protests against her were unconscious wishes of wanting to be a real boy. When he fought against other boys, it was not a small fight, it had to be a big one. When he was dirty, it had to be real dirt, because then was he a real man.

It was interesting to see what Alex had on his mind in his psychotherapeutic sessions with me. When I asked him to build a ship of some blocks, he at once stated that it was a warship, that he and I were on the same side and that we should shoot at the enemy. Another day when he was drawing a cat, he immediately drew another cat, because he said, "They have to fight." According to Alex everyone had to fight everyone else, until one or the other party was killed. It was evident that he was in a deep conflict, and from his standpoint every manifestation of life was a conflict and a fight. This conflict was deep down in him related to sexual intercourse, where, according to his imagination, not only the man but also the woman was hurt. The only way he could satisfy his own

30

sexual desires was through masturbation and exhibitionism. He used to walk around naked in the apartment exhibiting himself and desiring sexual gratification. When I asked him about it, he answered, "Why not, it's fun." "Only fun?" I asked. Alex looked at me and said, "Why not? There's no police around," and ran over to a book case in the office and started to pull out the books. After having thrown ten or fifteen books on the floor, he turned to me and said in a provocative way, "You can't do anything to me. Nobody saw me." In the next second he rushed over to me and said hurriedly, "Let's play a game."

This is so typical of antisocial children. They are nice and pleasant as long as you do what they want you to do, but as soon as you want to talk seriously to them or do something they do not like, they become rude, hostile and aggressive. This attitude Alex showed from the first day he was in treatment and it became more pronounced later on.

This attitude of satisfying his own desires immediately, rather than obtaining satisfaction from any relationship, is a cardinal point in any delinquent. We can understand this point a little better if we stop for a moment to see how the human being develops biologically and emotionally.

We are all born with biological drives, with certain instincts, regardless of whether we live in the slums or in the suburbs. Our personality structure does not exist in us from the first moment we breathe; it is developed in us through our contact with those with whom we live in infancy and childhood. Any child, wherever he is, can only watch and imitate those around him. He learns, and learns in great haste, from his impressions of his immediate surroundings. And since these impressions arise out of his emotions which in the beginning are unconscious, he is unaware of his own reactions and takes them for granted. Every child consists of a bundle of emotions at birth: he wants food; if he does not receive it, he cries; and when he has biological urges he lets go without any concern. Of course, he has also a nervous system and anatomical attributes, but all his functions and actions are dominated by his emotions.

We then see that what the child wants is immediate satisfaction or, as it is called, gratification. He cannot wait, he cannot postpone

31

his desires; he must have them fullfilled immediately; for him that is more important than achieving satisfaction from any object relationship. That he must have his wishes fulfilled at a moment's notice is the chief characteristic of any child, and for that matter of many people who call themselves adults. That they are impatient and cannot wait to have their wishes complied with may frequently be the stumbling block in their lives, and can be avoided only if they are aware of it. We see also another thing. A child's desires are originally tied up with biological needs, which if satisfied lead to pleasure, and if dissatisfied lead to pain. Human life rotates to a large extent around these principles, the Pleasure and the Pain Principle.

Every human being has as his conscious or unconscious goal the obtaining of pleasure and the avoidance of pain, but this goal is determined by his emotional strivings. These emotional strivings are rooted in the biological structure of man, and are always influenced by environment. As the child grows into adulthood, his emotions are colored, consciously or unconsciously, by his biological experiences in childhood. Thus the psychological phenomena present in everyone, whatever form they take as social and antisocial behavior, arise as a result of the interplay between basic physiological needs and the influence surroundings have on those needs.

This is a fundamental point we must always remember when we try to figure out human conduct. Alex was dependent upon his biological needs. His impulses required immediate gratification. For that reason he did not care whether he did right or wrong, as long as he could satisfy his instinctual demands. When he took money in the school it was to buy candy, and he did not care if he was discovered eating it. He was not even concerned about being caught telling a lie. What he really cared about was if he could have some immediate benefit from telling that lie. Because it was so impossible for him to postpone satisfying his impulses, he started to steal, became disobedient, unreliable and a troublemaker.

Those are not only symptoms of antisocial behavior; they are at the same time serious defects in the character of the individual. Wherever we find such faults of the personality, it seems as if the moral standards of the individual are defective. It is a question

32

whether or not this character defect is an earmark of the criminal. That is why it is so difficult to re-educate such an offender. He will resist any attempt at re-education. Whether you are friendly, firm, or severe, he will continue to lie, to do the opposite of what you want him to do, or not to do anything at all. This is just what happened in Alex's treatment, when he transferred his emotional attitude and behavior to me. Very frequently he came late to the appointments, always having a ready explanation. It was of no use to tell him to be on time, because at that period he was emotionally blind. It is this very blindness that takes many offenders off on the wrong road. It is no use to tell them not to be disobedient or not to play truant or not to steal. This language they do not understand because their own language is one of immediate satisfaction of their instinctual demands.

In the environment in which Alex was brought up his mother in particular had never exerted any constant influence upon his instinctual urges. Being inconsistent in her handling of him, she satisfied or frustrated him according to her own whims. We must here remember that a child's instinctual life originally is basically antisocial. Through the influence of the environment his urges become modified and he becomes a social individual. In Alex's case, however, his mother changed her attitude toward him several times a day, swinging from overdoses of motherly overprotection, which resulted in immediate satisfaction, to extreme deprivation, bringing about frustrations and anxieties. The results of this alternate handling were aggravated by the fact that his father was so much absent from home, and therefore could not exert a constant influence upon him.

But all the inconsistencies of Alex's mother were a pure reflection of her own emotional attitude which was a sadistic-masochistic one. On the one hand she was sadistic toward him; on the other, she permitted him to treat her at times with utter disregard, contempt and cruelty, thereby herself becoming masochistic. The crucial point, however, was that Alex adopted his mother's feelings in this respect. He himself became sado-masochistic. He liked to tease and plague his classmates, he tortured his mother with endless tricks and used to shock her by telling gruesome tales from school; he also tortured animals. On the other hand he accepted with some joy the punishment he received from her, when as it so often happened she ordered him to eat in the kitchen. While Alex with masochistic pleasure ate up all his food in the kitchen, his mother, alone in the dining room, was in deep despair. When he was punished, he gained enjoyment from it. In addition, when he did something wrong, it was so intimately tied up with his instinctual drives and with his basic personality make-up that his wrongdoing was only an expression of his sadistic-masochistic feelings.

This sado-masochistic relationship he transferred to everyone else, including me when he came into treatment, and toward anything he did, whether it was social or antisocial. It had reached the point where he had no feeling of guilt when he repeated antisocial acts. Whether or not he did something wrong depended upon whether or not he was going to be discovered. Therefore his usual answer, "Nobody saw me do it."

The case of Alex shows the fateful influence his immediate environment exerted upon his development and also what role his instinctual drives played in that process. His involved psychopathology made treatment of him difficult and prolonged. When he gradually began to improve, his attitude changed decisively to a positive one.

Not all juvenile offenders become as antisocial as Alex. But the juvenile delinquent in general is much more demanding than the non-delinquent because he feels, consciously or unconsciously, that he has been or still is deprived. It does not matter so much whether there has been an actual deprivation; it depends more upon his feeling that way, regardless of fact. The juvenile offender is the epitome of the fellow who wants to eat his cake and have it. Sometimes his behavior may take on a transitory form, and extreme demands coupled with other symptoms may disappear through psychiatric treatment.

A twelve-year-old boy, Tom, comes to my mind. He was very much attached to his mother until his brother was born. From that time on his jealousy of his younger brother made him resent her, although she apparently gave Tom all the attention she could.

When Tom's mother brought him a gift, she made sure it was not smaller than the one his brother received. Then Tom began to hate his brother so much that one day he beat him; when he was caught, he complained that it was the younger brother's fault. That same day some money disappeared, and Tom denied the theft. The following morning he sulked and did not want to go to school. The mother strongly suspected Tom of having taken the money, but he continued to deny it until one day he was caught stealing five dollars. That same night Tom had a dream that his mother gave him water instead of the chocolate he used to get. He screamed in his dream and woke up the whole house, and the next day he was brought to see me. In the following interviews and treatment sessions it came out that from the time his brother was born he had felt neglected and rejected by his mother. Although he first said that everything was "fine," he admitted little by little that since then he had felt that nobody cared for him, including his parents, and that he was a nuisance.

And that was just what he had made of himself. Since he could not have everything for himself, he might just as well not behave. His own instinctual cravings were so strong that he had to satisfy them at once. Tom was not aware of all this, and it took him a long time to understand his own emotional cravings.

We may be able to understand Alex's and Tom's trouble better when we start to follow the child's biological and psychological development, because here we may find many of the answers for which we are looking. Our basic question is why some persons have sufficient inhibitions so that they do not commit any crimes, while others are driven into crime for lack of these inhibitions. If a child is truant and steals some money, he does so for definite reasons, unknown to himself. If he cannot do in one way what he would like to do, he still has to do it and accomplishes it in another. And the way he chooses is frequently an indirect one. When Tom did not get enough attention, he chose another way of obtaining it, that of stealing money. Tom was used to being the center of all attention, something he regarded as natural until his brother was born. When the infant became a part of the family, Tom still remem-

35

bered that he once had been the only child who had all the attention, and that memory was tied up with the feeling of being wanted.

In the following pages we will use basically the concept of the personality which Freud first outlined. Although some may disagree with the way he thought the human mind acts or reacts, still his research of the personality structure has given us an insight into the working of the mind not heretofore achieved. He has thereby become one of the principal contributors to the understanding of how mental illness arises and how some conditions may be cured. It is most unfortunate that Freud did not have time to explore criminal behavior. In his long career of admirable endeavor, he wrote only one short paper in 1915 about crime. This does not mean that Freud was not interested in the subject; it means only that he considered the human mind and mental illness as his main subject, and this took so much of his time that he simply did not get around to concerning himself with offenders. Yet, Freud in his investigations came upon the theory that all our instincts are asocial and that they are endowed with energy which is called libido or with the Latin term "Id."

The knowledge that we all have instinctual urges is not anything new. The new thing which he emphasized is that the instincts possess energy which is constant. This implies that if, for instance, the sexual drive is repressed, it will come up in another form. The instincts constitute a force which makes itself felt whether we are awake or asleep; in the latter state they may appear as creations from our unconscious in the form of dreams. The important fact is that the drives have their root in the physical state of the body and vary according to its different physical status. While food is important for the hungry man, it loses its importance for the person when satisfied. The same is also true with sexual incentives. Thus, the source of the instincts is our physical condition, the chemical-physical state of our body. We can then explain the instinct as a need which makes a demand upon the individual's mind because the mind is tied up with the body. Since the body is kept in a chemical-physical tension, which has to be discharged, no individual can escape its consequences.

We then see that instincts are rooted in our biological make-up and that they influence our mind. The best way to understand the course such an instinct takes is to think in terms of our simple physical needs, as for instance hunger, defecation, or urination. The urge results in a specific action with consequent relaxation. In contrast to these instincts is the group of the sexual instincts which if they are not gratified in their original form may change their aims, or be repressed by the personality, and then reappear in different disguises. This does not mean that every psychological phenomenon is sexual, because there are other instincts beside the sexual, the aggressive ones. We cannot go into details here, but it is sufficient to mention that when we know more about the chemistry and physiology of the body, we will also widen our knowledge about the instincts.

We must keep in mind that every person is born with drives and that they act automatically. The infant is by and large a creature filled with instincts which are polymorph and sexual pervert by nature. Infantile sexuality shows itself in the form of sexual activities, not necessarily leading to sexual intercourse, but more resembling the activities which later play a part in forepleasure. According to clinical evidence we divide the pre-adult sexual period into three phases: the infantile, the latency and the puberty period. We know a great deal about the first and the last period, but little about the latency period which lasts from the sixth or seventh year until puberty. In this period sexual phenomena do not disappear altogether. In fact, we know of people living in certain primitive cultures which do not seem to have a period of latency at all. In our society, however, strong forces have been opposed to sexual desires so they have been curbed; this, among other things, may have created the latency stage. These repressing forces have also brought about shame and disgust connected with sexual life.

The antisocial acts of an individual have a bearing upon how his biological drives function. It is not exaggerated to say that all our laws have in effect been established in order to curb our biological instincts. Some law-abiding citizens are daily paying their price, not only in the form of shame and disgust, but also in the form of emotional disorder. They have by and large not been permitted to express themselves as children, and this lack of expression depends in the main upon the repression of their sexual desires.

What I am saying here is nothing new of course. But I have to mention it every day to well-meaning parents, who today should know otherwise but are themselves fixed in their own rigid feelings. To this lack of sexual and other types of expression is sometimes added sheer ignorance about the sexual functions. Just today I interviewed a forty-year-old man, who until his sixteenth year believed that his male organ was only for urination. He was shocked the day he learned that the organ also could be used for sexual purposes. A few weeks ago I talked with a twenty-three-year-old girl, a college graduate, who believed that a woman practically bled to death when she gave birth to a child.

In view of these examples which can be multiplied many, many times, how is it then possible for me to talk about crime and not mention the biological and psychological development every child goes through? It may very well be that some readers have asked themselves why I delve into details of the child's development. The answer is very simple: crime and for that matter, emotional maladjustment does not start suddenly, but insidiously with many forerunners. And some of these forerunners are expressed in the way the child develops psychologically.

The first stage of the infantile period is called the Oral Phase because the child at that time centers his main interests around the mouth. He puts all sorts of things into his mouth, he sucks his thumb; in short he displays during the first and into the second year of his life an oral activity which gives him a great deal of pleasure. This type of pleasure is partly sexual, otherwise we could not explain the great satisfaction a child derives from thumb-sucking, for instance. If he expected milk from his thumb, he would be disappointed when he did not receive it and would move his thumb from his mouth. When he continues to suck his thumb, it means that he receives pleasure from it. This oral eroticism we also see maintained in the adult in the form of kissing, smoking or drinking or in perverse activities. In smoking and drinking, however, are also additional stimulants which help decrease inhibitions so anxieties are overcome. Thus, the first stage is characterized by the child receiving food. His attitude now being mostly dependent during which he displays egocentric or narcissistic tendencies, he feels either accepted or rejected, depending upon his mother's attitude.

If a child is not weaned in the right way, or if he is subjected to prolonged breast feeding or allowed to suck his thumb for too long a time, or because of some unknown constitutional elements in him, he will be orally concerned for the rest of his life. If his oral orientation is severe, he will be inclined to excessive drinking, talking and eating, which has its root in the latter, or cannibalistic, part of the oral phase.

This latter part develops first after the appearance of teeth, at which time he is also more aware of the object, whether it is the breast or the thumb. At that time he may not only suck, but also bite, and the phase may then take on the character of sadism (oral-sadism). The symbolism of the cannibalistic part of the oral stage we find in some children is that they unconsciously want to devour someone, their mother, whom they dislike. Such special oral-sadistic fixation we find only in pathological cases, for instance in sadistic sexual offenders or in vampires. When they commit acts that are not only antisocial but also outrageous to the average citizen, they do so because they have gone through definite frustrations which have brought about oral-sadistic fantasies of such a magnitude that they cannot distinguish between those and their frustrating reality.

When a child, generally speaking, is denied normal oral gratification, he always seeks it. When he has had too much of it, the same is true. That is one of the reasons why spoiled children often become delinquent, emotionally sick, or both. Bob was thirteen years old when he and his mother first saw me. I had hardly started to talk to them when Bob put his finger in his mouth and started to suck. His story was one of poor schoolwork, truancy and nail-biting. His mother complained bitterly that Bob cried and whined for no reason just like a little baby. It was also very embarrassing for her that he sucked his thumb. At this point I found it necessary to ask her to leave me alone with the boy, which she reluctantly did.

Bob's voice sounded like a baby's. Before he answered my questions he frequently turned his head toward the door to the waiting room, as if he expected help from his mother. The next thing I knew my secretary called me from the outer office and said that Bob's mother wanted to speak to me. I told her that she had to wait until I was through with her son. At that point he started to cry. Between his sobs I heard him say that he did not want to go to school because the boys there were so "bad." He gave them so much, and he got nothing from them. When I told him that we were going to look into the matter, he automatically put his thumb into his mouth and looked happy.

Here was an extremely childish boy who was dependent on his mother for everything he did. As I later learned he had been over-indulged during the first year of his life and later on his mother had made a fuss about him and had seen that all his wishes were fulfilled. Bob refused to grow up. He was clinging to a powerful memory of the wonderful time he had had as a little child. All this was brought out in his treatment. He did not know it consciously, but deep in him lingered the idea of how good mother's breast was and how safe he felt there. This unconscious idea never left him. Instead it followed him constantly throughout his early and later childhood into puberty, and would have continued through all his life if he had not come for psychiatric treatment.

More important than not being weaned at the right time was the consequence that his oral drive laid the foundation for dependency and passivity which colored his whole character. Bob was orally fixated, as it is called. When he was generous to other boys, and they did not give him anything in return, he felt rejected and hurt, because he expected something from them. Bob believed, as many do who have the same character structure, that he was generous. On a deeper level, however, he was egocentric and his generosity was not without expectation of reward. Such an expectation also gave him that streak of optimism that is found in others with similar personality make-ups. In the end everything will be good, they think, for mother will help out. This was also Bob's attitude. He did not help himself because unconsciously he expected assistance from his mother. Yet, this also showed his unrealistic attitude, for one day when his mother was not present, he got into trouble by participating with two other boys in a clumsily performed holdup. Bob was on his way to becoming parasitic, an extreme character trait frequently found in confirmed criminals. We shall discuss this trait more fully later.

If a child grows up in a home where there is family tension, the situation for him will be particularly difficult in that oral or any other inclination may increase in intensity. This was the case, you remember, with Alex, who at times overate, a matter which his mother felt rather proud of. Alex's constant overeating, however, was only one side of his psychological development. Since he had also been frustrated in his demands, he refused to do tasks demanded of him. He had repressed these frustrations because he was in such a turmoil. His drives, oral or sexual, were thus cut off from the rest of his personality make-up. Left unchanged in his unconscious, the drives sent disturbing signals into his conscious mind, always demanding the same sort of gratification. When he masturbated or exhibited himself, he tried to repress these impulses, but they still pushed upward in spite of repression. Whenever his repressed desires came to the surface, his guilt feelings and anxiety which had first caused the repression became mobilized, pushing the undesirable impulses back into his unconscious. Resting there for only a short while, they again demanded satisfaction, thereby consciously and repetitiously provoking his Ego. Such repetition is a common phenomenon, and is one of the reasons why people of this type always repeat their actions including their antisocial ones.

Something more took place in Alex's psychological development, pertaining this time to the anal-sadistic stage. This phase lasts approximately from two to three and a half years and is concerned with the time the child is being toilet trained. Indifferent toilet training may make a child sloppy later on, while rigid toilet training tends to make him inflexible and stubborn, formal and sadistic, even suspicious, and may lead him later in life to compulsory paranoid behavior. In Alex was already laid the foundation for becoming a compulsory individual. He was toilet trained very early, and as we saw he was also cruel and sadistic, all of which could be led back to a fixation on the anal level. He was, as are all persons of his

41

type, extremely egocentric. When he got himself dirty at a time when he was supposed to be clean, it was a throwback, a regression to his anal stage, his unconscious wish to play with his feces. When he started bedwetting, it was unconsciously a substitution for masturbation. When he later stopped bedwetting, he began with masturbation. He started bedwetting because his mother did not permit him much pleasure while he defecated. She was always in a hurry, so the time in which he could enjoy the retention and expulsion of his feces was short lived. At that time the feces became to him the object of love and hate, just as in all children. His mother was proud when he could "make" and angry when he "pinched off."

Thus he began in an unconscious way to love or to hate his feces, almost in the same way as he would love or hate his mother or anyone else. Such a love and hate against one's own feces may seem incredible to the layman. But remembering that a child loves himself and either loves or hates all that he produces, we can see that this love and hate may extend to all other objects. The particular sadistic quality in Alex came partly as a result of his frustrating experiences and his pinching off his feces. Then too, when he was able to master defecation and become clean, he considered himself as a grownup and on the same level as his mother; therefore he could oppose her.

Let it be said in passing to the parent that a reasonable amount of toilet training is necessary for every child. Unless there are some other complicating factors, he will go through that stage without undue consequences. Let it also be said that we seldom find a person who is completely oral or anal. Just as the ages overlap in the development, so does the result. No individual has clear-cut character traits.

It is understandable that in view of the frustrations or indulgences the child experiences during the first years of his life, a great deal of hostility, hate and resentment will be aroused in him and be kept alive when he meets new disappointments. All these hostilities form a polymorph basis for later social and antisocial behavior, which is one reason why we have been compelled to go in detail about the child's development. But these hostilities become more acute and take on another character when, at about four years of age, he enters the genital stage, which lasts until he is about five. Around this time children become aware of their genitals and seek through them the pleasure they had previously sought through the mouth and anus. The boy turns his interest to his mother who represents to him all things—love, security and sexually speaking, a woman. She becomes exciting to him in a sexual way, and he resents and hates his father. In the particular case of Alex, we can see that he hated his father, not only because he sensed his mother also hated him, but because—as with all boys—he consciously and unconsciously wanted his mother for himself. Unconsciously the boy would like to get rid of his father, kill him if necessary, and take his own mother. In Greek mythology a youth named Oedipus did just that, unknowingly. This situation is referred to as the Oedipus complex. In the case of a girl child the reverse is true. She performs an about-face and becomes interested in her father. This is called the Electra situation or Electra complex and in it the girl resents, hates or envies her mother.

Both these situations may be complicated if there are several brothers or sisters in the family, each striving for the father or mother. This struggle for sexual supremacy, unconscious though it is, leaves its mark upon the children because it gives them feelings of guilt of which they are unaware. The frustrations, coupled with hostility and resentment which a child harbors, is part of the conflict. In the midst of that conflict are his sexual aggressive tendencies toward his mother, which are accompanied by guilt feelings and anxieties and which may lead to strong death wishes against his father, or in the case of a girl directed against her mother. More details about the peculiar reactions that may arise around the Oedipus situation will be discussed in Chapter VIII. Here it will suffice to stress that during the stages of the child's development much hostility is mobilized if not channelized, a factor to reckon with as a general cause of criminal behavior as well as of emotional disturbances.

That is what we saw in the case of Alex and Tom, and to a milder degree in Bob. If there is a tense home situation, as was the case with Alex, the hostility which is present in every one is multiplied. It expresses itself as a rebellion against the parents. Since

43

they consciously or unconsciously are considered by the child as authority, he resents and may even hate that authority, so he cannot identify himself with his parents. This lack of identification may, if certain circumstances are present, lead to disobedience and rebellion against them, and since the parents also are law to the child, he may expand his antisocial attitude into society. A boy tries to be like his father or whoever brought him up; if his hostilities are highly sensitized through his own biological and psychological development, these hostilities may bring his antisocial inclinations to the surface. A child is always reaching for warmth and affection—in short, security—and tries to hold on to whatever security he has. This means that every child to some extent feels afraid because he consciously or unconsciously feels his security threatened. Children who develop into offenders or who become mentally ill present these insecurities and anxieties to a higher degree than the average child.

Thus, because of the development the child goes through from early childhood, he experiences many a painful situation, or, in medical terms, a traumatic state. This traumatic situation is consciously or unconsciously always in his mind even when he is grown up, and it always brings about an acting out of this experience. When a boy commits a crime, it is not only to spite the law, but also because he is against his parents who laid down the law to him. This committing of an antisocial deed is a duplication of the emotional situation, the transference, between the offender and his parents. Consciously or unconsciously the child keeps always in his mind the basic relationship between himself and his parents, and he repeats that basic attitude later in life. In his relations to his parents, he wants to be gratified; if he is not, he feels rejected. All later behavior follows that pattern, thereby becoming repetitive, sometimes even taking on the color of a repetition compulsion. If this cycle is not broken, the child will later in life repeat over and over again what he did while younger. Alex's case shows this clearly. His mother's sado-masochistic attitude was reflected in him, so he did unconsciously to her what she had originally done to him.

It is also clear that when a child's development becomes distorted through some internal or external circumstances, so he cannot blend his instinctual drives with his whole personality, he becomes emotionally undeveloped. This means that the psychological development of becoming an offender is a long one. Our knowledge as to what happens to a child in the latency stage, between six and thirteen years of age, is still rudimentary, but it is possible that accidental happenings play quite a part here. Thus, criminalistic traits do not start suddenly in a particular individual, but are rather a carry-over of potentialities, which have found a responsive environment and where the environment has responded to the individual.

We have to emphasize that every factor which prevents the child from a healthy emotional growth will cause either juvenile delinquency and/or mental disturbances, or psychosomatic manifestations. For that reason anything that curbs the healthy development of a child is cause for delinquency. Inability to read can be such a cause, though it is frequently only a surface symptom based upon emotional difficulties. Sometimes, of course, reading inability is caused by organic changes in the brain; if such a situation is present, a child may become frustrated and may turn to antisocial activities. Children suffering from a physical handicap may become so emotionally warped that it may lead them into crime. Furthermore, children may become delinquent because of brain damage due to infectious diseases. Restless youngsters who cannot concentrate or pay attention, or who for no apparent reason get into temper tantrums, may be suspected of suffering from brain damage, if emotional disturbances in him or in the family constellation cannot be found.

Present views seem to indicate that the parts of the brain particularly involved in learning to control fits and anger, and in learning to concentrate and to pay attention, are those parts which are probably most exposed to injury by infectious diseases such as encephalitis.

Many potential offenders do not suffer from either a well-defined neurological condition or psychiatric illness. Some of them show compulsive behavior patterns, others suffer from phobias, others are rigid in their behavior. All of them are, however, emotionally undeveloped.

All the factors which bring about delinquency are by and large unspecific strains and stresses eliciting a panic or alarm reaction which, in a potential offender, may manifest itself in a crime. What really takes place is a disturbance of the emotional equilibrium which determines emotional adjustment. And this disturbance is caused by precipitating events. Thus, the transition of a potential offender into an actual one occurs through precipitating causes. In Alex's case there were several: overprotective and rejecting mother, rejecting father and rigid toilet training. In other cases, both for children and adults, these precipitating causes may be death of a beloved one, transfer from one school to another one, alcoholic spree, divorce, loss of prestige, rise of anxiety, homosexual panic, being the oldest. or the youngest of several brothers and sisters in a family, birth of a brother or sister, starting on a new job, etc. Sometimes it seems that a youngster's whole childhood and adolescence is a chain of precipitating causes.

What may be a precipitating event for one offender is not necessarily so for another. What happens to a child does not matter to him as much as how he reacts to a particular event. This reaction has a bearing upon the development of his Ego and Superego which will be clarified in the next chapter.

Here it is sufficient to state that there are no known specific factors that can start an individual into crime. From our studies at Columbia University over the past eight years, which originally were supported by a grant from The Josiah Macy Jr. Foundation, and from our research later carried out under the auspices of The Department of Mental Hygiene of the State of New York, it is evident that family tension plays an enormous role in the initial development of the emotional disturbances leading into crime or mental conditions or both. With family tensions and dissensions come infantile fixations leading into development of symptoms that are part of the general maladjustment structure of potential as well as actual offenders.

Although we could say that the term "potential offender" may not be a realistic one, since we all are potential offenders, such a term is nevertheless in order because it keeps us alert to the possibilities that a maladjusted person may get involved in criminal be-havior.

It must be remembered that the records of the Federal Bureau of Investigation for 1950 show that 28.9 per cent of crimes, such as robberies, larcenies, frauds, embezzlements, auto thefts and bur-glaries were committed by people under twenty-one years of age. It is also significant the increase of arrests in this age group was 7 per cent over that of 1941. This is only part of the picture of juve-nile delinquency. The spread of drug addiction among teen-agers is another side of a sordid picture. We have to remember that all these young people who commit crimes were once youngsters with small troubles that grew bigger and bigger.

We must face the important fact that the early signs of delin-quency which we are able to detect and diagnose may also be symp-toms of mental illness. The same symptoms may have many sources; just as fever is brought about by hundreds of causes, so truancy, undue aggressiveness, disobedience etc. have many causes. Above all, every symptom may be an outgrowth of the child's hostility and resentment, which if not channelized properly will be directed either toward criminal activity or emotional sickness.

We find then that these early symptoms may be the first signs of warning that something is wrong with a child. Parents frequently console themselves with the hope that their child eventually will grow out of it, but I must stress the importance of helping the child at once. If these symptoms are ignored, it is likely he will grow into an antisocial human being and end up as a criminal. Let us therefore delve into the intrinsic mechanism of his mind.

3

Crime in the Human Mind

A MAN is a member of society, of his community and of his
family. At the same time, however, he is an individual, but he
does not always act as one. All human behavior, including criminal
behavior, has these four roots, each of which influences the person in
its own way. Though these influences are external in their nature,
their effect is usually felt internally by every one of us. The interrelationship of these four forces is complicated, but this complexity
becomes more pronounced when we try to find the intrinsic mechanism of the human being.

One reason why it is so difficult to find out the working setup of
the human mind is that our knowledge of the basic structures of
our brain and body and their functioning is lacking. We have not
been able to solve the problem of crime because until recently so
few were interested in finding out what was going on in the mind of
the delinquent. Though we did have many data about the criminal
from the sociological and anthropological, legal, anatomical and
physiological point of view, we knew very little indeed about the
way he functioned and reacted. Many well-meaning sociologists
and anthropologists, not to speak of persons from the legal profession, have figured out causes for criminal behavior. But all these
attempts have been accompanied by the same faults: they have not
been able to come down to the problem itself, which is the criminal, because they did not have the tools with which to examine

49

him. They could examine him indirectly, either through the lawyer's eyes, or from the viewpoint of sociological or anthropological data, but not through the eyes of the offender himself.

To do this we need the assistance of the psychiatrist and the psychologist. Only the profession which basically deals with finding out how the individual functions biologically can have any hope of finding conclusive answers to why a person reacts in a certain way, be it with an emotional disorder or with a crime. Although psychiatry and psychoanalysis as a science may be considered to be in its childhood as compared to the much older sciences, such as sociology, law, anthropology or physiology, it has made great strides in uncovering some of the forces responsible for our behavior. As a matter of fact it has given us much more insight into the mind of the human being than any other science, which is only to be expected, the nature of psychiatry being what it is. As time goes by, more facts of the working of the personality make-up will be revealed to us. Our viewpoint may therefore change, in step with our scientific data. But that is what we see in any science; that it can change shows that it lives, because life is change. It can never reach a standstill; when life reaches that point, it means death.

Only vital knowledge which is fundamental to human behavior can therefore be used when we try to explain how a person becomes a criminal. We are facing the same difficulty here as when we try to find the reason why some people become afflicted with tuberculosis while others do not. All of us have one time or another been infected with the tubercle bacillus, yet only few of us acquire the disease. Nobody could give a satisfactory explanation of that phenomenon until we finally became aware of the fact that some people were sensitized, allergic to the tubercle bacillus; the degree of this sensitivity we believe, depends upon the constitution of the person. Today we may add that psychological factors can be involved in acquiring tuberculosis. These psychological elements make the organism acceptable or susceptible to the bacilli although of course the disease cannot exist without the actual bacilli.

We may apply the same general theory when a man becomes a criminal. A man with receptive criminalistic traits may, through some precipitating external or internal event, increase these traits qualitatively and quantitatively to such a degree that he becomes sensitized toward criminal influences. The result will be that he commits an antisocial act. Many times, though, the precipitating elements do not find receptive criminalistic traits in a person and therefore no crime takes place.

This means that only under certain conditions does a criminal act take place, and only after the individual for a long time has been exposed to criminal activities, or exposed to internal criminal thoughts or fantasies. Only then does he become sensitized toward criminal influences. However, this sensitization depends upon definite psychological processes which are rooted in the biological setup of the individual.

If a person commits a crime, or if he becomes emotionally disturbed or suffers from psychosomatic disorders, different factors enter into the resulting antisocial act or disease. What we can say at this point is that a selection of the particular manifestation takes place. A disease arises as a result of different factors in the person. There may be present a constitutional or a precipitating factor; there may be an emotional element, a psychological factor, or there may be present a non-psychological, physical factor, bacteria for instance, or a traumatic one. Finally a predisposing element may be present.

Since an illness can be caused by these various factors, we can also say that the disease can be a function of these different factors.

> If A is the constitutional factor
> B is the predispositional element
> C is the non-psychological factor, physical
> D is the emotional element
> E is the precipitating factor

we can say that the disease is a function of these different factors. If I stands for illness and F for function we may arrive at the following formula:

$$I = (F), \ A,B,C,D,E$$

A criminal act can also be the result of the various factors A,B,C, D,E, and a crime can be the function of these elements. Thus, if CR stands for crime, we arrive at the following formula:

$$CR = (F),\ A, B, C, D, E$$

Let me here say that it is not necessary that every factor be present in order for a crime to take place. One person may commit such an act, because at a certain age he is predisposed to crime, and therefore only a precipitating factor, such as being a lonely child, is necessary to elicit the antisocial act. In another individual a physical defect in combination with feelings of hatred, followed by a precipitating event, may be enough to elicit a crime. The one essential factor is the precipitating event which hits the person at the wrong time. But this precipitating factor is not always easy to find, particularly when the individual's whole life sometimes consists of a chain of precipitating events.

However, the main reason why it is difficult to discover these precipitating events is that they so often are thought to be external factors. Previous research has attributed so much to environmental and social elements as causes of criminal behavior. And as we have seen, the most important of those causes do seem to be located in the immediate or distant environment, but these external causes only appear more important because they can so often be easily detected. The intricate mental processes and reactions which may lead into criminal behavior or emotional disorders cannot be seen or felt by the examiner. The psychological mechanisms are not accessible to the naked eye, and therefore do not catch the attention of the researcher. Yet it is these minute mental processes we shall have to be concerned about if we would fully grasp the causation of criminal behavior.

That so many different elements present in the individual and in the environment may participate in eliciting a crime means that a multiplicity of factors go into its making. This multiplicity and the interplay between the causative factors must always be considered when we try to arrive at an understanding of criminal behavior. But this multitude means also another thing, and that is a most important one. Since this type of behavior is not caused by one factor alone, but by integration of several factors which change according to the situation and the way the person reacts, the causation of criminal behavior is a concept of relativity.

Only by keeping in mind the formative notion that the causation of crime is relativistic can we realize why it has been so difficult to find the causes of antisocial activities and why we have been so paralyzed in counteracting them. Previous research tried to focus upon certain factors which always were believed responsible for crime. This is not the case. It is not too much if I venture the idea that any cause can be considered a crime causative factor, and by the same token, this same factor in another constellation may bear not the slightest relation to causation of the crime.

We are dealing here with two sets of factors working upon and interrelated with each other. The first set of elements are external ones present in the environment and influencing the individual. The second set of factors are those present within the personality. The combinations of all these elements are numerous and vary qualitatively and quantitatively.

We can then formulate law number one in the science of criminology:

> A multiplicity of causative factors which vary qualitatively and quantitatively go into the making of criminal behavior.

Law number two:

> Since these causative factors differ from case to case of criminal activity, there can be no one rule given as to its causes. The causation of criminal behavior is a matter of relativity.

These laws seem natural and self-evident. Yet only those who work in the field of emotional disturbances and of criminal psychopathology will know how many unfounded theories there are as to the causes of antisocial behavior. And if there are many theories about one and the same matter, it means either that we know very little about it or that we do not apply our knowledge. In formulating these two laws I am trying not only to apply our knowledge of criminal behavior, but also to build a philosophy of etiology of delinquent activities. Only when we have such an etiology can we combat the static thinking with which we are still handicapped in the field of psychiatry and criminology. Only then will we have a chance successfully to make use of our knowledge in a realistic way.

These two laws lead to a third one, and that applies to the mechanism of the criminal act itself as performed by the offender. But before we can go further on that problem we have first to clear up as far as possible the constitutional factors in man and his relationship to his environment.

We cannot explain the working of the human mind in terms of constitution and environment. This is an outdated and a too-general concept which has proven to be of little value in our search for an understanding of how the mind operates. The same would be true if we tried to ascertain whether heredity or environment has the greater influence on the individual.

When we study mental sickness or criminal activities in their origin, we are again and again struck by the fact that hereditary elements are very much dominated and influenced by environment. Heredity gives a person opportunity to do things, while the environment determines what he does with his endowment. Under given conditions an individual will show certain characteristics due to certain inherited fundamentals. But that means that certain inherited traits and features create a disposition in him and that the influences from the environment can work within that frame. For instance if a child is emotionally unstable or has strong drives or feels out of gear with his family or the community, the environment may, if certain conditions are present, elicit criminal activities.

Much research has been done in order to throw light upon the relative influence of heredity and/or environment upon antisocial behavior. Rather sensational were the results of the investigation of "The Jukes," by Richard L. Dugdale, in 1877, and of "The Kallikaks," in 1912, by Henry H. Goddard, where it was claimed that criminal behavior was caused by hereditary traits, a finding we doubt very much today. Equally interesting were the investigations made by Healy and Spaulding, back in 1914, followed by later studies in which they could not trace any direct inheritance of criminalistic tendencies. If such inheirtance exists it may appear indirectly, as when the person is feeble-minded or suffers from epilepsy. In this and in similar cases, antisocial inclinations detour by way of certain mental conditions, but that does not mean that epilepsy or any other mental condition inevitably brings about crimes.

As recently as 1949, W. H. Sheldon published a book, *Varieties of Delinquent Youth*, in which he stresses the constitutional factors in the causation of crime, while he gives scant attention to the offender's interpersonal relationship. As a matter of fact, he even minimizes it. He emphasizes structure as the primary factor in human behavior. Although his anthropometric analysis is more refined than that of Kraepelin, it is impossible to understand how investigations of the structure of the body can lead to an understanding of the working of the mind, particularly when we deal with such a complicated aspect of human behavior as antisocial activities. Sheldon's belief that the structure is the prime mover in behavior does not help us very much, if he cannot tell us exactly how this structure utilizes and adapts itself to the environmental factors which the person encounters daily. No individual lives in a vacuum, and if the emotional relationships between people are eliminated from the considerations of human behavior, the conclusions must be sterile.

When we discuss heredity and environment as forces in producing crime the most essential matter to decide is: What is the most important characteristic of the individual? Some may say his body, others his intelligence, but very few will guess that his emotions are the most significant elements in him. And yet that is the case, generally speaking. Every person has consciously or unconsciously a goal in life. True, behind his goal-seeking tendency are inherited instincts. But when we keep in mind that our goals are constantly exposed to influences from our surroundings or from our emotional strivings, we realize that our aims become conditioned. It matters very little that a boy has a high intelligence if at the same time he hates his parents. His intelligence will not prevent him from committing a crime, while his hate may stimulate his dormant

55

criminalistic inclinations in certain situations. Therefore, instead of asking whether heredity or environment has the greatest influence on the person, we must rather first find out what the biological elements in man are, how they influence him, and what kind of environmental factors act as formative ones.

I have taken the time to explain the importance of biological and external influences on every person because much ignorance and prejudice about the way people behave and misbehave center around this point. The concept outlined here is a further development of the old heredity-versus-environment theory, and is possibly the most accurate viewpoint we have today. Only by including all pertinent factors which have a bearing upon the personality structure can we build a scientific psychology. Let me add that since psychological phenomena occur only in living organisms and form a part of all manifestations of life, the psychological phenomena follow the same law as the general laws of science. The fact that a psychological manifestation, such as immediate satisfaction of hunger or sexual desire, is governed by a special law, is based on the same sort of premise as that found in chemistry or in any other field of science.

The same also with criminal behavior. When we go over the history of criminology we find that extravagant claims have been made as to the causes of antisocial behavior. The adherents of the hereditary theories have not been able to make decisive discoveries which could prove the validity of those theories. On the other hand students of the environmental hypothesis have so far not been able to give conclusive evidence of their findings.

Social factors such as bad companionship, poor environment, broken-home situation, poor supervision, and many others have in turn been accused of being causative of criminal behavior. "Bad companionship" may be an accompanying but not a primary cause; "bad company" is in some cases responsible for the continuation of criminal activities. We have plenty of cases to show that many a crime was originally planned in prison. One prisoner learned from a fellow prisoner how to crack a safe, a newly acquired knowledge he used with great skill when he came out of prison. Poor environment has also been deemed the cause of delinquent behavior, but recalling that many good law-abiding citizens have come from equally poor surroundings, the theory does not hold. Neither can a broken-home situation be considered an original cause of criminal activities. Only indirectly may the broken home lead to crime by creating emotional tension among members of the family.

All these and other social factors have been claimed as causative of criminal behavior. No one, however, has been able to prove that criminal behavior has been due primarily to the influence of these or other social elements. The pertinent factors, the individual biological and the psychological ones and their interrelationship have not been put into focus. And yet here are located the driving forces which carry any man into action, including the antisocial ones. The way researchers have gone about finding the causes of criminal activities is the same as that of a man who investigates the driving power of his car by examining the body but neglecting to inspect the motor. By and large there has been an incredible waste of time, talent and money spent on research in criminology for details which have had little causative bearing upon criminal behavior.

One main reason is that much of this research has lacked creative composition which might have led us to certain keys which could have led in turn to the immediate causes of criminal behavior. Instead the research has been cumbersome and without rationale. Any work, and in particular research, must be done for a definite reason; if not, its human and social value is minimal. Much of the research in the field of criminology has been collecting data and attempting to correlate facts without putting them in the correct frame of reference because the starting point for most of this activity was wrong. With a very few honorable exceptions offenders were not examined from the psychological and biological viewpoint, which is the only fruitful starting point. No wonder, therefore, that most of the research stopped in a dead end street.

No wonder either that we know so little of what takes place in the mind of an individual when he commits a crime. For instance, we so often think of personality make-up in terms of heredity. When a father commits a crime of violence, one is apt to believe that the son, all other things being equal, would do the same because of inheritance. The son may have a constitutional predisposition toward violence, which does not mean that he inherits the same weakness as the parent, but only that he may develop the same tendency which may be evolved in the same direction. But that development depends upon the environment.

Instead of just asking why a person committed a crime, we should also ask what kind of needs and desires were satisfied in him when he committed it. The answer to that problem touches in the deepest sense upon the personality make-up of the offender who throughout his development is conditioned by his psychological make-up, by his past and present experiences and by the way he himself has reacted to these experiences.

We can think of three distinct ways in which a person may be led into criminal behavior. The first one may be that his criminalistic tendencies are exposed to antisocial influences all of which, under the impact of precipitating events, may lead him to commit antisocial acts. Or, because of his past experiences he may have developed feelings of guilt of which he is unaware and for which he unconsciously wants to be punished. The only way he can obtain that punishment is to commit a crime or put himself in some other embarrassing position, a matter we will hear more about later. A third way in which a man may be led to commit a crime may be in reacting to his surroundings by expressing his aggressiveness indirectly. He uses his aggressive emotional attitude to cover over his own weaknesses, and protests and rebels against anything which may get in his way. When the proper situation is present, this aggression leads him into criminal behavior.

In all three instances the person's criminalistic tendencies are mobilized to such a degree that he can no longer check them, and the carrying out of the action occurs either directly or indirectly. Whatever the mechanism, there will always be a working relationship between the personality make-up and the exposure. It is evident that a criminal act will be the more easily elicited the stronger the person's antisocial inclinations and the stronger the exposure. On the other hand, the less the degree of both these elements, the less the probability of crime. It then follows that in the performance of a criminal act a quantitative substitution takes place between the person and the environment to which he is exposed.

What the person does not find in his environment he tries consciously or unconsciously to find in his own make-up in order to elicit an action; and what he does not find in his personality traits he finds in the environment so an act can be performed.

Such an idea applies not only to criminal but to all sorts of behavior. A vivid interplay between the individual and his environment goes on all the time, resulting in an interchange and a quantitative replacement between him and his surroundings. The person, being a focus of action and reaction, is never static; he effects a dynamic influence upon the environment and vice versa. He seeks and exposes himself constantly to social or criminal standards; the type which he adopts depends upon circumstances and his personality make-up, all of which may or may not lead into criminal behavior.

In certain instances, then, an individual will succumb to his criminalistic inclinations. Those instances take place where there is an instability either in his personality traits or in the situation that confronts him. That is what we particularly find in a tense family situation. Because of this instability antisocial tendencies may increase in intensity and may be acutely expressed in a person's mind, which may lead him to a criminal act. A boy, for instance —and I have seen many of them—who has been living in a tense emotional home atmosphere may become sensitized to antisocial activities or to emotional disorders. In such a child there is always one form or another of emotional deprivation which he will try to repress. But in the process of repressing these painful experiences, he will at times become aggressive, a conduct which is always accompanied by anxieties and guilt. If he has not developed enough of a conscience structure, he is the potential offender who, under pressure of precipitating events, may commit a crime. If this behavior is repeated, this pattern becomes fixed so his personality traits are always ready to accept any criminal exposure.

When such a boy has developed enough of a Superego structure, he will be able to cope with his antisocial tendencies; or if he is unable to handle them, he may develop signs of a mental condition. This latter statement should not mislead the reader into believing that all that we do or don't do is centered around our conscience.

When I use that term here, it is only to focus attention upon one particular component in our personality make-up which, for psychological and historical reasons, has come to be of great importance in our daily life. More important even than the conscience is the inner relationship between the Ego, the instincts and the Superego. As a matter of fact we will not be able to understand how a criminal act takes place unless we go into the motivations which govern every act and the development of that particular structure called Superego. Since many of man's motivations are related to his conscience, particularly when it comes to criminal activities, we will first see how the personality develops.

As mentioned previously we are all born with instincts, or the Id as it is called technically. Besides the Id we also have an "Ego" and a "Superego." This does not mean that our mind is divided into three separate compartments or sections; these three names have been given in order that we may fully define their overlapping functions. We do not know where they are located in the brain, although much of the Ego is located in the cortex and its connecting association fibers. Cortex is phylogenetically the most recently developed part of our brain and determines to the largest extent our intellectual capacity, while the Id, which is possibly related to the midbrain, is one of the oldest parts of the brain. Even if the cortex is removed or most of it damaged through general paresis, for instance, the organism may continue to live, although mostly carrying out instinctual reactions. This fact alone shows how powerful the instincts are. Where the anatomical subtract for the Superego is we do not know. Again, these three titles refer only to the function of each; structurally we do not know where one begins and the other ends.

We are not born with Ego; it is not standard equipment. We develop it. So it is also with the Superego.

The Ego is what makes up a person in the sense of turning him into a personality. None of us knows anything when we are born. Through the Ego, which develops from our instincts, we gradually become aware of things around us. We start among other things to see, to hear, to listen and to taste. In short, we become more and more aware of the world around us. We become aware of reality, and what is more important, we start to test it. If we, as infants, do not get mother's breast at once or if, later on, as adults, we cannot get the job we think that we ought to have, our Ego gets into action. The Ego tries to bring our desires and needs into harmony. It tries to find gratification for us by compromising between our different, frequently conflicting desires. What this Ego does, besides being responsible for our acquired knowledge of keeping clean, eating only at certain times and being polite, is teach us how to establish relations between ourselves and the outside world.

This is the beginning of the Ego in the child and it develops slowly, hand in hand with the evolution described in Chapter II of the oral, anal and genital stages. The Ego, being in essence the self, is also the personification of reason; it is created and grows through experience, often called common sense. During the child's early life he adds experience to experience. He starts to say "I," which is the Ego. But his Ego is not completely conscious. Through everyday living it becomes partly unconscious, because there are so many desires left in the Id which are painful and vehement to his personality. And here we begin to meet with some of the difficulties that face us in attempting complete adjustment within ourselves. As a result of learning, the Ego has become to know that it must not have "desires" such as resentment or hatred, or even sexual ones; so the Ego often rejects impulses from the Id which are still in the unconscious mind or "Pure Id." These impulses are the primitive, a-social and a-moral impulses, the wild and untamed ones within us which constantly seek relief.

Thus the child already has its biological desires at odds with the social demands of his life. A civil war rages within him. He is constantly driven by a desire to do one thing or another, very frequently a sexual one, and these desires, whatever their nature, are pounding and weakening his Ego, constantly tempting and inciting him. But the Ego does not give in easily. The child has learned that he must control his impulses, suppress or inhibit them. When this process has been going on for some time, he inhibits them automatically and "forgets" about them. He represses them. That part of his personality, or that force which compels him to control himself, is called Superego. Popularly the Superego is called conscience, but the words are not synonymous. The Superego is a broader concept and is in part unconscious, while conscience is a faculty employed consciously.

The Superego is frequently stronger than the Ego. It is our red light, our stop sign. One patient described it to me thus: "I have a strong policeman in me." The Superego is our judge within us that says, "Thou shall not." It goes over and beyond the Ego in stopping Id impulses, for the Superego is at times more than reason; it is law, and frequently a primitive law which often knows no compromise. Thus, the Superego comes into existence in much the same way as the Ego. The child, having only instincts, seeks to express his instinctual desires in their most natural, primitive form. The parent tries to teach him otherwise. The child in the beginning may not adhere to this teaching; but little by little he accepts his parent's wishes because, after all, this is the easiest way. In case he does not obey, he is punished and feels guilty or has a sense of shame about his behavior. In the end he makes the parent's wishes his own, and so much do they become a part of himself that he no longer thinks about them; they become unconscious.

Whereas originally his parent's rules took form as an external pressure, something to think about and remind one's self of, they now have become a pressure from within. While there previously was an external conflict between parent and child, the conflict has now moved within his Ego and the new forming part of the Ego, the Superego. The Superego, then, like the Ego, is not an element which is merely on the surface or conscious. It permeates the unconscious as well.

The Superego starts to take form in the child's early years as a result of his parents' modes of living and morals. When he grows older he becomes influenced by the standards of the community and society; the extent of this influence is a result of his identification with these authorities. In this development religious and other ethical influences also play a part, all becoming a stabilizing force in the individual. Without doubt the moral life, though the standards differ, must also include the mental aspects of the individual, a matter we will hear about later.

We might ask how a person would act without an Ego and a

Superego. In the event that they were to be destroyed, that person would become disorganized and psychotic. If his Superego should be partially or fully impaired, his inhibitions would disappear and he would become impulsive and apt to become an offender.

The peculiar phenomenon is that the Superego in a person criticizes not only a criminal act he has committed, it also censors his mere intention or desire to commit it. The proof of this is that conscious or unconscious fantasies or thoughts about committing a crime may give rise to a sense of guilt. We can thus see that the Superego has been interposed between the Id and the Ego in order to help out the Ego, thereby serving as a defense against unwelcome desires which otherwise would reach the Ego and possibly destroy it. The Ego has to be assisted and the Superego does that by frequently posing the question whether the former should follow its desires.

Let us picture the psychological structure of the personality make-up then as the great reservoir of instincts surrounded by the Ego which is in contact with both the instincts and with the external world. The Superego to a large extent controls the Ego and gives in only when its moral standards permit. The Ego is the only fully conscious part of the personality, while the Superego is partly conscious and partly unconscious.

According to this we might be inclined to believe that an impairment of the Superego always takes place when a man commits a crime. However, this is far from the full story. If a criminal act always took place because of a damage to the Superego, it would be very easy to explain not only every crime, but also how to prevent every criminal act. We are faced with the problem of many children who have been raised in a good environment, have gone to good schools and who have belonged to the so-called correct circles, but who, in spite of having been given every opportunity to learn social values, have turned into criminals. On the other hand, we also know of those who have been raised by parents with poor ethical standards and yet have become law-abiding citizens.

If we consider the Superego only as one among many links in the development of antisocial behavior, this seeming contradiction makes sense. The Ego tries to harmonize the various impulses between itself and the Superego. If, however, the latter is too strict and the Ego too lenient, or the other way around, a struggle goes on between them, each pulling in its own direction. As the child grows, a merging normally occurs between these two elements, but that is just the time when his strong, powerful instinctual drives make themselves felt and they complicate the blending of the Ego and the Superego.

Both Ego and Superego must, within certain limits, be independent of each other. Thus the confluence between them must enable both to act in relation and yet independent of each other. Where there is an antisocial pattern—as with Alex, who was not able to identify himself with his mother and father and thus could not internalize their demands in himself—we see an example of the lack of Superego formation.

This parallel we also find in Alex's relationship to his teacher. As always happens in the child's development when he is of school age, he identifies himself with his teachers or other people in school, with the result that the Superego is widened and broadened and becomes in a way independent of the parents. Alex, though, as the reader will remember, only tranferred his original sado-masochistic relationship to all other people. The consequence was that his personality was in no way enriched, although he received some satisfaction from school relationships. For that reason it was very difficult to re-educate Alex so that he could develop social values. This lack of re-education indicates that one important part of his development also took place in the latency stage.

More important, perhaps, is that this lack of Superego formation is in some way related to a poor development of the Ego. And that impoverished Ego comes about because the personality has failed to develop.

We may now better understand the difficulties which confront us when we try to explain the actual criminal act. When a man does not commit a crime, it is because he has developed resistance against perpetrating it. This resistance is to a large extent located in the Superego and depends upon its development. But since a crime may not necessarily depend only upon Superego formation, we may surmise that other mental processes take place in conjunction with those of the Superego. Our question then is: When are criminalistic inclinations transformed into acts?

We have here to distinguish between two definite separate factors. One is motivation, the other one is the motor act. The first one is a conscious or unconscious psychological process intimately tied up with our biological make-up, while the latter is mostly carried out with our muscles and depends upon our motor control.

The first factor, motivation, varies to a considerable degree because the perpetrator of the act most frequently does not know the reason he committed the crime. Since an overwhelming amount of unconscious emotions go into the making of crime, we must penetrate deeply into the human mind in order to be able to trace the origin and the path of the criminal's processes.

All criminal behavior is a direct or indirect manifestation of aggression. This aggression whatever form it may take, may be an expression of the sexual or other drives. Everyone has aggressive tendencies; thus the inclination toward crime is present in everyone. That a man does not commit a crime does not mean that he is void of antisocial tendencies. It simply means that he is able to cope with these inclinations, sometimes by sublimating them, at other times by turning them against himself, thereby producing emotional and physical symptoms or both. Sometimes again he is able to overcome his criminal tendencies and lead them into constructive channels.

At still other times, the aggression may present itself only in the form of an individual's fantasies and dreams during which he kills or hurts his beloved ones or his enemies, but which he never carries out in reality. Such people frequently suffer from mental disorders, but so may persons who are considered normal. Some vegetarians, for instance, may often have bloody dreams about annihilating or hurting others, all of which is a result of a reaction formation in their personality make-up. Whatever form human behavior and action takes, it is dynamic and involves human tendencies which in essence are also dynamic.

We may note in passing how difficult it is to distinguish between an offender's fantasies, which may lead to antisocial activities, and those of a neurotic or psychotic person who does not commit any criminal acts. We may guess that the potential offender has more aggressive and revengeful fantasies and daydreams directed against others, whereas these manifestations in the neurotic and psychotic individuals are of a more egocentric quality. The latter possibly derive more pleasure from their own self-aggrandizement in their fantasies.

In trying to consider the criminalistic impulses which occur in the mind of a person, we have to think of the desires which arise from the instincts and which have met with the approval or disapproval of the Ego or the Superego. This means that the carrying out of a crime depends upon how the Ego and the Superego react to the impulses, but that again can depend upon the way in which these personality elements have been conditioned to the environment and upon the situation into which the individual enters.

As we mentioned previously, a man who has experienced emotional and social upset is more sensitized to antisocial activities and emotional disturbances than one whose development has been relatively free from such influences. This sensitization, which is instrumental in transforming potential criminalistic tendencies into actual ones, can be seen at an early age. Most children have at one time or another done something which can be considered antisocial, even if mildly. Many childhood memories center around the "fun" children have had when, in the absence of their mothers, they took some pennies, apples or a piece of cake they were not supposed to. They took these things mainly because there was no parent around, no Superego present. However, among these children there were possibly one or two who did not take anything, either because they were timid, or because they had developed some conscience or resistance against such ideas.

This is a very simple example and shows criminalistic inclinations brought into action at an early stage of the child's development before a complete formation of the Superego has taken place. The significant matter is that it was the situation that elicited the antisocial tendencies, a fact we find in all types of crime, as the following case will show.

Two boys in their twenties were talking over the details of robbing a bar, when another fellow, Harry, whom they knew only

66

slightly, passed them on the street. They intimated that they were planning a "stick-up" and asked him if he would act as a look-out. Harry went with them at once; the other boys walked into the bar, while he stood outside. As the two others were robbing the patrons, a patrol car pulled up. Harry yelled a warning; the other boys left the bar by a back door and Harry was shot by the police when he tried to run off. On the one hand we can contend that if Harry had not met the other boys he might not have been in-volved in the crime. On the other hand it is understandable that the situation was intimately connected with himself. Harry could have said no to the boys' request if he had wanted to. That he did not shows the connection between him and the situation into which he brought himself even though the situation in itself pre-cipitated the crime. This means that we have to count situation as a special factor in any crime.

When we have these three factors, criminalistic tendencies (T), situation (S), and resistance (R) entering into any criminal act, we are able to formulate law number III thus:

> A criminal act equals the product of a person's crim-inalistic tendencies elicited by the momentary situation, all of which results in his mental resistance being so decreased that he carries out the criminal act. This law can be put into a formula:

$$C = \frac{T + S}{R}$$

A man's criminalistic tendencies and his resistance against them are always potential in nature and may result either in criminal acts or in socially approved behavior. A crime is the outcome of the person's antisocial tendencies which are produced by the momen-tary situation against the pressure of his mental resistance. The sum total of the factors T, S, and R is always constant, and depending upon the strength of the tendencies or exposure of the situation and the person's resistance, the crime will take place. The mathe-matical formula I have suggested is a concept which is useful in un-derstanding criminal behavior. But it can also be seen very readily that this formula really covers all sorts of human behavior. If we substitute H (human behavior) for C we arrive at the same formula

$$H = \frac{T + S}{R}$$

Since every person has a different personality make-up, each with his own personality traits, and since there are thousands of situations and many degrees of resistance, great variety as to the causes of criminal behavior is indicated. This is one more reason why we can maintain that the causes of crime are relative. The great imbalance existing among these three factors may enable us to explain why a person becomes a criminal when, for instance, his living situation changes. The very fact of moving, not only from a good neighborhood to a bad one, but also from a bad to a good one, may in many instances cause a man to be maladjusted socially and personally and, depending upon personality make-up and situation, it may lead him into antisocial activities. As soon as a change takes place in the balance between the individual's resources and what the situation demands of him every minute, he will run the danger of being out of place and thus must act with vigilance.

To determine a person's resistance against committing a crime in any given situation is difficult when we remember that the resistance arises from two roots, an intellectual and an emotional one, both intimately connected with the Superego formation and its relationship to the Ego. When mental activity is decreased, the resistance is lowered accordingly. We find this to be the case in conditions of general fatigue or in certain mental diseases where repressions are at work, in illnesses caused by alcohol or drugs, in certain kidney conditions, epilepsy, diabetes or in encephalitis. In the ensuing interplay between intellectual and emotional elements, the inhibitions decrease as the resistance is lowered. The Superego is here the dominating figure, not only because it is the descendant of the parents, but also because it is punishing and threatening the Ego to make it do only good deeds, not evil ones. The result of its commanding role is that one person feels guilty when he has committed a crime, while another individual has a feeling of well-being after a deed well done.

The interesting point is that the aims of the Oedipus complex continue to live on in the Superego. Freud once said the Superego is the heir of the Oedipus complex. Since the Superego is originally developed from the Id, this may explain why it is so strict and opinionated and irrational, all of which can be overcome only by the Ego. The resistance to committing an antisocial act therefore depends to a large extent upon how the person has been able to solve his unconscious incestuous desires. This does not mean that crime arises just because of an Oedipus situation per se, but also because of the factors that caused the unsolved complex and all the psychologically and socially abnormal processes it brought in its wake.

Because of the outspoken role of the Superego, we will hardly find any man with only antisocial tendencies. The exceptions are profit murderers and gangsters. But the large mass of offenders all have mingled social and antisocial inclinations. As a matter of fact we do not find any individual who has one pure thought or emotion isolated. Every thought has its opposite thought, every emotion its contrary one, every idea its converse. This ambivalence exists to such a degree in some persons that their thoughts and emotions are so pitted against each other they are in a morbid state of doubt and completely unable to act. They are caught in their own yarn; trying to check their own aggressive tendencies, they become hesitant, afraid and shy, which may lead them into a complete removal from their real world. That is what we see in people suffering from schizophrenia. Expressed in another form and following a different type of mechanism, we see this defense against their aggression present in people suffering from compulsory obsessional behavior or from a milder form of neurosis.

In contrast to persons who, because of strong Superego development, are caught in their inhibitions, there are those we mentioned previously who commit antisocial acts impulsively because their Superego structure and their Ego evolution has been faulty.

When a criminal act takes place, strong emotions are discharged in the individual. Any man who commits a crime is, with the exception of the profit murderer or gangster, in an emotional conflict filled with anxieties and guilt feelings. This emotional discharge is a leveling off of the panic or alarm reaction every offender experiences when he commits a crime, and is in many cases felt by him as a momentary relief, often followed shortly by feelings of guilt. In case he does not feel relief, he tries to create it by going perhaps to a baseball game or movie, which serve to relieve anxieties and guilt feelings with which the Superego beats the Ego. The emotional discharge brings his mental balance back to the level where it was before the crime was committed.

The factor T does contain not only the individual's aggressive inclinations, but the indirect aggressions as well. We must not always think of criminal acts in terms of explicit break-through of aggressions, because we have also indirect expressions of aggression. Direct and indirect aggression is found not only in criminal behavior, but in all walks of life. Socially approved aggression we find to a varying degree in the work we do, or in any performance of art. Aggressions which do not have social approval vary in degree, too. Lying and stealing are not as serious as lynching, rape or murder. We see a high degree of indirect aggression where the person has turned the aggressions against himself, as in the alcoholic or the suicide, or in certain types of crime where because of unconscious guilt feelings, the criminal has committed the crime in order to punish himself, a matter we will take up in the next chapter.

Aggressive tendencies appearing indirectly we find expressed as protest reactions, or as hostility, rebellious in nature, directed against any person, or as projections. The formula

$$C = \frac{T + S}{R}$$

therefore will cover all criminal acts taking place as a result of release of suppressed or repressed aggressive tendencies. There are, however, crimes that result from indirect aggressive manifestations, and it may be argued that the law does not cover these antisocial acts. A criminal act may, for instance, sometimes be committed when a person has become aggressive as a defense. His character was originally passive, but earlier emotional experiences conditioned him to be aggressive. When he is faced with a threatening situation, he expresses his aggressiveness by loud protests, bullying, rebelliousness or an outward criminal act. Such indirect aggressiveness has been established basically in the individual when he was a child, possibly in the oral period. Beneath his aggression we may, therefore, find passivity frequently of an oral nature and the result of oral aggression, a point which has been stressed by Schilder-Kaiser and Bergler.

Basic passivity which has been turned into aggressiveness is a manifestation found not only in criminal but in other human behavior as well. It only shows how deep-seated human emotions are and how difficult to reach when we try to treat them. All aggressions are not, however, oral in nature. They may be anal, anal-sadistic, sexual, or a blending of all of them. Even when passivity is present behind the aggression, it still does not alter our theory that in one way or another some type of break-through often takes place. How else can we explain the manner in which aggressions can express themselves in criminal behavior?

We find this also verified in the nature of the aggressions. Every aggression has a main potential; it is never at rest, it is always seeking to express itself. But this is possibly more important: aggressions not accepted by the Ego and the Superego are repressed. Those which are not suppressed or repressed, break through.

As a result of my research over a period of four years, supported by The Josiah Macy Jr. Foundation, I have found that the emotional reaction occurring in a man when he commits a crime can be comparable to the body's reaction to a disease. The Ego, in conjunction with the Superego and the instincts, acts and reacts upon criminalistic stimuli much as the body acts when it is exposed to a prolonged infection; a soil is created favorable to the development of defective behavior. This does not mean that crime is an infectious disease. Crime is a condition of defectiveness, either biological or environmental or both, and the nature of this defectiveness is either qualitative or quantitative. The quality of a rejection or of some other traumatic event may bring about criminal acts if these factors are sufficiently great. Or if the type of the particular agent is strong enough in itself, it will to a large extent decide whether a potential offender will develop into an actual one.

Since any disease can limit a man's usefulness to himself and society for a shorter or longer time, we can say that every disease is a social one; and since it operates within the frame of his psycho-biological make-up it is also psychological. The same is true for crime. Thus we can say that crime is a psychobiological and social disease caused by a defectiveness. This defectiveness leading into criminal behavior follows certain laws, some of which I have tried to formulate here. Other laws we may only surmise, and still others we do not know at all. If we knew all laws governing all human behavior, we could predict with certainty the way a man would behave five or ten years from now, and we would be able to prevent any illness within the frame of human conduct.

In judging human behavior we must not look only at the external circumstances which lead to any act. People invariably do so because these factors are on the surface, but they forget the intrinsic mental processes, mostly unconscious, which are to such a great extent responsible for man's behavior. These processes are imbedded in the psychobiological frame of the individual which guides many of the actions he performs, including the antisocial ones. This guidance takes the form of motivation and constitutes the intrinsic force which impels man to action.

4

The Psychology of the Criminal

A N EMOTIONAL pattern has been laid down in every individual, the make-up of which is determined not only by the instincts and the Superego, but also by the Ego itself. Through both
biological and external influences these three elements have been
conditioned so the personality can act according to purpose. This
purpose is hidden in many instances; as a matter of fact, it is very
rarely that the individual really understands every reason why he
does this or that. Frequently, when a crime is committed because
of apparent gain, we believe this to be the true motive, but it is far
from so. Only by delving into people's behavior can we see the great
difference between the surface motive and the real, which is often
beyond their comprehension.

The reason for this lack of understanding is that all behavior is
colored by emotions and emotional conflicts which cover and interfere with the individual's thinking; therefore he cannot see
the causes for his actions. Sometimes the causes are so repressed that
under usual circumstances he will have no chance of reaching them,
much less understanding them. Take the case of Richard for example.

Richard was a shy, thin, good-looking boy. He was in prison,
convicted of three robberies. In my first interview with him, he
told me, before I had a chance to ask him questions, that he committed the crime because he was drunk and therefore did not know

what he was doing. He sat there before me fumbling with his cap.

"Is that your whole story?" I asked.

He looked down saying nothing.

"Don't you have more to say?"

"My girl left me," he blurted out.

"What happened then?" I asked quietly.

He looked at me, looked away and started to talk in a distant voice: "When she broke off with me, I was blue and nervous. I took a few drinks; I felt so lonesome, terribly lonesome. . . . All night I couldn't sleep. The next morning I began walking around the streets; then I saw a doctor's shingle and went into his office. When I sat in his waiting room, I didn't know why I had come there. When I talked to the doctor, he asked me what was the matter with me; then he said I was nervous and that I should go to a hospital. I got scared, I couldn't understand what he meant. Where was I going to get the money from? He gave me some sleeping tablets, and I went home and went to bed.

"The next morning I was jittery and jumpy. I kept thinking of my mother and father all the time. I couldn't go to work so I stayed in the house, couldn't eat anything, kept turning the radio on and off. My father told me to get some fresh air, but I went to bed instead and woke up late next day, too late to go to work. That evening I went to a movie, but left before I had seen the second feature and walked home. I sat down on the bed and tried to think; my thoughts whirled around and so I went out again.

"I didn't know where I was going. Then I found myself in a park and I saw a man coming toward me. In a second I put my hand in my pocket and made him believe I had a gun. 'This is a stick up,' I told him. 'Where is your money?' He was scared, and so was I. But he gave me the money, and I ran.

"I found a bar and had a few drinks. I was still scared, but felt a little better with money in my pocket. Two girls sat next to me; I tried to talk to them, but I couldn't get my steam up. Then all of a sudden I was sore as hell, and let them have it. They wouldn't answer me even when I told them I was not drunk. That's all."

"Isn't there any more?" I asked.

Richard looked at me, and said quickly, "When the girls left, I followed them. They tried to get away from me, but I hurried until I caught up and then asked for their money. One girl gave me her purse, but the other began to scream. I took the purse and ran."

Beads of perspiration appeared on Richard's forehead. I could see from his face that he was going through an emotional upheaval. His eyes filled with anguish. A long silence followed.

Finally I heard him murmur something unintelligibly, so I asked, "Were you afraid, Richard?"

"I was terribly afraid."

At that point I did not want to interrupt him so I sat quietly waiting for him to talk. His head was bent, his chin touching his chest, his body limp. He sat like that for quite a while, then he raised his head and looked away.

"I was afraid, and horrified about myself. Never had I done such a thing before. I knew those girls."

"You knew them?"

"Well," he answered more quietly than before, "I knew them in a funny way . . ."

He stopped for a few seconds; I saw that he was struggling to find something in his memory. He closed his eyes, his lips were tight while he tried to figure out what had happened to him. I realized vaguely that he might have a clue for the robbery of the two girls. He then opened his eyes, looked at me without seeing me and stammered, "I don't know them—well, maybe I do."

I asked, "And what happened after you had robbed the two girls?"

"I walked around the streets; I was terribly afraid of being caught. I don't know where I was, but then I saw a man pass me. The street was empty; it must have been in the middle of the night. Before I knew what I was doing, I had walked up to him and asked for his money. He said that he didn't have any, and when I asked again he hit me. I got angry and hit him back, but then I got frightened, pulled away and ran. The man followed me. On the corner a policeman grabbed me, took me to the police precinct and put me in jail."

75

A long silence followed and then he said, "I can't understand what got into my head, I must have been out of my mind. The whole thing has been a nightmare."

"How do you feel now?"

He did not answer, he only shrugged his shoulders.

Let us look at his report: Parents of average means, middle-class people, father hard-working until three years ago when he became disabled through an accident at his job. When that happened, Richard, at the age of seventeen, quit high school and had odd jobs for the next three years. Every week he brought home his earnings and gave his mother most of the money, keeping only a small sum for his own pleasures. Even with the compensation his father received for his disability, the family, including Richard's sister, could barely get by. Later Richard obtained a job in a manufacturing plant, where he met a girl and fell in love with her. They became engaged, but could not marry because he had to support his parents and his sister. He kept postponing their marriage, until the girl in disgust broke their engagement. He then became depressed and committed the robberies.

These were the "cold" facts as ascertained from the report. Very simple explanations for his crime, too, much too simple. The boy became depressed and committed the robberies. In this report, as is so often the case, there was no attempt made to penetrate the surface. Why did the support of the parents take partly the form of self-sacrifice and self-annihilation? Of course, to support one's family is both necessary and commendable, but as it developed in this instance, things had gone too far and were completely out of control. Under the smoke screen of sacrifice Richard became a sort of hero for his family. Here was a good boy, who seemed to give his family everything, including his future. When the story first broke in the newspapers, the headlines were: "Self-sacrificing Boy Becomes Robber," "Boy Jilted by Girl Becomes Robber."

In subsequent interviews and psychotherapeutic sessions the full story could be unfolded so we could see the true motivations of Richard's actions. But at the time the fateful events took place, he did not know the driving power behind his actions. Let us see what this driving power was.

Since early childhood Richard had been his mother's pet; she gave him all sorts of affection and love, spoiled him and made him into the most important human being in the family. When his younger sister was born, his mother's attitude changed somewhat, but he still was able to get her attention by ingratiating himself with her and giving in to all her wishes. The result was that he repressed and suppressed his own desires for the welfare of his mother, father and sister, the last being only incidental but nevertheless troublesome. It did not help matters that his father, until the accident, had been rather a disciplinarian so Richard quite naturally drew closer to his mother. The more afraid he became of his father, the more he depended on his mother, which resulted in a strong identification with her. His deep attachment to her made it impossible for him to marry his girl friend. Yet the excuse for constantly postponing the marriage was that he had to support his family.

Richard himself believed this to be the case and when his girl friend broke with him, his whole family was on his side and berated her vehemently. He became depressed, not only because of the broken engagement, but because he felt guilty about his behavior toward the girl. These feelings of guilt (unconscious in this case) are the usual reasons for mental depression. But Richard's guilt feelings were in part a result of the repressed hostility he harbored against his father and sister. He had never been able to express his resentment and hostility against them, but when his girl friend broke with him, it served as a precipitating event and turned loose emotions which had been hidden in him too long. The result was a chain of events that he could not master. After a preliminary emotional upheaval he went out drinking. This served not only as a preparation for his antisocial acts, and not only as means for "drowning his sorrows," but also as a way of getting rid of his inhibitions, unconscious though they were. As the evening developed, this loosening of his inhibitions paved the way for releasing his aggressions. He needed desperately to get rid of them, no matter against whom they might be directed. He was now out for revenge and when he saw the man coming toward him in the park, he found a suitable object. What Richard really wanted to get at was his father, who was not around, so he robbed the man in the park.

Richard was scared after the robbery, but to his surprise he had for a short while a feeling of relief. After he had had a few drinks in the bar where he met the two girls, the tension started again to gather momentum. It was quite striking that during our first interview he had some emotions about the girls, even though he did not really know what they meant to him. In subsequent psychotherapeutic sessions he finally realized that the girls stood for his sister or his mother and sister, and that he wanted to harm them. This holdup against the girls apparently did not give him enough satisfaction, so he held up a third person. The interesting point here is that the man hit Richard, and that Richard hit him back. If he had been smart, he would have run at once instead of hitting back, but he got so angry that we must suspect that he was driven to do so by a stronger force. Such an idea was also confirmed when at the beginning of the treatment he spoke about several dreams, the main theme of which was that he was hitting a man. One such dream was almost like a nightmare, and he woke up from it in a sweat. The next day he related in a rather excited and disturbed way that the man he had been hitting was his own father. In a flash the third robbery became clear to him. He could also see now why he had committed the first robbery, and why it gave him temporary relief, notwithstanding his guilt feelings about it.

So hidden had been his hatred and resentment against his father, and so dutifully had he behaved toward him, that he had completely repressed his ill feelings. But this hatred went much too deep to be explained merely by Richard's support of his father. The clue to it, we may find in the same dream, where he was hitting a man while protecting a woman. This man was a father figure, and the woman of course was a mother figure, a conflict which was related to his unsolved Oedipus situation. This could explain his protective attitude toward his mother, his not wanting to marry somebody else because he unconsciously desired her. But these desires were also mixed up with resentful and hostile feelings against her which, in addition to his hatred of his sister, may explain his robbing the two girls. Yet on the surface everyone, including Richard himself, thought that he loved his family. So he did, in a fashion. It was his unconscious feelings against them that drove him into crime.

In summing up this case we find the motivations for Richard's criminal acts were quite contrary to what was apparent on the surface. Furthermore, his aggressions were directed against substitutes, not against persons he really wanted to harm. When he wanted to hit back at his mother and sister, he robbed two innocent girls instead. This substitution of one person for another one happens frequently in criminal acts, and for that matter in many social ones, too. This may sound somewhat enigmatic to the layman, but such a substitution mechanism is often found in many of our actions. For that reason many people are surprised when they hear of an apparently fine young man committing a crime; perhaps he himself is surprised at having perpetrated a crime, the nature of which he cannot grasp. When Richard was afraid after he had committed the crime, it was not only because he might be caught; it was also fear of realizing that he, who was regarded by everyone as an admirable young man, could commit a crime at all. He himself did not know that he had such potentialities. Through psychoanalysis we found the reason for his antisocial act, and also the symbolic meaning of it.

It is important in this connection to note that Richard's crime took place on an unconscious level. As we have said before, many of our actions occur without our knowing the real reason for them. It cannot be stressed enough that our emotions effect and interfere with our intellectual processes. In general, we can say that a man within certain limits uses his intelligence to rate and test the situation around him. He tries to test reality. He also has another way of looking at the world because his childhood and adolescence have given him a mental image of his surroundings based upon his instinctual desires, wishes and fears. He also tests the world around him through his childish eyes, through his own emotions; whether they are desires or fears, they always color what he sees. He looks at things very much the way he wants to look at them, not the way they are in reality.

This cardinal point of looking at things the way we want to see them has been one of the great puzzles of human psychology. It is also one of the greatest obstacles man has in achieving a picture of reality. The emotional processes through which he arrives at his viewpoints serve also as a basis for his actions, including the anti-social ones, and are so ingrained in the individual that he for the most part believes that he acts in accordance with the dictates of his intelligence.

Nothing is further from the truth. If human beings acted with their intelligence, many things with us personally and with the world at large would be quite otherwise than they are. Man within himself would then be largely without conflicts; he would know just what to do and do it at the right moment. He would never expose himself to trouble of any kind, and there would be no wars. Everything would be peace and quiet, perhaps a little too quiet. Every act would be carefully calculated in advance by the individual so there would be a minimum of impulsiveness. There would be little excitement of any kind and there would be few, if any, pleasant or unpleasant surprises, no startling or electrifying events, because the moment of the unforeseen would be gone. The astonishment which gives so much flavor to life, not to speak of the bolt from the blue, would be gone forever. In short, life without emotions would be dull and boring as love without fire.

When we remember that the evolution from reptiles to human beings has taken about one million years, it seems likely that the development from emotional beings into men equipped only with reason would take such a long time that, practically speaking, there is no risk of our developing into people using intelligence exclusively. For a long time to come many will go on having emotional outbursts, becoming emotionally disturbed or sick, or committing crimes of all types. What we must try to do is reduce emotional interference with our actions to the utmost minimum so that we can act rationally to the utmost maximum. Which means that every person has to grow up emotionally and act in an emotionally adult way. That is basically the aim of all education. A completely mature man would therefore be an individual who knows to the largest possible extent the motivations for his actions. Very few of us do. Into every action, unknown to the person, go several motivations. Sometimes through prolonged psychoanalysis—but frequently not even there, because of extreme personality difficulties—it is possible to trace the complex psychological processes which motivate both the emotional attitude and the physical behavior of a person.

Although motivation for human conduct is complicated because of the unknown qualities and quantities of emotions involved, there have since olden times been two criminal actions which have been universally condemned by members of even primitive society —homicide and incest. Two laws, which dealt with totemism, prohibited touching totem companions of the other sex because they were sacred or dangerous. Incest had to be forbidden because of its universal temptation and also, according to the anthropologist Bronislaw Malinowski, because it was incompatible with the establishment of the first basis of culture. Since homicide and sexual intercourse with certain persons were forbidden, we can deduct that they were prohibited because of men's powerful desires. People in primitive society were afraid of the evil powers which they believed were incorporated in the taboo, but such a fear was only a reflection of their own fears. That is, they were afraid their own homicidal tendencies might overpower them and make them commit criminal acts. They had to protect themselves against those of their inclinations which they recognized as antisocial; they did so by raising barriers against them.

So automatically did this occur that they accepted these ring fences as customs. Later on these customs developed into laws, many of which became "commandments." The only way these barriers could be eliminated was by carrying out certain ceremonies in the form of atonement or purification, asking the gods' forgiveness for their crimes. Interestingly enough, we see today the same ceremonial behavior in persons suffering from certain mental disorders, such as obsessive compulsive neurosis. Because of their deeply ingrained guilt feelings they are doing the same as their brothers did in primitive society.

This example may show that members of primitive tribes did not possess any personal valid motivation when they bowed to the customs of taboo. They repressed certain inclinations and "forgot" them, though they were still present in the unconscious. Their criminal tendencies could be checked only by their own fear. If they transgressed their customs of taboo, it was done without any conscious motivations on the part of the doer. Also since man in primitive society believed that his behavior in general was decided by fate or some divine guidance, there was no reason for him to have a motivation for his actions or to try to find an intention for his behavior. Such an attitude naturally led society only to seek and punish the criminal, a principle which still is practised today.

There is still another reason why society did not look beneath the surface to find the motivation of the criminal. When the primitive tribe punished the offender, the members of that group felt that they too were responsible for the crime and therefore had to suffer. Filled with fears for their security, resenting and hating the criminal, they reacted violently against him as if they had one single mind, or a "common soul." It has been believed that this collective mind or "collective unconscious," which in our time has been put forward with so much bravado by Jung, consists of the total sum of the experiences, superstitions and myths a tribe or a nation has gone through from its earliest origin. This is in contrast to the individual unconscious which is a result of personal experiences. What we can say is that, in order to know man's motivation, we must know the culture within which he lives.

When we talk about motivation it can only mean the motivation a person possesses when he carries out an act. When we analyze an individual, be he social or antisocial, we will find the motivation for his act was personal indeed. But our society, I repeat, is still concerned primarily with apprehending the culprit so he can be given what he deserves. The psychiatrist and the psychoanalyst cannot be satisfied with merely catching the criminal. They also want to find out the motives for his crime; only by understanding him, can they enable the offender to understand himself, so that possible future crimes can be prevented.

What we have said here leads us to one significant conclusion: A person's behavior leading into crime can be understood only in terms of his past. And that past is responsible for the fact that a man, when he commits a crime, is driven into it largely by unconscious forces. He may believe that he knows the motivations, but if he does, he knows usually the least important ones. The powerful motivations which are the actual motor behind the act are repressed and forgotten. Also these motives are irrational. As a matter of fact, when we think of criminal behavior, we are again and again astounded to see how senseless and purposeless it frequently is. Altogether, the question of what happens in the mind of the criminal just before he commits a crime is hard to answer because, judging from our present knowledge about antisocial behavior, the psychological processes started to work in an antisocial direction long before the crime actually took place.

The following case may show not only a forgotten past, but also the irrational motivations present in offenders and in many other citizens who make up a great bulk of our society.

John is forty. He is serving a prison term for grand larceny. He was the oldest of three children; his father was a well-to-do business man, who used to take many chances in business deals. When he died suddenly, the family found itself in poverty, and John had to leave college in order to go to work. John had never been close to his parents, since he had been sent to boarding schools and in the summer to camp. Although he had made good marks, he was known to have temper tantrums when he did not get what he wanted. He had only one friend in college, and they kept pretty much to themselves. Rarely did they make dates with girls, and the impression grew that they were homosexuals. A heated quarrel took place between them, and John's friend left college. Shortly thereafter John himself had to leave, and he found a job as a salesman. When he was twenty, he married and seemed to be happy. He gave up his job as a salesman and started a small business of his own, which for the first few years seemed to be a success.

Then at the age of twenty-six he began to bet on horses. Up to that time, according to his statements, he had never known what a horse race or betting was. Then one evening some friends asked him to join them at the races, and he lost ten dollars. One week later he returned to the race track in order to regain his loss, but instead he lost another twenty dollars. He then became a frequent visitor at the track, sometimes winning, mostly losing. Within a short time he developed the habit of going to the races every evening. The racing forms became his most important reading matter, and he figured out an elaborate "system."

During all this time he did not care at all about his wife or children. He stayed at his business only in the morning and then went off to the race track; gradually he lost his business for good. After that he stopped gambling at the track for about three or four years, lived through some meager times during which his wife divorced him. He found a job, was able to pay off some of his debts, and lived with his wife again without remarrying her. At that time he had completely lost interest in horses and enjoyed himself at basketball and baseball games; according to his story, he did not do any gambling.

Then he started to bet on horses once more. "I tried to fight against it, but I felt driven by something within me. I began to place two-dollar bets with a bookmaker, and I was lucky. In a few days I had won thirty dollars, and I forgot to fight against betting. I played, however, only on Wednesdays, because that was my lucky day. Then I lost two Wednesdays in a row, and I switched to Saturdays. One Saturday I won two hundred dollars. I went home and told my wife about it because I wanted to be truthful with her. She bawled me out, and the next day I went out to the race track and started all over again. That day I lost every dollar, but it didn't matter to me; what really upset me was that I had lost my good luck. The following Sunday I borrowed some money and lost everything. Next day was a work day. I felt low and came in late. There were some big sales in the shop, so I 'borrowed' a few hundred dollars. I made some excuse to leave and started for the race track. It was raining hard, so when I arrived at the track, there were no races. I thought of the money I had taken and felt so badly about it I hurried back as fast as possible to the store, which was already closed. Now I could not put the money back, and I would be discovered. When I came trembling into the shop the next morning, the loss of the money had not been discovered. Then I thought: Why should I give it back now? So I waited, which was a big mistake, because I went out that evening and played numbers and lost every dollar. That week was a black one. I did not think of my home, only about the money that I had taken. The following Saturday I 'borrowed' some more, because I had to play in order to win back what I had lost. But my luck was gone. . . ."

He continued to take money for a period of three years, was discovered and sent to prison. During all that time he had never taken a day off for vacation, so when his embezzlement was finally revealed, everyone was shocked. In the court his fine work record—not a day's absence from work—was brought out. Now, however, everyone realized that he had stayed in the shop all year round because he did not dare let anyone else see his books. So excited had he become about gambling that he literally let everything else go.

This excitement we find in John and other gamblers to a greater or lesser degree is in type similar to sexual excitement. John had done just one thing about which he had felt guilty all his life. As a child he had either masturbated with himself or had had someone else masturbate him; that was the explanation of his one close friendship in college. When he had told his wife that he had won two hundred dollars, it was not really because he wanted to tell her the truth, but rather to let her know that he had had luck. Luck is of great importance to the gambler, because it means not only that he wins the game, but also that fate or God has permitted him to win. But that in turn meant, in this case, that the gambler unconsciously felt he had been excused for his wrongdoings when he masturbated. This is natural when we remember that conflicts about sexual matters often cause the most trouble because of the taboo surrounding sexual life.

In a man like John, brought up in a society and by parents who did not approve of his masturbation as a child, such a conflict more than any other created guilt feelings. He had to try to find some way to bring about forgiveness, which he thought he received when he won at gambling. John had felt guilty all the time because of his masturbation for which he had to be punished, but this wish for punishment was unconscious. When he continued to lose money and stole more in order to cover up his losses, he put himself in a still worse position, thereby punishing himself even more. The greatest fulfillment of his unconscious wish was that he was sent to prison.

It may sound strange to the layman to be told that gambling unconsciously has a root in masturbation. But if we think of the fact that both are a kind of playing, it is more understandable. The purpose of play is to get rid of emotional tensions. Since these tensions built up constantly in a child, he repeats his play over and over again, whenever he feels like it. In this meaning, masturbation in a boy during childhood or puberty is like playing for sexual excitement. The boy becomes acquainted with this experience, then tries to learn to control it. When a man starts gambling, that also begins as a sort of play. Another similarity is that in many forms of gambling as well as in masturbation the person uses his hands. The reader may know the story by Stefan Zweig, "Twenty-four Hours in a Day," in which the movements of a gambler's hands are described in detail; when a woman notices his hands at the gambling table she falls in love with him. Having lost his money he promises to leave town with her. Through several mishaps, she arrives too late at the station. In despair she returns to her hotel, walks into the casino, and stops suddenly because she sees her lover's hands at the table.

But this is not sufficient to explain a passionate gambler like John. Gambling may mean that fate has to be provoked; fate has to decide for or against the person. When John gambled desperately, it was obvious he could not possibly win back all the money he had lost; he was letting the gods decide. His early winning he consciously or unconsciously considered a promise that he would be protected against any losses; his continued gambling, which resulted in steady losses, meant that he thought that he could force fate to do what it ought to do for him, to make him win. Thus, when he said that he was fighting the gambling, he was really struggling with fate, trying to convince it that he had to win. So blindly did he follow this idea in betting on the horses that at times he really thought that destiny was indebted to him.

But such an idea was related unconsciously to the notion that it was his father who owed him a debt. By leaving a thing to fate John was unconsciously letting his father decide the outcome. It will be recalled that until his college days he had accepted all his money from his father. When he died, John felt deprived not only emotionally, but of money as well. In his later life he repeated the pattern: whenever he had money he had to reject it, which he did unconsciously by losing at gambling. He lost not only to punish himself but also to ingratiate himself with fate, or in other words, with his father. What finally happened with this man is what almost always happens to the true gambler: he was ruined.

That is what gives gambling its haunting character. The Broadway musical, "Guys and Dolls" depicts memorable scenes in which the gamblers try to find a place where they can have a crap game. Finally they end up in the sewer, where all but one gamble away their fortunes. The haunting music and the macabre dance imparts to the audience an unforgettable impression of gamblers caught in the struggle of death.

John was completely unaware of what was behind his actions; he did not understand that his gambling was an expression of trying to come to terms with his father. His behavior was impulsive, and in that respect we could say that he suffered from an impulsive neurosis. Because of his strong Superego structure he had the unconscious need to punish himself. His conscience bothered him at certain times, so he was loaded with guilt feelings; at other times he stole money as if his Superego did not function at all, a characteristic of the impulsive neurosis.

This case and, for that matter, all the cases we have described leave us with the important lesson that no emotion is forgotten. If it does not have the proper outlet, it will seek another until it is expressed indirectly without the person being aware of it. This is what happens in everyday life. The way these emotions express themselves depends upon how strong the person is (that is, how efficient his Ego functioning is), upon the strength of his instinctual drives and upon the quality of his Superego. Depending upon the interplay of these three elements and the effects of the environment, the individual's emotional attitude and his accompanying motivations are molded.

Keeping in mind that every person is led by his own goal and emotional strivings, that point alone may indicate that every motivation is accompanied by one or several, often contradictory, emotions. If we were able to measure with a scientific apparatus the feelings present in motivations, we would be able to detect even the faintest sign of emotion. People believe that the intention of an act in its entire course is an intellectual process, but that is not so because the intellectual process is instigated by an emotion, either in the form of a desire, fear or hate, or some other tone of feeling. It is with these feelings that the individual grows up, though of course they may change in quality.

It is, therefore, only by probing into an individual's past that we are able to trace the real motivation of all behavior. This shows also how intimately connected the mind of the person is to his act and how closely his emotional pattern is tied with everything he does. Contrary to the old theory that crime has simply to do with breaking of the law, we can truthfully state that it is a form of emotional expression. Every person acts in accordance with his emotional expression, whether in the way he becomes physically ill, gets into accidents, chooses a job or selects the crime that he commits. Regardless of his conscious intentions, his biological structure accompanies him in every path of his life, infringes upon his intellectual functioning and makes him do things his intelligence has told him to avoid, all of which leads frequently to irrational behavior. And this goes both for the criminal and the law-abiding citizen who becomes his victim.

Any action a person performs is in the deepest sense an attempt to adapt to a certain situation. In accordance with his molded personality make-up and his biological structure, he chooses— within certain limits—his own work. The criminal does the same when he commits a crime. The person is an active partner to his act. In the same way we find that a man becomes a lawyer, physician, cabdriver, printer or anything else, the selection depending upon his personality striving; so also does the offender select his particular type of crime. Sometimes we do find a man who commits robberies, rape and larcenies. But this combination when found in one person has a definite hidden meaning to him, which corresponds to his emotional make-up. The only possible exception to this rule is found in a person we call a genuine psychopath, who combines in himself all sorts of personality traits and whose instinctual drives are so strong and Superego so weak that he will commit all sorts of crimes. But even in this case he follows his own make-up.

The over-all impression of the way an offender selects his criminal activity is found in the process by which he singles out the crime he is going to commit. This process of picking out the criminal act is conscious as far as the planning goes (if it is planned) and as far as its actual carrying out is concerned. But even the planning of a particular crime may be done for reasons unknown to the perpetrator. Furthermore, we do know that a certain timing and a certain combination of circumstances must coincide with one or several personality traits in order to set the person into action. We could therefore say—and I am sure this is also in the reader's mind—that the selection of a crime depends upon the circumstances. We hear too often that a criminal is a victim of circumstances. As a matter of fact, this is one of the answers I usually receive when I first interview an offender. Only a few days ago a twenty-year-old boy said this to me when he was explaining his offense, a rape. He told me that he and a girl went to several bars together. Later he and a friend of his took the girl and her girl friend into their car, where they had sexual intercourse.

After he had given his story, I tried to lead his attention to the fact that he had invited the girl.

"That's so," he answered, "but she was willing. I didn't drag her with me, she came of her own accord."

"But," I said, "you went to that bar and became acquainted with the girl. Isn't that so?"

"Yes," he answered, "but shouldn't a guy be permitted to go to a bar and have a few drinks? And," he continued, "it was Friday evening and I was through with work for that week, and I like to have some drinks."

"You like to drink?" I asked.

"Yes, sir," he answered firmly, "I like to drink and eat."

"Well," I said quietly, "if it had not been for the fact you like to eat and drink, you might not have gone to the bar."

This offender did not know how truly he stated his own situation when he said that he "liked to eat and drink." That was the crux of the whole matter. Of course drinking and eating are not manifestations that always lead to crime; only when they appear in exaggerated form and in a certain constellation with a particular personality make-up and a certain situation will a criminal act follow. In this case there is little doubt that the offender himself had created the circumstances of which he became a victim. He put

89

himself into the situation and was at least an active partner in it, a point he finally understood.

We may also mention the victim. She claimed that she had been raped; she showed a few bruises on her face, but the fact that she was with the man the whole evening, that she consented to take a ride in his car, shows that she herself was in the game. At least she ought to have known, being twenty years old, that in their half-intoxicated situation, he did not invite her just for the sake of the ride. But that, she says, is what she thought. What apparently took place in her own mind is that she herself wanted to have sexual intercourse, but after it was accomplished she felt guilty about it, told her father what had happened and he informed the police, whereupon the young man was apprehended.

Rounding out this case, we may ask whether the alcoholic intoxication was not instrumental in bringing about the rape. The answer is affirmative, but—and when I say "but," the reader will answer there is always a but with a psychiatrist—we can also say that the alcohol served as a device to overcome the offender's inhibitions and that he consciously or unconsciously was striving to do that in order to be able to have sexual intercourse. The same can be said for the girl.

Beside showing that the offender himself creates the circumstances of which he becomes the victim, this case also reveals that the victim, unconsciously no doubt, seduced the offender, a point we will take up in Chapter VIII.

Here we must emphasize that in general there is a much closer relationship between the offender and his victim that is believed. The case of a nagging wife comes to mind. She was married, as would be expected, to a passive, quiet man who did his job, came home in the evening, quietly ate his dinner, read his newspaper and puffed his pipe. Once in a while he went to a movie while she enjoyed herself at a woman's club. Every evening before going to bed she berated him for all the things he did not do, and usually he was given the same lecture in the morning before he left for work. Once in a while he talked back to her, but being invariably stopped by her stream of words, he would slam the door behind him and walk out. Invariably too, he came back to the house, apparently feeling unhappy about being on bad terms with his wife. But the quarreling continued between them. That is, she argued and he kept silent until one day when he was, as usual, eating his dinner in the kitchen she started with her bickering. When, for one moment, she turned her back to him, he took a heavy plate from the table and hit her so hard on the head she collapsed. That she was not killed was not his fault. He would have killed her if he could because that was his intention.

When she came to, she was startled and shocked. He, on his side, was as shocked as she about his behavior and tried to ask forgiveness. What they both did not know was that she unconsciously had been inviting the treatment her husband gave her. She was, so to speak, flirting with being assaulted although she was not aware of it. In her quarreling she frequently taunted that he would not dare to touch one hair of her head. In the end he touched more than one hair.

Interesting as her personality make-up is, perhaps his was more curious. He was a masochist to the extreme. During his long life with his wife he had become bitter, but rarely expressed it. He tried to rebel against her, but always in a passive way, either by ignoring her arguments and leaving the house or by shutting himself completely off from her and living in his own world. The outstanding point in this case is that he had to resort to violence in order to assert himself. He could not break away from her as any average man would have done, but had to stay with her like a martyr. His crime therefore reflects his masochistic personality; he could only perform a crime in which his masochistic traits could be expressed. On the other hand, he would not have committed the crime had it not been for the type of wife he had chosen. We can say that they both were victims of their own personalities. They were fitted to each other as the key to the lock.

Therefore, when we consider the motivation of the criminal, we must also keep in mind the victim who stands in the delinquent's path. Many victims frequently ask, although unconsciously, that some criminal act be carried out against them. We can think of the man who often goes out on a spree and every so often is robbed. He complains bitterly to the police about how inefficient they are since they do not protect him against robbers. Still he continues to be robbed. As we will see later, this whole problem between criminal and victim has a bearing upon prevention of crime. Here again we must emphasize that the delinquent person acts according to the trends of his personality. When a man becomes an accountant, it is for definite psychological and social reasons. For the same reasons he may start a criminal career with embezzlement and not with stealing a car or raping a woman. Another man with a dull intelligence, for instance, who cannot become an accountant, may commit an elementary crime, such as stealing a car, but he will not be able to carry out embezzling.

This selection of crime has to do not only with the personality make-up, but also whether the perpetrator is a man or a woman. It is interesting that certain types of crime are preferred by women, for example, shoplifting. As a matter of fact, shoplifting is the only type of crime which is more prevalent among women than among men. Other types of crimes frequent for women are infanticide, poisoning, extortion and kleptomania. Undoubtedly this prevalence is connected with the biological structure of the woman and the particular cultural influences to which she has been submitted. It has been asserted that crime is more prevalent among men than among women; at least the statistics have shown this to be the case. But I wonder whether it is so. Firstly, it is a question whether all the crimes women commit are reported. Men try, in general, to be benevolent toward a woman if she commits a crime and therefore hesitate to arrest her. And unless her crime is a hideous one, a jury or a judge will be unwilling to convict her. Furthermore, because of women's particular work, they have often access to the performance of antisocial acts which are denied the man. By poisoning food, or by being in immediate contact with children, they may commit crimes which are not easily detectable. Or they may be involved in illicit relations with men who, because of their position, cannot expose them. Or, as Pollak has stressed in his book, *The Criminality of Women*, women tend to take on the position of informers, or receivers of burglarized merchandise, and are often not discovered.

Women seem to participate in crimes which are performed in a cunning way, and that may reflect to some extent their personality structure. However, some men are capable of the same cunning, and that is an important point. The difference in type of crime committed by the two sexes, does not depend upon whether the person be man or woman, but much more upon how masculine or feminine is the individual. No man or woman possesses 100 per cent masculine or feminine traits. Notwithstanding their anatomical difference, men and women consist of a mixture of traits. We find women who are aggressive, forward and domineering; on the other hand, we find men being meek and passive, afraid of their own shadows and behaving like timid females. I am aware that many of woman's qualities have been developed through cultural influences, but these influences would not have a chance to grow if they did not find a fertile soil. Although we cannot today prove scientifically what are definite feminine or masculine traits, we do know in a roundabout way the significance of these features. (The reader may refer to my book *Mind and Death of a Genius*.) What we can say is that every man and woman oscillates between male and female characteristics; we may also add that every person has a basic personality make-up which tends to go in the direction of one or the other of the sexes.

The question is whether we can affix the origin of criminality in a person to his sex. Except for such a crime as abortion, I wonder whether there are any particular criteria of crimes committed by women. Even here we have to acknowledge that abortions are performed by men. When we think of prostitution, we find this too among men. It shall be noted though, that certain biological factors such as menstruation, often accompanied by emotional upsets, may be concurrent with criminal activities; if this is the case it may sometimes be that the woman tries to "deny" her menstruation and such a psychological denial frequently expresses itself in pains and emotional imbalance. Statistics here cannot prove anything. To decide the relationship between menstruation and criminal behavior, we would have to have individual case history of the offender, including her emotional relationships, in order to establish the connection between her monthly period and her crime.

It has been claimed that, since women are able to hide their emotional reactions better than men—a manifestation believed to be related to their ability to conceal their reaction in sexual intercourse—they are therefore more apt to deceive people. Such a deception can be used as a device in carrying out antisocial activities. Against such an argument it can well be stated that homosexual men frequently carry out their acts in deep secret, just as some women do as prostitutes.

Again, the distinction between male and female crime made upon the basis of anatomical differences is incorrect. Regardless of whether the offender is a male or a female, we have to look at psychological characteristics rather than at anatomical attributes. But this indicates that the particular psychological make-up of a man or a woman is the pivot around which their behavior rotates. Yet, in reading through material about offenders I have been unable to find one place where it has been stated that we, in a psychological sense, all are mixtures of male and female characteristics. If we do not discard the old statistical cleavage between man and woman, we will not be able to understand the actions and motivations of any social or antisocial person. We can then realize that a particular crime does not take place because the criminal anatomically is a man or woman, but that it depends upon how these characteristics are blended in the individual concerned. A great deal of research will have to be done here because, except for broad generalities, we have only a scattered knowledge of what male or female characteristics are.

What I have said here may tend to show that, whenever we deal with motivations, we are handling forces in the human being which often are beyond the reach of the individual so that he behaves in an irrational way. Instead of speaking about the psychology of the criminal, we should rather speak about the lack or absence of the psychology in him. Since a psychic reality exists in the same way as a physical one, man's unconscious forces have to be recognized as motivations in any actions the individual performs.

These unconscious forces play so much havoc with all persons that many offenders commit crimes without knowing about it themselves so they can be punished. Their desire to be punished stems from strong guilt feelings, most often related to "crimes,"

94

frequently sexual ones, committed when they were small children. If they are not caught, they may dream of being arrested, even imprisoned. One inmate with whom I spoke recently told me that for years before he was sent to prison he frequently dreamed that he was imprisoned. These strong feelings of guilt may transform people into criminals because they unconsciously want to be punished.

5

Psychosomatic Disorders
in Antisocial Behavior

W E HAVE seen that human behavior is governed by our biology and the emotions and motivations which arise therefrom. Beneath all our actions are emotions, which, conscious or unconscious, pierce through in all our deeds. In each act we perform there is always present an emotional matrix. As a result our emotions mold our personality pattern and our actions, including the antisocial ones. When the emotional pattern is disturbed, the person becomes maladjusted. Every human being is subject to this phenomenon. The outcome of this maladjustment differs from individual to individual and depends not so much upon the type of his inner conflict as upon the way he can or cannot cope with it. But the mental processes with which he tries to handle his situations are largely unconscious.

Clinical experience has shown us that each individual reacts differently. Not only does he act and react to the external situation, but also to his bodily needs which are or are not satisfied. In short, he reacts by feeling either frustrated or gratified. We can therefore say that man can be considered a psychobio-functional organism who responds in different ways to the environment. It is interesting and significant that while we frequently have only one criminal in a family, a brother may develop a peptic ulcer or some other bodily disease and another brother may suffer from a neurosis. Yet, those three brothers have lived in the same life situation and all have been exposed to the same stimuli. In another instance—and I am now drawing upon my research project conducted between 1944 and 1948 at the Psychiatric Institute of the Department of Psychiatry, at Columbia University and supported by grants from The Josiah Macy Jr. Foundation—one youngster became antisocial, his elder brother was psychotic, while his sister suffered from a psychosomatic disorder. We cannot explain an offender's antisocial activities merely by saying he is, for instance, the oldest or youngest in the family, but rather by a certain pattern and a personality reaction together with circumstances which in due course brought about his criminal behavior. My theoretical reason for this different outcome—confirmed in the study and now made known to the general public for the first time—was that a crime, a neurosis or a psychosis or a psychosomatic disease, was determined by the different personality structure, by what kind and how great the individual's traumata had been and by his reaction to these traumata.

I have stated before that the previous personality make-up determines how an individual will react to a certain situation. If a person has previously shown emotional disturbances to a slight degree, these emotional upsets may develop further and result in more serious mental conditions, including psychosomatic disturbances. The same is true for the criminal. In an article written in 1948, "Psychosomatic Disturbances and Their Significance in Antisocial Behavior," I stated: "In the same way as the reaction to the disease depends upon what the personality was before the onset, so also the reaction to the crime depends upon the type of personality traits before the antisocial act was committed." The individual's biological needs and feelings have a direct bearing upon his personality reaction.

It is here necessary to explain the term "psychosomatic." The word is a combination of "psyche" which means spirit, soul or mind, and "soma" which means body. "Psychosomatic" would then mean "mind-body." The term indicates that there is a bisection or a dichotomy between mind and body, but this is not so. Every bodily illness influences the person's emotions to a greater or a lesser degree, and any emotional disturbance, faint though it may be, interferes with the biological processes of the body. The term "psychosomatic" is an unfortunate one, and in a lecture a few years ago, I coined the term "psychobiotic" which does not sound so abrupt as "psychosomatic." Whatever term we use, we must remember that the function of the mind depends not only upon external influences, but also upon the physiological and chemical processes in the body in the same way as feelings (such as hostility), frustrations and instinctual satisfactions depend upon environmental and biochemical changes. This is true of all of our actions, social as well as antisocial. We can say, then, that a psychosomatic illness is a disturbance of bodily functions related to emotional conflicts which are frequently of an unconscious character.

The idea that mind and body are interrelated in their functions is an old one, and goes back to the "Father of Medicine," Hippocrates. The new element in our concept is that psychobiotic disease is a disturbance frequently associated with unconscious feelings. This is a revolutionary discovery, because when taking into account the unconscious emotions, the whole concept of psychosomatic diseases became broadened so much that we today can say there is hardly any disease which does not have psychosomatic components. That it should have taken over two thousand years to develop the conception of psychosomatic illnesses is due to the fact that we knew so little about our unconscious feelings. Only after Freud had explored that part of the human mind and put that knowledge into a useful system, were we able to apply this concept to the fullest extent.

It is already common knowledge that peptic ulcer, migraine, asthma and a host of other conditions have an emotional element. The reader may remember also that I earlier mentioned tuberculosis. What is not so well known is that emotional upsets have been recognized as etiological factors in many cases of menstrual disturbances, infertility and in "False pregnancy" (pseudocyesis). In the latter cases it was found that the women had an intense desire for or were fearful of pregnancy. In these and in similar conditions it is believed that the emotional disturbances act through the intermedium of the endocrine system. In other instances we find individuals who are prone to accidents which are related to their unconscious feelings. The main point is that we find emotions acting

99

upon our bodily functions in all fashions without our being aware of it, and bringing forth bodily and mental, social and antisocial disturbances.

The widened concept of psychosomatic disturbances and their biological and psychological roots puts our view of human behavior, social and criminal, in a different light. This was one of the starting points in my research where we tried to find the relationship between emotional maladjustments with or without delinquency as they took place in schools and home; we also tried to ascertain the emotional relationship between the school, family and the children. Here we shall deal with the psychosomatic disturbances. (For other aspects of this research see Chapters VI and XII.) We had known for quite a time of cases where an individual wants to do something specific, but because something unexplained happens to him, he cannot carry out his wish. Everyone may have heard of the man who wanted to scold his employee because he was not doing his work properly. The employer was a sensitive and proper man, and he had grown up with the idea that it was improper to scold anyone. Instead of scolding, the employer started to cough. On the one hand he wanted to scold, but could not; on the other hand he wanted at least to say something. So he made a compromise with himself and, as a result, he coughed.

With the help of the psychosomatic concept, we will now return to a problem we have dealt with previously, and that is: What makes a person receptive to crime? To answer this question, we have to determine to what point and degree the individual's personality development has become warped.

To this end we started our research at the New York State Psychiatric Institute in the special out-patient department, organized for and devoted to the particular study and treatment of personality and behavior disorders of children and their families. We began to examine, treat and follow up many complicated cases of children and adolescents as well as their brothers and sisters and mothers and fathers whenever the latter was feasible. The cases were referred to us from principals and teachers of public and private schools, parents and psychiatrists, and from different agencies such as The Jewish Board of Guardians, Children's and General Sessions

Court. In addition, we also examined neurotic or psychotic patients who did not show delinquent attitudes and who were used as control patients and their family members who were referred to us from the Psychiatric Institute.

Many were children who had played truant, had showed behavior disorders, had failed or misbehaved in classes, or had shown exhibitionistic tendencies. Others had committed petty thefts; still others were kleptomaniacs. Whenever necessary, the case was hospitalized in the Children's Department at Psychiatric Institute.

Each case was examined medically and psychiatrically, the latter according to the method of associative anamnesis, a technique first outlined by Dr. Felix Deutsch in 1939. In the cases we undertook, the patient was asked to describe his life experiences and was encouraged to talk freely of whatever came into his mind. When a point bearing upon his emotional attitude was touched, a salient question was asked and that elicited new associations. In order to utilize such a technique, the patient must have a positive attitude toward the examiner. That means that the emotional relationship between them, or as it is called transference, is a positive one. This same method was used in examining the available members of his family, and control patients and their families. What we tried to uncover in these examinations was medical and psychological facts and their impression upon the person, in order to determine his personality make-up.

The way any patient states his symptoms or the way he reacted to them, as he tries to recall them the first time, may vary from the way he later recollects the same events. The reason for this changed opinion about our impressions is that we usually want to see things in accordance with our wishes, not according to the way they really are. The associative anamnesis tries to avoid a rigid listing of facts in the history and attempts rather to follow the emotional stream of the patient, much in the same way as a patient does when, during psychoanalysis, he gives free associations. Using this method of examination, it was startling to see how frequently the delinquents complained of bodily disorders of one type or another, and how constant their emotional upsets were.

Beside psychiatric-psychological examinations, a battery of psychological tests, including those of the projective techniques, such as Rorschach (ink-blot) test, were given not only to the patients themselves but also to their family members, so that we could evaluate the psychological make-up of the latter as well as the family situation. As far as I know, this is the first time that family members of the patient have been given these tests in a comprehensive way. In addition, the social workers interviewed each patient and his parents, foster parents, guardians or those with whom he lived, made trips to their homes to investigate them and to their schools in order to talk over with the teacher a child's behavior.

The technique we used was team work, the psychiatrist, psychologist and psychiatric social worker dealing with the same case, each case being followed up by all of them. This is the technique used by Child Guidance or Orthopsychiatric clinics.

We also made a physical examination of the patient including X ray of the gastro-intestinal tract and determination of the basal metabolism. Frequently it was difficult to do the latter because the patient was fearful and sometimes even refused to have the tests taken.

Interested as we were in the diagnosis of our cases, we were more concerned with their treatment. Since we worked with individual cases as well as with members of their families, our treatment was intensive, some being given psychotherapy two to three times a week.

Almost all the delinquents had, during either childhood or adolescence, suffered at least once from bodily disorders of a psychosomatic nature. The exceptions were two young homosexuals who denied ever having suffered from psychosomatic illnesses. These two, however, were unco-operative, hostile and antagonistic, and it was difficult, if not impossible, to obtain any reliable information from them. We may therefore disregard them. All the control patients who were mentally abnormal and in need of treatment, but who had committed no crimes, showed to a greater or lesser degree manifestations of psychosomatic disturbances, but these signs did not seem to be so solid and dense as they were in the delinquents.

We can here note that we did not use any so-called normal persons as comparison, because it is extremely difficult to find an absolutely normal person. Also, even if we had succeeded in grouping together those who would be considered normal, we might in the final analysis have found that they were abnormal.

When we examined the members of delinquents' families, we found that psychosomatic disorders were constantly found either in the mother or father, or in one or more of the brothers or sisters. This was in contrast to the control patients in whom the psychosomatic disturbances did not show up so often.

In a cross section of about 150 delinquents and non-delinquents we found that diseases of the gastro-intestinal tract appeared in 55 per cent of the former and 45 of the latter. Skin afflictions occurred in 17 per cent of the delinquents and 5 per cent of the non-delinquents. And while we found that 20 per cent of the former were prone to accidents, this was true of only 10 per cent of those who were law-abiding citizens. We also found delinquents suffering from psychosomatic disorders of the cardio-vascular system, of the respiratory tract, of the nervous system, and some who showed symptoms of two of them.

The numbers given here may be small, but they still may indicate a trend showing considerable presence of psychosomatic disorders in delinquents and in the members of their families as compared with non-delinquents. Significant also is the appearance in the delinquents of psychosomatic disturbances located in the gastro-intestinal tract. The same was also true of the non-delinquents, but to a lesser extent. It may show though, that the gastro-intestinal tract is the system through which a delinquent's emotions are most often expressed.

When we found psychosomatic disorders, we also encountered distorted emotions in the home situation, such as resentment and hostility, or hatred and rivalry, always coupled with either over-protection or overindulgence. If we ascertained symptoms of defense mechanisms such as aggressiveness or bullying, or some other outward expression, physical symptoms were present or appeared later. The emotional and physical manifestations frequently went hand in hand, and were often immediately apparent. These phenomena gave us an excellent opportunity to look for the relationship between emotional attitudes and the existence of antisocial behavior.

I cannot go into all the interesting and significant cases we have seen, but I would like to cite from the life of Mike, who was fourteen years old when he first came to our attention. During the preceding three years he had been frequently truant from school, had done a great deal of stealing and during those times had stayed away from home. When this antisocial behavior had continued for about two years, he developed a severe condition of rheumatic fever with cardiac signs, which kept him in bed for several weeks. When he apparently recovered, he went back to school, which he attended only for a few days. He then started again to be truant and had a recurrence of the fever which lasted for a week. In the next six months he had several recurrences of fever, lasting four or five days. When he was again well enough to attend school, he became involved in several thefts, and his mother finally agreed with the school's recommendation that the boy be sent to an institution.

He stayed there for a year, with only minor infractions of the rules, and was then sent home over a weekend as a tryout. Hardly had he been home a day before he developed fever, fatigue, headache and some cardiac symptoms. He was returned to the institution, and the fever subsided. He stayed there for another half year, then returned home. After three or four weeks at home he became ill again with the same symptoms, and was sent back. When he was seventeen years old, he joined the Navy, which indicates that his rheumatic condition had cleared up.

We will be able to understand this case when we learn that Mike and his brother lived with their mother and that their father had left her. She was an obstinate, nagging and aggressive woman who demanded much of her children. Because she had to support her boys, she could not be home when they came in from school, so they were left pretty much on their own. No doubt the lack of attention and supervision played a part in developing the antisocial and psychosomatic symptoms. The relationship between Mike and his mother was tense, and there was a great deal of fighting between the brothers which did not help the situation either. Mike himself was tense, jealous and aggressive and always tried to bully his younger brother, who seemed to be his mother's pet. When fights with his brother led to fights with his mother, and when he was finally admonished that he had to stay away from the younger boy, Mike had to find new means to attract her attention.

The way he chose was to play hookey from school. In the beginning it was not discovered; at least, it does not seem that the mother was completely aware of it, and that may indicate that she in all truth did not care so much about Mike. But when his truancy became associated with thefts, the school took the matter up with her. She pleaded with Mike, and when that did not help, she scolded or threatened him. For a few months everything seemed fine, but then one day he developed symptoms of a rheumatic fever as we have described. His illness shocked his mother tremendously. She quit her job and was around Mike all the weeks he was in bed. He liked to have his mother home, particularly at school time when his brother was not there. But when the time came to return to school, Mike had several arguments with his mother. The "sweetness" he had displayed while he was sick was gone, and instead there was the same aggressive boy as before. He again became truant, started to steal, and the new circle with fever, etc., began all over again.

In reality, while Mike was aggressive, he showed also many anxieties; he was afraid, and tried to cover his fears by bullying his brother and other boys. At the same time he was also seeking his mother's affection, which he did not get. To say that she was a cold woman does not do her justice, because she had to go out to make a living. That she did not understand her children is another matter, and that she was compulsorily demanding of them is a thing we can comprehend because she tried to do for them what her husband had left undone. She had, however, no concept of what they really wanted. In all her actions toward them, particularly toward Mike, she was not only a disciplinarian, but drove him almost as if he were a lifeless object. Mike reacted to that. Instead of living up to his mother's expectation, he became a "bad" boy, which was his revenge for not getting the love he wanted from her. The first manifestations of his rebellion against her were playing truant and stealing. In doing so he attained one of his aims, which was to attract the attention of his mother. But this attention was short lived, so when truancy and stealing failed, he became ill, which was another way of obtaining attention. Of course, both his antisocial behavior and his psychosomatic disturbances were phenomena of which he was unaware, though his way of getting revenge over his mother might have had a conscious root.

Mike's sickness was a desperate attempt, almost the last one, to attract his mother's attention. His illness was only part of the picture of an emotional tension in his family, the other part being his antisocial activities. Interestingly enough, the brother did not develop any such manifestations. It is significant that as soon as Mike left home for the institution, he stayed well for some time, and while there, did not display any psychosomatic symptoms. It is equally interesting that when he was to visit his mother, he broke several rules as if unconsciously he did not want to go home. When he came home, he developed the same psychosomatic signs although in a weaker form.

While we see here that the psychosomatic disorder developed after the antisocial symptoms had appeared, two types of manifestations came to the fore, all from one and the same person. The underlying factor in this case was emotional tension in which Mike found himself and which pervaded the whole family situation. Imbedded in his emotional tension was anxiety which possibly had been instrumental in producing his antisocial behavior and psychosomatic disturbances. Anxiety being an expression of the various amounts of tension present in the individual, it may be believed to be the device through which disorders of function of behavior and/or bodily disorders are produced. This anxiety and the way it is expressed depends upon the personality make-up and upon the conflict the person finds in himself as a result of the fears, aggressions or frustrations, desires or revengeful feelings he had developed. The way we express ourselves depends a great deal upon our anxieties. Our being able to handle a situation depends to a large extent on how we cope with our anxieties. Although we, of course, have to handle the situation itself, basically, when we deal with it, we handle our anxieties.

We put our energy into what we want to obtain, and that was certainly the case with Mike. As we have previously stated, the energy in us—the libido—is constant and strives to express itself. When Mike could not express himself sufficiently in the form of playing truant and committing thefts, he resorted to producing psychosomatic symptoms.

I have refrained so far from mentioning that Mike also showed some faint signs of a neurosis. But these were kept in the background because his antisocial behavior and the psychosomatic disturbances dominated the picture. He had, so to speak, no use for developing a neurosis because his criminal activities and his bodily disorders served his purpose very well. When we remember that a psychosomatic disorder in general may arise from emotional conflicts, solved only halfway or not at all because the person's psychological needs are not satisfied, we will see that Mike's emotional needs were always pitted against a domineering mother's will, which was rather of an authoritarian character. When he started with his antisocial activities, he was emotionally maladjusted. It was reported that he always had been a complaining child and that he always stayed close to his mother, which indicates that he tried to be close to her but was rebuffed by her. When he started school, he became more frustrated because now he was farther away from her. When his criminal activities did not seem to satisfy him any more, and did not seem to bring him in closer contact with his mother, he became physically sick, and that appeared to do the trick, at least for a time. Mike did not forget that his illness had kept his mother home, and that feeling seems to have followed him in the ensuing years when he suffered from the fever.

The psychotherapy he received in the institution helped him to see his difficulties, engrossed as he was in his mother. He was unable to express his resentment and hostility against her whom he considered unapproachable. He could therefore only rebel against her indirectly; but in expressing this rebellion he also diverted his energy into channels which were psychosomatic in nature. He took his whole body including his mind into account in trying to over-

107

come his emotional difficulties. His first reaction to his school environment had been that of antisocial activities; when they were not sufficient, he had found an outlet in psychosomatic disturbances against himself, all of which came about because he felt emotionally deprived.

Another case was that of a girl, Kate, who had been arrested and put in jail several times for thefts. She was the youngest of a family of one brother and two sisters, who had good positions. Kate's father was sickly and lived on a pension, so her mother had to support the family by keeping roomers. The mother was a rather domineering person, intellectually superior to her husband. Because of this background there was much bickering and quarreling in the home during which Kate overheard her mother saying that her father had been promiscuous. Kate was quite sick as a child, and suffered from mumps, scarlet fever and pneumonia for which she spent many months in the hospital. In the next couple of years she had boils on her arms and legs which required lancing and which also kept her in the hospital. Here, however, she seemed to feel happy. When she grew older she had diarrhea a number of times, each bout lasting for a couple of weeks. She also suffered from menstrual pains for which she was given treatment.

When Kate was about fifteen, she ran away from home with one of her mother's roomers, who left her stranded in a large city where she took to drink. In the course of two years she developed quite a taste for alcohol. Then her mother came to town and took her home, where she stayed for a few years. Then Kate moved East and stayed with the younger of her sisters, who in the meantime had received professional training. She married, and everything seemed fine. Then one day she walked into a store and stole a few dresses. At the trial the judge gave her a suspended sentence. In the course of a year she took several articles from stores and from acquaintances, for which she was sent to jail. When she finally was seen by us, she had again been charged with theft.

Kate was an attractive, somewhat stout girl, who was distinctly passive, although one would not think so at first glance. Physical examination was negative except for elevated blood pressure. It was noteworthy that perhaps more important to her than her parents was her sister with whom she was in strong competition. At first, when Kate talked about her sister, she always praised her, sometimes too much, so that we received the impression that she hated her, a fact which she later admitted. Kate tried to outdo her sister, and to be the one to get the most attention. Since she had disliked school, in contrast to her sister, she had become ill in all sorts of ways. Of course, one can hardly help it if he gets mumps or pneumonia or some other infectious disease, although one can do something to protect oneself, for instance, stay away from the infectious sources. But Kate did not do that. Whenever her sisters or brother were sick, she was sure to get the same disease. She was able, thereby, to attract the same attention as the others. But she enjoyed being sick. When she was in the hospital, she did not want to go home, and if she came home, she used all types of devices to get back to the hospital.

It is evident from Kate's personality make-up, that there were a great many self-sacrificing elements which tended to make her feel content even when she was plagued with all kinds of diseases. Her character traits were deeply masochistic and expressed themselves in various types of behavior and in emotional and physical sicknesses. On the surface she was smiling and amicable, but this was coupled with a great deal of gluttony stemming from a strong oral aggressive drive which covered many of her actions. So pronounced were those oral tendencies that they covered her self-punishing inclinations which had been instigated by her guilt feelings. These guilt feelings were in turn the result of strong hostilities and resentments she felt in particular against her sister. Interesting in this respect is that Kate's thefts often took the character of kleptomania in that she stole articles which did not have any value for her. This self-punishing mechanism brings about manifestations of criminal activities and/or psychosomatic disturbances, depending upon the situation.

Thus, in childhood Kate reacted to her environment by displaying bodily disorders of psychosomatic origin, which followed her through early adolescence and adulthood. Since her sister made her feel rejected, Kate developed fears and anxieties and reacted to this rejection by attempting to obtain attention so she could be taken care of by her family or by someone else. To be taken care of fitted well also into her passive personality, which reached its extreme expression when she became sick, or when she became drunk, or when she stole. Thereby she put herself in a position of a little baby who always had to be cared for and who always had to be given attention. Whether she became ill, or whether she committed crimes—in either case she had to be taken care of. Her crimes and illnesses thus served the same purpose.

In this case, as in so many others seen during our research, psychosomatic disturbances and criminal activities were interchangeable. Sometimes we found delinquents who, when they committed crimes, did not display any psychosomatic signs; it was when they were in prison they developed these symptoms. One such case was that of Nick, who had been charged with thefts for which he had served several sentences. I cannot go into all the interesting details of his case, but shall give only the high lights.

Nick's father was a heavy drinker who was very severe toward the boy. When Nick was eight years old, he started to stay out at night with the result that his father punished him severely. As a child, Nick was seriously ill several times and his mother's sister, in whose home he grew up, became overprotective toward him. He witnessed upsetting scenes between his father and a woman who later proved to be his real mother, but who was married to another man. Nick did not learn about that until he was thirteen. Several times he saw this woman thrown out of his home by the father who got angry when she visited them and brought candy for Nick. When he was eight, he stole some money from a small girl, and that incident initiated him upon a long career of antisocial activities. Nick described to me how, when he committed his first theft, he was thrilled; he felt it almost like a physical elevation which lasted as long as he stood there taking the money. It was almost like "having an orgasm." He had the same feeling when he first drove a car and the first time he rode a bike. At this same age he started masturbation.

When at thirteen, he learned that the woman whom he thought was his mother was only his stepmother, he reacted by misbehavior and stealing in school so he was expelled. Shortly thereafter, Nick

110

was involved in several thefts while drunk and was sent to a reformatory for about a year. While there, he developed facial tics
which lasted for almost an hour several times during the day, and
which increased when it was noticed or when he was teased about
it. When he left the reformatory, he started his stealing anew and
the twitching diminished or stopped.

Two years later he was back in the reformatory and his tics reap-
peared and lasted during the whole of his stay. Within the next few
years, Nick was in and out of the reformatory four times. During
imprisonment, his facial twitching persisted; upon release, he reverted to stealing and the twitching disappeared. When he was
paroled he received psychiatric help; he fell in love with a girl and
married her. The gratifying result was that then his symptoms
practically disappeared, or at least became so rare they did not
bother him.

Apparently two factors were responsible for the fact that
Nick's psychosomatic disturbances were overcome in the main—his
psychoanalysis and his marriage. When he left the institution for
the last time, he entered into a family situation in which he felt
more secure and where, in contrast to his previous family life, the
emotional tension was less. It is interesting that his treatment
brought out the fact that Nick's dreams and fantasy life always
centered around a frustrating character—a woman or women figures—who could be identified as a mother.

His fantasy life was intimately connected with the type of
thefts he committed. He always stole from containers or boxes—
slot machines, telephone boxes or purses. He developed the technique of snatching purses into a fine art. He had always yearned for
his mother's love and affection, which had been denied him since
she married a man other than his father. When his desperate attempts to regain her love were unsuccessful, he tried to regain
something that symbolically stood for his mother. When he broke
up a slot machine or telephone box, he had no idea that as a con-
tainer it could be compared with a uterus which symbolized his
mother. During his treatment he realized this, and he then understood emotionally that his stealing was in reality a seeking of his
mother.

The pivotal point in Nick's case is that his facial tic during imprisonment alternated with his stealing when he was free. In his emotional deprivation and his desire to regain his missed love, he had developed neurotic-like symptoms with self-punishing tendencies which led into antisocial activities alternating with psychosomatic disturbances. His tics seem to have been a vicarious expression for his crimes. His oral orientation, as revealed by his drinking, showed itself in the nature of the facial tics; they were originally oriented around the mouth in muscles which functionally have some connection with the chewing movements of the jaw.

It is noteworthy that Nick was looking and waiting for a mother who could take care of him; he finally succeeded when he found himself a wife who was able to fulfill his needs in this respect. Notwithstanding his criminal activities he was a passive type of man, a passivity which was intimately related to his oral drive. This passive, dependent, conforming person we find quite frequently among thieves and embezzlers who select this type of crime as an expression of their particular instinctual urges which are so closely allied to their oral drive.

Among the delinquents we saw were many who were prone to accidents. We examined fifteen of them, mostly children who had been in all sorts of accidents which were expressions of a self-punishing mechanism. It was characteristic that several of them did not display so much anxiety as we would expect; they were rather of the blundering type who "happened" into or who "dared" themselves into accidents. Among the children we found that most had been truant from school or had committed some thefts without really developing an antisocial character. All of these youngsters, many of whom had sought help in child-guidance clinics or outpatient departments of hospitals, were investigated thoroughly as to their family background. It was surprising to find how many of their parents or grandparents had themselves been prone to accidents. It was evident that the child living with this type of parent might have been predisposed to develop the same form of sickness. This form of identification with his parent might, at least to some extent, reflect some identity on the part of the child with his father or mother, an identification which possibly was instrumental in preventing him from forming an antisocial character.

Although, as mentioned previously, we also found psychosomatic disorders among neurotic and psychotic patients, such disturbances among the delinquents seemed to be more intense. The reason for a more solid infiltration of the psychosomatic illnesses in the delinquent person and members of his family was found to be due to a different type of emotional tension in the family. Although family tension was present in both groups, in the offender's family it was usually of a greater degree, possibly because of his greater hostility. The reason for this may be that the neurotic persons in the non-offender's family have been usually subjected to a stronger Superego influence than in the offender's where ethical training frequently is at a minimum. Because the delinquent individual's hostility is often uninhibited, the tension is expressed more freely than in the neurotic or psychotic family, although of course there are exceptions to that rule, which we will take up in the next chapter.

In many of the control patients the psychosomatic symptoms seemed to lessen or disappear and in their stead we saw paranoid signs or other manifestations of projection. In the delinquent, on the other hand, the psychosomatic disorders occurred instead of their crimes, in fact seemed to be a substitute for their antisocial tendencies and acts. We found that their psychic energy, their libido, alternated. In one period we found an emotional or mental disorder and in another period an antisocial act took place, all of which reveals that a quantitative replacement occurred.

Since we found the psychosomatic disorders so massively present in the delinquent and among members of his family, we have to question whether or not his anxiety has become to a greater or lesser degree infiltrated in his bodily structure and has called forth a bodily disorder. This particular circumstance leads us to ask whether these psychosomatic disturbances may not help determine the degree of susceptibility to criminal behavior. We have pointed out that if the individual's instinctive energy is not modified, the Ego will be weak, unable to function well, and the Superego formation will be disturbed. Since we have assumed that the presence of psychosomatic illness or an emotional disorder is a question of a quantitative replacement of energy or libido, and since we find psychosomatic disorders allied to antisocial activities, it follows that these manifestations reflect a certain emotional state. In the cases we have described we saw that a certain antisocial development of the individual's character had taken place. This character deformation is to a high degree responsible for a person's becoming receptive to criminal activities.

It is interesting in this connection that August Aichorn in his famous book, *Wayward Youth,* speaks of a state called "latent delinquency." He comes to the conclusion that during this state there will not be overt criminal behavior unless a deformed character structure of the individual already exists. This distorted character we found in the cases just here mentioned; and what is more interesting, we found it together with the extreme presence of psychosomatic disorders, reflecting a certain emotional state interwoven with the person's deformed character. I have in my previous writings stated that there must exist a susceptibility to criminal activities. The presence of psychosomatic disturbances in an offender is a new device of his to cope with energy he does not know how to handle. Those people who constantly develop psychosomatic symptoms in order to ward off certain difficult situations reveal that to a large extent their character is involved.

We shall have to raise the question whether we can relate certain personality structure with psychosomatic disorders to certain types of delinquent individuals. Experience has led us to assume that certain types of offenders, as, for instance, those suffering from epilepsy or with an epileptic temperament, behave in an overtly aggressive manner against person or property. We have previously noted that each person selects the type of crime he commits and that this selection depends upon the form his instinctual development took and how much of an imprint this development left upon the formation of the Superego structure and upon the evolution of the Ego. These elements, together with environmental situational factors which bring about the emotional state of the individual, decide overwhelmingly what type of crime or what type of psychosomatic disease or any other form of illness he chooses. Thus we cannot say conclusively that a personality disorder is the cause of criminal activity any more than we can say that a personality disturbance *per se* may be the cause of psychosomatic disturbances. The emotional state rather than the personality type determines the form of social or antisocial behavior, and this emotional state, being the result of a long development, is tied up with the emotional tension in the family.

In a way we can say that the person's psychosomatic disturbances are to some extent antisocial in that he incapacitates himself and puts himself consciously or unconsciously apart from other individuals. It is true that while he shows psychosomatic symptoms, he may also commit antisocial acts; on the other hand, he may display bodily disturbances without committing any crimes. But these disorders which seem to be so deeply imbedded in the structure of the individual must have gone on for a long time in him. Since these psychosomatic disturbances are so constant in their presence, it indicates that they express something within the person which is characteristic of his make-up and follows him as shadow follows light. Only when there is a quantitative substitution will there arise symptoms such as antisocial behavior, or other types of emotional expression. This brings us to the conclusion that the appearance of psychosomatic disturbances depends mostly upon a character deformation. This deformation may not necessarily be so pronounced as to change the individual into an antisocial character. Psychosomatic disorders may be rather a defense against antisocial inclinations and can be considered the first step, or another step, in trying to handle a certain situation.

I do not know whether the reader is aware of the implications of what I have just said. The psychosomatic disturbances seem to take a middle place between antisocial activities on the one hand and neurotic and psychotic manifestations on the other, and to link all three emotional expressions together. In the psychosomatic illnesses are incorporated mental and bodily disturbances, while in the neuroses and psychoses are present mainly emotional features which give the particular emotional conditions their characteristics.

The significant point in our investigations is that the whole mechanism of the antisocial person is interwoven with his emotional and physical actions, including the antisocial ones. That indicates that criminal behavior is an expression of human behavior and that neuroses, psychoses, psychosomatic disturbances and antisocial behavior must be considered to be on the same line of human conduct and one, although a different, aspect of human activity. Delinquent behavior is not thus a concern only of the law, but to a higher degree a concern of human beings who should create human institutions which will take this concept into consideration.

Furthermore, we can say that the emotional maladjustment and the psychosomatic disturbances are the results of a faulty development which has taken place at an early stage of the individual's life. It is reasonable to believe that this basic failure is related to the deformation of the person's character which again is tied to his Ego. It must be stated that character is not the same as personality. By character we mean that structure of man which determines his behavior, in short the way he carries out or fails to carry out his actions. A person may, for instance, be aggressive or passive; he will solve his problems either by carrying out aggressive actions, or by complying with the situation without saying or doing anything about it. Character depends to a large extent upon the way the individual goes through the developmental stages.

Because a child lacks understanding of himself and evaluates reality according to his emotions, he is unable to establish constant values and therefore tends to be an unstable character. At least he changes character, so to speak, from day to day. When he becomes an adolescent this same change of attitude occurs although he basically acts according to the way his instinctual urges have developed. We may then say that character contains the individual's basic or predominant set of emotional attitudes and functions which decide his social or antisocial behavior.

The character formation takes place in the child's early years and tends to develop in one rather decided direction, depending upon his instinctual forces. Character deformation seems also to be prevalent among those offenders who show psychosomatic disturbances. We can here object and say that this deformation is related rather to the antisocial than to the psychosomatic aspect of the individual, but as was pointed out previously, the psychosomatic disturbances are so persevering and solid that they possibly must be considered a constant earmark, and that earmark is the person's twisted character. We are then able to point out that a mutual indicator for psychosomatic disturbances and criminal behavior is to be found in the individual's character traits. We may conclude that the common denominator for disturbances both in bodily functions and in social behavior is to a great extent related to the deformed character of the person.

We may now better understand that the complicated psychological processes which take place in the mind of the offender as the result of a personality reaction are by and large reactions which may be compared with those found in a *disease*.

For the first time, this research gives us the reasons for a better understanding of the individual's social and antisocial behavior. For the first time, we are able to build a bridge between *social* and psychobiological functions.

This is a fundamental approach. Up to now we have been unable to bridge man's functions and social manifestations, the reason being that the social scientist was interested mainly in what occurred in society while the medical doctor was concerned with what happened to his patient. Only indirectly, through public health, did the medical man become important to society as a whole, by eliminating epidemic diseases, for instance, or controlling water supply. The physician was a person who by and large knew more and more about man, but less and less about the society in which he walked. The social scientist, for his part, was able to gather many significant data about society and its many institutions, but knew little about the man who lived and breathed in that society. In particular, his knowledge of the working of the mind of the man was minimal. A gulf existed between the medical doctor and social scientist, and it was reflected in their concepts of man's and society's functions. What both missed is that man does not live in a vacuum, and that society cannot function without man.

That a person becomes ill is in general of concern only to himself and his nearest ones. Society as such is not interested very much in his disease, unless it so incapacitates him that he must be publicly supported. However, if the individual, instead of becoming physically ill, commits a crime, then society considers his deed an attack upon itself and tries to see that he is apprehended so he can be punished. Although the crime may have and often does have a quite different meaning to the offender than to society, society feels threatened and must punish. To the delinquent person, however, his crime had a definite although frequently hidden meaning. This difference in outlook was enough to furnish a starting point in investigating the merits of the citizen and the virtues of society. It was difficult enough to find the intimate connection between man and society, but that difficulty was increased immensely when it came to ascertaining the relationship between the criminal and society. This difficulty was enlarged because old prejudice and obstinate ignorance made people believe that the offender was apart from all life.

The history of the offender is that of his meeting with the law as the only expression of society and its interests toward him. It was when medicine was on the march that the delinquent person first became a part of the doctor's orbit, but only when he was physically or mentally sick. By and large society forgot that the offender was an individual human being and that he could not be pigeonholed like some kind of garden seed.

I have tried to show that each man acts in accordance with his personality make-up and that his working medium is his family, community or society at large. That part of the historical development is hardly history because it is so recent. But we could not go further in our studies until we started to investigate the relationship between criminal activities and psychosomatic disturbances. In my research I had to choose a function or an expression of man which was present both in the mind and in the body. That expression was a psychosomatic disorder. We had all too long been puzzled by the fact that we had been unable to combine the individual's psychobiological activities with the social ones. One reason for this may have been that we did not know of a common expression from mind and body of man until we found it in the psychosomatic disturbances.

When we find other common denominators for social and human activities, we shall be able to establish a real basis for understanding human relations and social and antisocial actions. These projected findings will possibly have to be performed by medical men and will put medicine in its just place.

6

Crime and Mental Illness

WHEN, in 1925, I started my clinical clerkship at the Royal Norwegian University Clinic in Oslo, we were one day making the rounds with our professor. He was at that time in his sixties and we considered him old, although thinking today of my own age I believe he was young. The professor was comfortably seated in a chair while we were standing around listening to him, when we suddenly heard high screams in the corridor. We all rushed out and saw a young fellow running toward us with two men in close pursuit. The frightened young man took refuge behind us. At that point the professor asked what was the matter. The pursuers explained that the young man was a criminal whom they had been trailing for several days. They had seen him walking into the hospital and had orders to take him to the police station.

One of the detectives started to walk behind us to catch the man, but the professor shot out like lightning and placed himself between them. "This man is a criminal," said the detective in a determined voice and made a grab for him. The professor stood straight as a ramrod and retorted, "I have no criminals here, I have only sick people." And pointing, he added one word: "Go!" The detectives looked at each other, turned around and left slowly.

As it turned out, the much sought-after man was a patient in the out-patient department. He suffered from a peptic ulcer and had that day come to the clinic so he could be given proper care and, incidentally, be protected against the police.

Never will I forget that little scene many years ago in the corridor of the hospital. The professor had no criminals, he had only sick people. At that moment I did not realize that some years later I myself was going to occupy my time and efforts with sick people.

I shall not go into the legal complications surrounding the case. Here I would like to raise the question: Are there any normal criminals? Is it possible that a man would choose to become a robber or a murderer, become imprisoned, possibly die in the electric chair, if he had another way out? Of course, we don't know what constitutes a so-called normal man, but even if we are unable to delineate him, we should at least try to limit the frame within which the normal man functions. Let it here be repeated that we do not know where the border is between the normal and the abnormal mind and its functioning. The reason for this is twofold: Firstly, our behavior is governed largely by laws to which we try to adhere; but within these laws there is much room for conduct which is not and could not be covered by any law. A painter or a writer, for instance, who puts down his ideas on canvas or on paper may to the average man appear abnormal, and therefore is often viewed as obscene or immoral while a decade or a generation later his productions are considered well within the framework of the normal man. As a matter of fact, much of the history of creativeness is filled with men fighting against bigotry and set opinions. Beethoven was in his time considered a revolutionary; although he could hardly be considered a normal man, he still produced music which probably will live forever. Today Beethoven is a very much respected man whose music is played in the best circles. That which is within easy grasp of the average man and can be easily understood is accepted at once; in particular, this is the case when the matter follows the thinking of the majority of the public. This is not the case when new thinking is advanced. Surrealism, for instance, which deals so much with the unconscious, has not as yet been accepted because it is not understood, and the painters themselves are often considered odd or queer people. Yet it is not inconceivable that one day soon surrealism will be completely accepted.

We see the same reaction in any other field, in medicine, politics, etc. There has been one exception and that is the delinquent. He has been considered something outside society for a long, long time and has simply not been reckoned with when human behavior in general was considered. Normality or abnormality was not discussed; he was a criminal.

Another reason why it has been so difficult to determine the border between normal and abnormal functioning is that we have not had the proper tools to investigate the minds of the persons involved. True, as time has gone by our tools have been perfected; in addition to our basic psychiatric examination we have developed psychological tests which started out as a sheer measuring of the intelligence, but later evolved to embrace the emotions as well. Beside the Binet-Simon Test and the Bellevue-Wechsler Test, both measuring the intelligence, we have the Projective Personality Test, the Rorschach, Szondi and Thematic Apperception tests; of the Concept Formation-Tests, the Hanfmann-Kasanin and B.R.I. Sorting Tests are often used. That we use those tests does not mean that through them and through our technique of examination we can ascertain all pertinent data about the human mind; we still have a long way to go. Only in the previous chapter did I mention the associative anamnesis as a valuable means of obtaining data particularly about the patient's emotional relationship and emotional attitudes.

Beside the matter of tools for the psychiatric-psychological examination, it was also of concern that the psychiatrist frequently was not given enough time for the examination. This point came very vividly to my mind when, at the end of 1948, we were in the process of examining sex offenders at Sing Sing Prison. Probably for one of the first times in the history of psychiatry, we gave ourselves enough time for a thorough examination of the offenders. Although a psychiatric examination can go on indefinitely because we will always be able to uncover new data, in our investigations here we were at least able to ascertain findings which put the offender in quite a different light than before.

While previously it was believed that many offenders did not show any mental pathology, recent investigations have revealed that from 10 to 20 per cent of them have been mentally ill. While

123

Charles Goring, in 1913 (*The English Convict*), stated that many criminals were mentally defective and that one factor in the etiology of criminal behavior was a defective intelligence, other researchers in this country claimed that mental abnormalities were present in 60 per cent of the offenders. B. Glueck who worked with prisoners at Sing Sing found in 1917 that 12 per cent were mentally diseased, 19 per cent had a psychopathic personality or were constitutionally inferior and 28 per cent were mentally deficient, while one of our most distinguished psychiatrists, Dr. Winfred Overholser, Superintendent at Saint Elizabeth's Hospital, Washington, D.C., found in investigations begun in 1939 and carried out over a span of fourteen years that 14.9 per cent of all prisoners examined under the Briggs Law in Massachusetts were found to be frankly or suggestively abnormal mentally.

Early investigators put undue stress upon the intelligence factor of the delinquent person. They could not understand, and many do not yet realize that the prevalence of mental deficiency found in imprisoned offenders might be due to the fact that they got caught more easily than the intelligent ones. Therefore, the mentally deficient criminal would more often be jailed and, consequently, would turn up more frequently in the statistics. Another point was that if the offender was not outright mentally deficient, then his intelligence was thought to be lower than that of the average man. This too is a fallacy. The examination of the delinquent depends not only upon him but also, within certain limits, upon the examiner's attitude and the care with which he carries it out. In our own test material, we have invariably found a higher I.Q. in the offender than did other examiners. In some cases it has not only been a difference of a few points, for instance from 68 to 75, but as much as from 68 to 88.

In this connection, it is interesting to note that we have thought that a great many sex offenders are mentally defective. Of course, many of them are, but many more suffer from a mental disorder other than mental defectiveness. We found that of 102 sex offenders, 7 were of very superior intelligence, 18 showed superior intelligence, 6 had a high average intelligence, 50 had average intelligence and 18 were of low intelligence. It is true that these offenders were selected as to their crime. Many of them were rapists who were found to be rather intelligent; only a few were exhibitionists among whom we do find many with a low average or mentally deficient intelligence. Nevertheless, these numbers are at least an indication that the offender is not usually an intellectually deficient person. He is deficient, but the deficiency is rather an emotional or psychobiological one.

In all my experience I have not been able to find one single offender who did not show some mental pathology, in his emotions or in his character or in his intelligence. The "normal" offender is a myth. When I speak now of a criminal, I do not mean the man who once commits an inconsequential offense. In my opinion he is not so much an offender as he is a sufferer from some mental abnormalities, although the law might not say so. A few judges have now come around to considering a harmless first-time offender with leniency, which may indicate that the law acknowledges mental aberrant behavior. There is no doubt that if we had sufficiently refined methods of examining delinquent persons, we would find that all of them suffer from some form of mental disorder. I have always claimed this to be the case, but I did not expect my prediction to be so completely fulfilled when we examined the 102 sex offenders. (See: "Report on Study of 102 Sex Offenders at Sing Sing Prison" as submitted to Governor Thomas E. Dewey. March 1950.) Here we found that each one suffered from a deep-seated mental abnormality, either a psychosis, neurosis, a character disorder or another form of an emotional disturbance.

Again, I hasten to repeat that those were sex offenders and, therefore, the conclusions cannot be applied to the general population of offenders. But these numbers are highly suggestive. Furthermore, many of these criminals had committed, in addition to their sex offenses, crimes of other types, so all in all these numbers might still have a great deal of bearing upon the relationship between crime and mental abnormalcy. Let us remember here the findings mentioned in the previous chapter when our research ascertained that all of the subjects showed mental pathology in one form or another. That the larger percentage of them were children and adolescents shows that this pathology starts at an early age and that it is deep-seated.

Our investigations have, in this respect, resulted in findings which have not been revealed so pointedly by other researchers. This is due in part to the fact that we have taken more time in our examinations and have supplemented them extensively with data derived from other methods of investigations. In this respect, our research can be compared with the invention of X ray. Prior to its use many people had fractures which were never discovered because they could not be seen or felt by the physician. Prior to our recent investigations, offenders suffered from mental illnesses which were not detected because of insufficient methods. Our investigations which are also used by other researchers constitute a sort of X-raying of the human mind and are a means of revealing hidden illnesses not detected by the naked eye. It is only fair to add that X-raying the human mind is only an analogy, and, like all analogies, is only partly true. Emotions and motivations cannot be seen; we are aware of them only when the individual is carrying out or has carried out his action.

The important point is now that as we go along and examine persons suffering from a mental illness or individuals who have committed crimes, we will have to change our concept of the various mental disorders. For instance, the lay public believes that a man suffering from schizophrenia (popularly called split personality) should show symptoms of delusions or hallucinations. These symptoms, however, appear mainly in the paranoid form of schizophrenia where ideas of persecution dominate the picture. A man having signs of a simple schizophrenia may have these symptoms, but only very vaguely, almost in passing. So faint may they appear that only a detailed and careful psychiatric observation for many weeks, coupled with a minute psychological testing, can reveal these manifestations and the underlying pathology. In several of these offenders there are present neurotic-like traits, (pseudoneurotic schizophrenia) a neurotic overlay which may confuse an inexperienced observer.

When we consider the core of crime and mental illness, it is well to remember that an overwhelming amount of unconscious emotions goes into the making of an offender. The same is true of a neurotic or a psychotic. The overt difference, then, is that a criminal turns his aggressions outward and often gets locked up, whereas in other forms of mental illness the person turns his hostilities inward and thereby in one way or another locks himself up. In short, a neurotic or a psychotic individual locks himself up, while an offender is locked up by others.

In crime or mental disease, be it a neurosis or a psychosis, the same layers of emotions are acting, but to a different degree and in a different constellation. There has been a great deal of discussion as to why a certain individual becomes an offender instead of developing into a neurotic or a psychotic. Alexander and Healy in their book, *Roots of Crime*, as well as Aichorn, could only state that we did not know the reason why one person became neurotic and another a criminal. They have, however, pointed out that early deprivations predispose a man to becoming a delinquent.

Emotional deprivation is of the most crucial importance in anyone's life and must be considered a significant factor in producing an antisocial and an emotionally unstable individual. Returning to my study cited in the previous chapter, when we examined delinquent individuals together with their families and compared them with patients not manifesting delinquency, we found much more family tension in the case histories of the former than in the latter. This tension between the family members was frequently extreme, with hostility and hatred accompanied by bickering, nagging and quarreling. Sometimes this emotional tension was not so easy to detect, for the defenses were pronounced and difficult to break through. When we had dealt with the family and with the children awhile, it was possible to see how a mother or a father quietly dominated the children, how a child dominated her parents, or how one child was preferred over another one, or how jealous one was of another; how one brother quietly teased his sister, or how the one daughter who became delinquent not only felt rejected, but was herself extremely demanding and rejected everyone else. In the wake of this emotional tension, went emotional deprivation.

Frequently, therefore, we had to seek the emotional tension

within the family and found it present as a strong undercurrent which colored the behavior of the family members. (The reader may refer to my paper, "Family Tension, Basic Cause of Criminal Behavior," *Journal of Criminal Law and Criminology*, Vol. 40, No. 3, Sept.-Oct. 1949.)

A typical case was that of a young girl, Jean, who came to us when she was eight years old. Her parents were bright, in particular her mother, who was also artistically gifted. When they were first referred to us, the report from the agency indicated that the parents were very happy with each other and, therefore, could not understand why Jean had become such a nuisance in the school. They were considered model parents in their community and took an active part in the community life. They were members of the scout group, of the welfare group and of the church and were so busy covering meetings that in order to attend them all, they had to divide them up between them. Frequently it happened that when the mother went out to a meeting, the father came home and shortly thereafter went out to another meeting. The woman professed to love her husband dearly, and he in turn loved her.

We were at a loss at first to understand what really took place in that household. Our only lead was that Jean did not do her work in school, that she often was truant and used such obscene language that her classmates refused to play with her, all of which was confirmed by her teacher when we interviewed her. When Jean continued to write obscene words in her books and on the walls and also became a disciplinary problem, she was referred to an agency who investigated the famly as well as the child but could not find anything particularly wrong about them. Jean was bright so she was able to follow the class work although she had not done any homework for a long time.

In my first interview with the mother she looked rather unhappy, but not more so than could be explained by Jean's behavior. She repeated again and again that she could not understand why the child behaved as she did, because "we are a very happy family; my husband makes a good living, and there is no reason for Jean to be the way she is." She then related all the activities in which they participated and when I suggested that perhaps Jean was jealous and felt rejected by them because they were so often away from home, she laughed it off, saying, "The children are never alone."

I let her talk, but no significant details came out which could give me a clue to all their trouble, until at the end of the interview, I asked her, more out of despair than anything else, if she had had any dreams.

"Dreams," she answered, startled. "Yes, when you ask about that, I had one dream a few days ago." I had no need to ask what the dream was about because she continued immediately: "I dreamt that a man came toward me and embraced me." She looked straight at me scarcely realizing what she had said.

When a few minutes had passed and she did not say any more, I asked whether she knew who that man in the dream was.

"Oh, yes," she said hurriedly, "he was a man to whom I was engaged before I met my husband."

The words had hardly left her mouth before she started to cry bitterly. Then she told me between sobs that she had been engaged twice before she married her husband. He was her third choice, not even her second choice, and she married him because that was the thing she had to do since, according to her father, she could not stay unmarried. The marriage had been a failure from the start because she found out very soon that she did not love him. She hated him and resented him, only spoke to him when he spoke to her. For several years they had not had any sexual relations with each other, and when the whole community spoke of her and her husband as "model parents," it was an outright lie. She had tried to bury her hostile feelings against her husband, and tried to avoid him as much as possible. That was the reason, contrary to what the neighbors thought, why they chose to attend different meetings of the community activities.

That the parents hated each other and consequently had quite opposite ideas about how Jean and her brothers were to be raised brought about many clashes between them, but of a nature so subtle that the mother and father were able to deceive the whole community and the referring agency. The parents tried desperately to hide their differences from Jean but did not succeed, because she resented the way they ordered her about and was angry at being so

129

rejected by them. Her greatest rebellion was probably against the way her parents acted toward each other, because she realized unknowingly that they did not love each other and therefore did not love her. Her protest was against her lack of love, which resulted from the lack of love between the parents. They had permitted their resentments and hatred to grow; their emotions had become so twisted that, on the conscious level, they had no idea of the root of their unhappiness. They had tried to suppress what they did not like to face, and without their knowing it, had developed contempt for each other. All of this resulted in an emotional tension which could not be seen on the surface, but only felt. And the one who felt it most was Jean.

Ignoble emotions such as these, kept hidden long enough, can be covered up with rationalizations, but they break through sooner or later, and when they do, the result is disastrous.

Jean reacted severely to the home situation. Being emotionally deprived, she sought her own ways which led her to alienate herself from her parents and to commit antisocial acts.

Behind all emotional difficulties there is to be found some childhood deprivation, some wound which has caused the mind to twist and turn until a neurosis, psychosis, psychosomatic disorder or some other disorder such as a criminal one sets in. In criminal behavior we find the supreme emotional family tension and emotional deprivation, and therefore the supreme wound, which results in the supreme final reaction.

Fundamentally, I have found that more than the economic or social position of the family, the *emotional* relationship between parents and children influences character development. Our experience proves that family tension, even of a subtle nature, breeds criminals. Homes where there is bickering and nagging cause children to tighten up with resentment and hostility, resulting in their rebellion against authority and their responding to delinquent stimuli. It is this hostility we have found so pronounced in every offender. If it does not take an outright form, there may be a tendency to spiteful revenge or resentment or jealousy, but always the hostility is turned against someone else.

When this hostility for one or another reason cannot be turned outward, the child may direct it against himself as we have described previously. That is to say, stresses and strains within the developmental period can cause a child to become physically as well as mentally ill, and also to strike out with antisocial acts. Therefore, a person can, because of childhood traumas and an intolerable home atmosphere, develop a neurosis or psychosis, become physically ill or even commit a crime.

The reason, then, why one individual develops into a criminal, and another one shows signs of emotional or physical disorder, may lie in the family tension. Since the emotional tension in the family hangs together with the emotional state of the individual, it is logical to think that criminal activities reflect a family tension definitely different from that of the neurotic or psychotic individual. When this is the case, we cannot treat the delinquent person as an individual but as a member of the family, who lives and functions within that unit, a point we will take up in Chapter X.

On the surface the offender has much the same background as the mentally ill person, but when we probe into the emotional relationships and study the degrees of emotional tension, we are frequently struck with the difference between them. The difference in tension can be understood when we remember that the neurotic or psychotic person is raised in an environment where there has been at least some development of a conscience or some regulating force bearing some resemblance to moral standards of human conduct. It is true that frequently we do find among those people a strongly developed Superego structure, which often tends to lead them into a suppressive or submissive rather than an uninhibited way of life. That is, by the way, one reason why some people become either neurotic, psychotic or physically ill; they have never learned to express themselves.

In the delinquent family, therefore, we find uninhibited emotional expressions with heated discussions and emotional outbursts which give the tension here an acute color. This is in contrast to the neurotic or psychotic family where the tension is by and large more inhibited. Of course we do sometimes also find these acute signs here too.

This tension among members of the offender's family brings in its wake the deformation of the character of the person which makes him into an antisocial individual. The main characteristic of the delinquent person is that his character formation has deviated from the average individual. This character deformation varies in degrees and accounts to a large extent for the difference between the seriousness of the individual offences.

Before we can consider further some of the mechanisms we have uncovered in those who commit delinquent acts, we first have to go into some of the most frequent forms of mental illness, psychosis and neurosis.

It is quite normal for all of us to have daydreams of one kind or another. It is when the daydreams have us that it is abnormal. That is, so long as we keep our dreams within bounds and do our jobs and face reality, we do not need to worry. We have then developed toward the Reality Principle and adhere to it. When we, however, become slaves to our dreams and thereby live in a world that centers only on ourselves, there is a need for concern. The psychotic person does this so that he is completely shut off from his surroundings, from reality. He cannot communicate with people around him, because he has withdrawn from them into his own world with his own dreams. We find him shy, without friends, unable to express his feelings since he has repressed or suppressed them. The result is that he gets more and more withdrawn, so he becomes completely narcissistic.

Such a person may go along for a long time and live his life without anything happening to him, but he is unable to form any emotional relationship with anyone. These people always live on a superficial emotional level. They are lone wolves. They may live with you without your knowing them and their knowing you. They dream about themselves, about carrying out great deeds and becoming heroes or martyrs. The connection between such a man and the surrounding world is very thin, and so it happens that when this thin tie suddenly breaks, then he breaks off any link with reality and he lives by himself. He is psychotic—most frequently, though not always, of a schizophrenic type. But not all psychotic persons are schizophrenics, since there are many types of psychosis.

A person may develop such a psychosis if there is great stress and strain which he wants to leave or cannot stand; he then tries to withdraw from reality and withdraws too far.

Into the making of a schizophrenic person go certain definite experiences in childhood and adolescence and/or possibly some unknown constitutional factors. The one earmark of a schizophrenic person is that he cannot identify himself as a man or a woman. He forgets who he is and what his name is. One patient I saw some years ago insisted that he was "Mrs. Smith" and that he was the "mother" to his children.

Schizophrenia is a major psychosis; a neurosis is often called a minor psychosis. The psychotic is completely absorbed with himself; the neurotic is absorbed to a lesser extent. The main difference between them is that in the neurotic individual there is no break with reality. A neurosis differs from all other diseases in that it is characterized by a disturbance of the functioning of the individual. While in a physical disease one or several organs may be sick, in a neurosis the co-ordinating center of the person, his Ego, is disturbed. The central element in a neurosis is that experiences we have had in infancy, childhood or early adolescence are repressed. As we have said before: No emotion is ever forgotten; if it does not have the proper outlet, the emotion will seek another way out, until it is expressed unconsciously. The main symptom of a neurosis, and for that matter of a psychosis, is that the person finds himself in a conflict. Both the neurotic and psychotic person come into being when their repression or their suppression has not been successfully mastered.

In the course of a neurotic illness we find symptoms of a psychogenic nature, that is, manifestations which arise in the mind of the person and prevent him from doing his work, or plainly speaking, from functioning. These symptoms are, for instance, fear of heights or open spaces or fear of traveling from home. Such phobias are irrational and to a large extent incapacitating. Other signs can be hysterical paralysis, washing mania, impotence, frigidity, etc. All those symptoms can be in a lesser degree present in people we call normal. What is significant is that most of these neurotic persons are able to stay within the law. The obsessive-compulsory individual who harbors pronounced hostile feelings has a strongly developed Superego and, therefore, shows most frequently a rigid conduct which keeps him within the boundaries of the law.

The normal person or the individual who tends to keep within the law without developing any predominant neurotic signs have this in common with the offender: they both try insofar as it is possible to make their dreams come true. The difference is that the so-called normal person tries to do it in a logical and methodical fashion; the offender does it without regard to anyone else but himself, while at the same time overlooking the reality factors. Then too the fantasies of the well person and the criminal are of an altogether different nature. Whereas the adjusted person frequently has constructive dreams, the offender often has dreams of wanting to hurt to make up for his own hurts, in effect to take what was kept from him before. By the very method he uses, he also proves his need for punishment for his evil deeds.

There has been altogether too much literature on the market— and bland acceptance of it what's more—to the effect that offenders act out their aggressions and therefore get rid of them all. According to this theory, they throw all their hatred against the world rather than against themselves. Thus they are set apart as a special *kind* of person. Nothing could be further from the truth.

To begin with, although the offender against society may seem to rid himself of his hostilities by acting them out, he does so only for the moment—a release, incidentally, that neurotics and psychotics do not have because they are too inhibited. However, with each new crime an offender builds a thicker wall between himself and society, which makes it more difficult for him to live in this world. In addition, he also has going on within him those temptations and desires to which he does not and cannot give expression. Therefore, rather than a simple release, he has his original fantasies, the acting out of them, the punishment received therefore, and still more fantasies to torment him.

Since a neurotic or psychotic disorder takes place because the individual's suppression or repression has been unsuccessful, we might say that, objectively speaking, the criminal is a normal person inasmuch as he rids himself of his emotional tension by giving vent to his feelings.

The fact that the delinquent person is in conflict with himself and with society is demonstrated by his constant repetition of his crimes. If through every crime he tries to liberate himself from his emotions, then there is obviously an accumulation of emotions within him that are seeking release and an answer to the conflict that goes on within him.

Sometimes I wonder how much proof we must have to show that offenders do not merely act out their difficulties and thereby rid themselves of them until next time. Rather than a simple mechanism in the minds of those who step outside the law, it appears that there is an involved one indeed. There are many deep and devious workings within this sphere of life that are seldom evident on the surface. I do not need to remind the reader about our findings previously mentioned, that the offender and/or his family is more often physically ill, that his anxieties seem to be greater, and that he very often commits a crime because he unconsciously desires punishment. It is an old and all-too-true theory that the criminal often returns to the scene of his crime.

To put it simply, we could say that a man becomes neurotic, psychotic or shows psychosomatic disturbances because he does not dare to express himself in a general way or is afraid of expressing outwardly his asocial or antisocial desires. People who do not act out their criminal tendencies (and these are very often the ones who sit in judgment on those that do) find a substitute expression in mental and/or physical illness. Many neurotic, psychotic or other manifestations can be considered vicarious expressions of antisocial behavior. The mental and physical symptoms an individual manifests is to a large extent the price he has to pay because he does not have the guts to express himself. These symptoms are signals of a man in distress and indicate that his Id impulses are fighting with his Superego. This does not mean that his conscience is wrong, but that somehow his Superego is too strict for him.

The offender too does not have the guts to express himself at the right time and in the right place, and all the mental, physical and antisocial signs express a maladjusted individual.

Actually, it is normal to express hostility if kept within limits and to act out one's aggressions. Were it not for the fact that the so-called criminal is so irrational, both in his method of committing crime and in the various neurotic symptoms he shows, the fact of his acting out his conflicts would mean that he was normal.

The constant characteristic we find in criminals is their overwhelming abnormal emotions and effects. That they possess and give in to these emotions is due to the original existence of severe emotional and social pathology in their early home lives. They all show the effects of having parents one or both of whom were sadistic and dominating. If the parents themselves ignore the law, the child will then either imitate them by doing likewise; or he might possibly rebel by becoming exceptionally good, and later showing his opposition to his parents by becoming ill or breaking the law. The latter again demonstrates the irrationality of criminals.

The offender, then, might be said to be a person suffering from a mental disturbance; or a mentally disturbed person might be said to be a criminal. Intrinsically they are practically interchangeable. The over-all surface difference might be said to be that a criminal is more outwardly maladapted to society. His actions, resulting from his emotions, place him in a sort of twilight wherein he acts in a way that he should not, and yet deep down he feels he not only can act, but he must and will.

It is extremely difficult to point out the different and the similar characteristics of the mentally sick person and the delinquent, particularly since we frequently find offenders who also show symptoms of a neurosis or a psychosis. Yet, for the last few years I have found it helpful to call my students' attention to the different criteria of the criminal and the emotionally disturbed individual. Let us, therefore, start with the differences between the neurotic person and the criminal.

1. The neurotic person has within him a conflict which he turns completely against himself by producing emotional or physical symptoms. Although the criminal frequently turns his aggressions against himself, he most often turns them against society and thereby attacks or injures a second or third party. He will not renounce his antisocial tendencies, but will try to see them satisfied, if only in a symbolic way. Here too, the crime is more important for the unconscious than the conscious.

2. The neurotic individual suffers from conflicts which basically are always related to the sexual drive. As far as we know today this is also true of many neurotic offenders such as kleptomaniacs, fire-setters or sex offenders and some people who commit crimes because of guilt feelings for which they unconsciously want to be punished. In most other cases a criminal's acts are tied up with his Ego functioning, his Ego drives, if such an expression can be used, and with the aggressions thereby called forth.

3. The neurotic person is satisfied with a desire in his fantasy while the criminal must transform his fantasy into action in order to be gratified. As a matter of fact, the main neurotic symptom and also a symptom in psychosis is a substitute satisfaction in fantasy. Though there is a great difference between criminal fantasies and the actual carrying out of a crime, antisocial fantasies, as pointed out before, are most frequent in those suffering from a neurosis. An individual with homosexual leanings, for instance, may be pre-occupied with such fantasies but not actually carry them out, while a neurotic homosexual may have such fantasies and carry them out in reality. As we will understand, it is a question of whether he follows the Pleasure or Pain Principle. Fantasies are really ideas with which the person is preoccupied. The offender may elaborate them and ultimately carry them out, while the neurotic person goes over and over them in his mind and simply lets them stay there.

4. In the neurotic individual, the Superego is strongly developed, as seen particularly in the obsessive-compulsory neurotic person. These persons are strongly inhibited because their Superego is over-developed and that structure checks their instinctual drives. In contrast to this evolution of the conscience, a faulty development of the Superego takes place in the offender so that he is over-whelmed by his instinctual impulses. Compared with the obsessive individual, the delinquent person's Superego is small. Even in those neurotic persons who commit crimes because of strong guilt feelings and therefore give the impression of an extremely strong conscience, the Superego should rather be considered hypertrophic and hollow because of constant exposure to their strong unconscious instinctual drives.

5. Strongly connected with a faulty development of the Super-ego in an offender is also the faulty development of his Ego functioning. Not only does he have an undeveloped Superego, but his Ego is weak as well, all of which leads to a faulty formation of his character, the formation of an antisocial character. When we talk in a general way about a criminal, we most often say he does not have any character. In one sense this is correct, because he has no guide within himself. He yields to the side where the pressure is heaviest, and even if no stress is present, he may suddenly take off on an adventure without too many scruples. What he really does is to commit acts against others. His Ego and Superego being weak, he has developed on the contrary an antisocial, a destructive character. The antisocial character is the earmark of the delinquent person.

The character of the neurotic individual is by and large normal—as seen in a hysterical person—or he reveals an overdeveloped Super-ego—as seen in an obsessive-compulsory person.

6. This different development of character takes place where there is family tension present of a particular type and degree as described before. The acute family tension with emotional outbursts is instrumental in bringing about an antisocial character in an individual; under stress and strain, he will develop rather into a criminal than into a neurotic person. If an individual shows criminal tendencies for instance late in his teens, it is not because he suddenly became a delinquent at that time, but because he has suffered from a distorted character formation which has been hidden since his childhood. Where threats of punishment alternate with overindulgence, the latter being caused by the domineering member's guilt feelings, it will, as pointed out before, bring to the fore an antisocial character. If, in addition, he has suffered from early emotional deprivations, this development will be furthered.

I want in this connection to mention our comprehensive research at Sing Sing, which dealt with sex offenders (See *Report to Governor Dewey*) and which showed that all offenders had experienced in their infancy or in their childhood devastating emotional deprivation. That many of these people were deprived financially was not so much of a trauma as their being deprived of emotional warmth for a considerable length of time. Some of these young men were spoiled and overprotected. Such an overprotection works in reality as a deprivation because an overindulged child will on certain points have to give in to the domineering parent. Interestingly enough, while we find that offenders in general have had one or more predominant traumatic events in their lives, the sex offenders we examined had experienced several of these events spread out over a whole life span through early and late infancy, early and late childhood and adolescence. Charlie, for instance, was brought up by parents who were both alcoholics and had violent fights between them. I quote from our report to Governor Dewey: "First time a social worker visited their home, the mother threatened to use her small baby as a weapon with which to strike the social worker. That baby was Charles. When he was eleven months old, his father was sent to the workhouse for kicking his pregnant wife in the stomach. The children were taken to an orphanage. Soon afterwards the mother died of alcoholism.

"The baby was later returned to his grandfather, who was a brawling drunkard like the baby's parents. Then he dwelt with his father who lived with a succession of women. It was recorded, when he was four, that he had witnessed his father's sexual relations with two different women.

"His earliest memories, confirmed by documents, are of the continued beatings his father gave him. He ran away several times, and was beaten soundly when brought home. He remembers that he was always running away and never knew where he was running. From the age of twelve to sixteen he lived in an orphanage and an institution for juvenile delinquents, from both of which he ran away numerous times, to live by petty crime.

"At thirteen, he had sexual relations with a girl in the orphanage, but even before this he had begun practice of sodomizing younger boys.

"At sixteen, on request of his custodians, he was sent on to a State School for delinquents with a maximum term of three years. A year later he was released on parole.

"He had been at liberty a month when a policeman picked him up for trying to persuade a little girl to go into a cellar with him.

139

Then he confessed that a few days previously he had taken the five-year-old daughter of an acquaintance into a basement and sexually abused her. Probably he had committed offenses against other little girls and boys. He said he saw nothing wrong about this. He had no pangs of conscience about that type of act. He was sentenced, to serve from five to ten years in prison. . . ."

In this case Charles' Ego had become distorted. Because of his incessant frustrations and his strong instinctual drives, his character became crippled and antisocial.

This is an extreme case of emotional deprivation, but recalling that a child is sensitive and that very frequently it is not a question of how much he is deprived in reality as of how much he feels he is deprived, then we may understand that a character deformation will arise if a child has lacked even a reasonable amount of gratification. An antisocial character originates in a person who either has strong instincts and has experienced early emotional deprivation, or in an individual where this deprivation constantly alternates with gratification.

7. Delinquent persons seem to suffer a higher degree of psychosomatic disturbances than non-delinquent ones. In particular, we find a higher incidence of psychosomatic illnesses in the family members of the offender than in the neurotic or psychotic non-offender's family. The psychosomatic disturbances are often used as an excuse to commit criminal acts, and sometimes these disorders occur vicariously with antisocial manifestations. These physical illnesses seem to be located in the gastro-intestinal tract more often in the offender than in the neurotic or psychotic non-offender. More research to validate this finding is necessary.

I have tried here to give the differences between delinquent and neurotic behavior. For the sake of clarity I have not mentioned those offenders who also suffer from a neurosis or those children who show neurotic signs and at the same time have committed criminal acts, a point we will take up in the next chapter. Now let us look back at the many similarities between neurotic and criminal behavior.

1. The neurotic patient and the delinquent person both suffer from a conflict which is similar in type and most frequently of an

unconscious nature. In both cases this conflict comes to the fore because of the struggle between society's demand upon the individual and his instinctual drives.

2. As a result of the conflict, neurotic or delinquent symptoms arise which are irrational in nature in the neurotic person, and most often are irrational in the criminal. That means, the emotions of the offender are so powerful and dominate his actions so much that they give the impression of being irrational in nature.

3. Since both the neurotic and the delinquent person show an irrational emotional attitude which is also reflected in their actions, these acts have a symbolic meaning. The pains which a hysterical patient may feel or, for instance, Nick's stealing can only be understood in terms of their symbolic significance. In the same way, a homicide of a stranger may to the unconscious of the murderer mean his father or brother. In the Oedipus legend, Oedipus believes he has killed a stranger. In reality, that is in the reality of the unconscious, it is his father.

4. Both the neurotic person and the offender have stopped growing emotionally and have therefore become fixated at the pregenital levels, or if they have grown emotionally, they have regressed to those stages.

5. All neurotic persons reveal guilt feelings, a manifestation we find present in many delinquent persons.

6. The neurotic and the delinquent individual show a great deal of narcissism. The neurotic person is engrossed in his conflicts and in his own emotions and has little interest, if any, in the world around him. The same is true with the criminal. The neurotic individual is to a large extent asocial in that he is preoccupied in his desires and wishes with all sorts of deeds which because of his neurotic condition he cannot carry out. The delinquent person performs his antisocial act without consideration for anyone else but himself. Frequently, he is completely unaware of the pain, or loss of property, or damage in general he may inflict upon his victim.

7. Both the neurotic and delinquent individual need one or more precipitating events in order to produce neurotic or delinquent signs. These precipitating events are also necessary to bring out a

141

psychosis or psychosomatic disturbances. In all these four conditions, symptoms and emotional disturbances have been present for a long time, but one or more precipitating event, that is, one either outside or inside stimulus is necessary actually to bring into being a neurosis, psychosis or psychosomatic disturbance or delinquent behavior.

That these precipitating events may also be of internal nature shows in the following case. A young man who was somewhat mentally upset was drinking with another person in a bar, when the latter suddenly started to make homosexual propositions to him. The young fellow became frightened because he was overwhelmed by his own homosexual leaning. He left the bar in a hurry, and that same evening committed rape upon a woman, probably in order to assert his own masculinity, a motivation of which he was unaware. This, then, was a precipitating event arising from outside stimulus that provoked the man's own emotions. But the stimulus came fundamentally from himself, not from the other man. A well-adjusted man would have rejected the homosexual proposition and thought nothing more about it.

When we think of the similarities between a neurosis and criminal behavior, there is no wonder that delinquent behavior has been taken for neurotic conduct and vice versa. Particularly is this the case where there is a tie-up of criminal behavior and neurotic symptoms, a manifestation we find frequently in juvenile delinquency. Although we find that neurotic individuals commit crimes, it is more frequent to see criminal acts influenced by neurotic symptoms. This being the case, we can understand how manifold and how varied the different types of offenders are, and it becomes more complex when we see that many offenders are psychotic. But about that we will hear in the next chapter.

7

Delinquent Types

THE way a person reacts to emotional shocks and situations is a reflection of his own personality make-up and has to do with a certain mental and sometimes constitutional predisposition to one or another form of behavior. When we follow the emotional and intellectual development of the specific individual, we are able to explain his behavior in terms of his personal traits and his mental condition. The intimate connection between the person and his actions leads us to understand his behavior, but this does not necessarily mean that every form of an act always reflects a specific mental condition.

When a man commits an outrageous crime, we may surmise that the individual suffers from a deep-seated mental disorder. If a man goes berserk and kills a number of persons as, for instance, happened in 1950 when a man in New Jersey shot down several people in the course of one hour, I ventured the idea at once that he probably suffered from a paranoid schizophrenia, a thing every experienced psychiatrist would say. I pointed out also that I had not examined the killer and that my diagnosis was based only upon the way the murders took place.

Although it is difficult if not impossible to determine accurately the influence of abnormal mental processes in the motivation and execution of an act, including the criminal one, we can still maintain that the crime is part of the offender's abnormal state of mind. But when it comes to the point where there apparently are no abnormal findings present, we cannot say how much pathology enters the picture, the reason being that we do not have a satisfactory

143

hypothesis which can explain what is normal and what is pathological. This is but another reason why it has been so difficult to classify criminals; we have failed to find definite criteria which could tie different offenders into the same groups.

In the course of time various investigators such as Lombroso, Enrico Ferri, von Liszt and others have tried to outline a classification of offenders. The classifications have varied to a large extent because their basis has differed so widely. It is worth-while to remember that Lombroso, in addition to his basic idea, "The Born Criminal," classified criminals in three groups: the insane criminal, the offender by passion and the accidental or occasional delinquent. Fritz von Liszt, another outstanding criminologist, divided offenders into instantaneous, improvable and unimprovable ones, but this classification does not take into consideration the psychotic irresponsible offender and is not fully concerned with the abnormal criminal in general.

The only fruitful viewpoint in grouping offenders is the etiological one. If we can find in the person the causes for his criminal acts, then we have a sound basis for a classification. One expression of this etiology is to find out how often a crime is committed, a point I stressed in *Crime and the Human Mind:*

"Regardless of how much of the personality is involved in the perpetration of the act and regardless of how much the social situation is entangled, there is one element that stands out, and that is the time factor—how often the act is committed. This has a bearing upon the nature of the personality and type of situation in which the offender finds himself." (p. 93)

Today, however, we are able to go a step further for we have learned more about criminal behavior. Yet such a classification rigidly presupposes that each delinquent individual is examined carefully. Even with such an examination, it may be difficult to decide to what kind of category the offender belongs, or whether he suffers at all from an abnormal mental condition. We found that difficulty with Al.

At seventeen, Al had been convicted of larceny after he had passed several bad checks amounting to a large sum. In our examination, we found that he was fearful and timid, and rather belligerent and antagonistic toward his parents. He had a slight sinus condition which was always worse when he was upset about anything. Thus, on the surface everything seemed almost all right with him except for his offense, which was a rebellion against his family situation and furthered by his own personality make-up.

Al's mother was a borderline psychotic, his father was suspicious to the point of being paranoid, and his sister was a mental defective. Al's aggression was mobilized when his father objected to his attending college and proceeded to watch Al's every move for fear he would put his energy and efforts into an education rather than into an ordinary everyday job. If it was good enough for Al's father, it should be good enough for Al, the father reasoned. And while the father reasoned, Al reacted inside until finally one day the inside reaction became too much for him: he struck out, thereby hurting his father for his unjustness and at the same time getting, though in a distorted form, the attention for himself that he had for so long desired. This was Al's first offense; until that time he had been a model boy. Usually I am very suspicious about anyone who behaves in such a way that he is an example for everyone else. There is no 100 per cent "good" boy, if that is the case, then the idea suggests itself that this "model boy" or "model person" tries to take on a front in order to hide his weaknesses. Although this was not so explicit here as we will see in another case later, still this very factor was one of the leads for considering that Al suffered from a neurosis. But I could only arrive at such a diagnosis after much probing.

Our classification should therefore be based primarily upon the causation underlying criminal behavior. Healy and others have tried to do the same and were to a large extent able to group the causative elements of the so-called "normal criminal" which, in their opinion, were responsible for his antisocial activities.

It should also be added that Alexander and Staub have tried to establish a classification of offenders along the same lines, but combined with the criminologist's viewpoint. One important aspect for the basis of this classification is how much the Ego of the offender participates in the antisocial act. While they differentiate between accidental and chronic criminals, they divide the latter group into several other categories. (See: *The Criminal, the Judge and the Public*, London, 1931.)

Mention should also be made here of Kate Friedlander's classification of juvenile offenders (*The Psychoanalytical Approach to Juvenile Delinquency*, pp. 186-187, London, 1947) in which she classifies delinquents according to their antisocial character formation, organic disturbances and psychotic Ego disturbance. This is a well-thought-out grouping which is amplified in her constructive book.

Valuable as such classification is, we must ask one question: What causative factor or factors bring about criminal behavior? There is possibly no single cause which cannot be explained as a reason for delinquent behavior, and on the other hand there is no single cause, with the possible exception of antisocial character, which cannot be thought of as a reason for a mental condition. We therefore have to go a step further. Not only can we consider causative factors of criminal activities as a basis for their classification, but the causative factors in conjunction with the mental make-up of the offender. These two factors are so closely linked that the one cannot be considered apart from the other. Saying this does not mean that we will not have difficulty in establishing the classification. Human behavior is never clear-cut. Just as life is never black or white, even if some people would like to believe that, so also human conduct has many colors and variations, one sort of behavior indiscernibly overlapping another, always reflecting the diversity of the human being.

We cannot always carefully categorize disturbances within the human mind, and departmentalize people as though they were subjects one studies in school. It may be true that a person predominantly shows his emotional conflict in one certain way, yet it is always within the realm of possibility that he will show some conflict to one degree or another in various ways. Thus he may be an offender against society, be ill through physical disturbances, seem to suffer from a character disorder and yet appear to be highly neurotic. He may also, on a very deep level, show psychotic traits.

The one important difference here is that intrinsically an emotionally ill person is either neurotic, psychotic, a victim of character disorders, or suffers from some other clearly defined or ill-

146

defined psychiatric condition. He may have one of the disorders plus physical disturbances—in fact he probably will; and he may have any one of the disorders and commit crime. But he will not be neurotic and psychotic, or psychotic and suffer from character disorders, or any such combination. For one of these mechanisms cannot go into the other. They may seem to at times, but this is merely because in the process of growing up slight fixations have occurred which have continued to exist. But so also has the original and intrinsic mechanism, which is why we say one cannot go into the other.

The main and most important factor for us to keep in mind in dealing with any classification of criminals is that those involved, i.e., the offenders, are first of all people. Secondly, that they are individual people and thus cannot be thrust helter-skelter into a large bag. Each person acts in accordance with his own conflicts and his own personality.

To be a little clearer and more specific, a person can show character disorder traits and still suffer many anxieties and guilt feelings. Thus he can have more of a character disorder than anything else, but still show on the surface some neurotic traits as well. Even a few genuine psychopaths are obsessive-compulsory for intermittent periods of time. Obsessive-compulsory behavior is neurotic in that it stems from an inner drive, centering sometimes around extreme Superego and early emotional fixations. While controlled by it, the offender is under the morbid influence of irresistible ideas of impulse which cause him to act contrary to his conscious will at the time. Oftentimes we see offenders who suffer from a very apparent neurosis such as an anxiety hysteria or, in other words, acute and uncontrollable state of anxiety caused by an unrealized emotional situation. Through various psychological tests and a psychiatric examination, however, it might develop that he has an underlying schizophrenia. This would quite naturally mean that he was basically psychotic, and therefore not really neurotic as his outward behavior indicated.

I think it not difficult to realize, therefore, that more often than not offenders against society are offenders against themselves as well. Moreover, they often use their ailments as an excuse for their aggressions. The classification will, therefore, have to depend upon a careful examination of the offender so that we can find the most significant traits in him.

In considering this classification it would be good to keep in mind the psychological development every person goes through and the fact that the way this evolution takes place leaves a mark upon him. Of all the offenders I have seen, every one has been fixated at one or more stages of his development. Some are orally oriented, in that they strive for immediate satisfaction through the mouth, and frequently for omnipotence. Others are anal sadistic, cruel and suspicious. Others do not show any signs of conscience, while still others have some kind of mother fixation, be it strong attachment to or a deep dislike of the mother, which may have turned them to homosexual practices.

Then too, we must remember that the particular type of criminal depends upon the interrelationship between his Ego, Superego and Id impulses.

1. The first group of offenders are those I designate *the momentary ones;* they could also be called the situational, accidental or associational offenders. They commit an antisocial act once or twice, and frequently thereafter if a situation presents itself. They are those people one would be inclined to call the "normal criminal," although this is not so. In delving into them, we find them to be rebellious, antagonistic and spiteful but on a superficial level. The majority are juveniles who have been raised in homes with family tension present and who want to express themselves and frequently do so by committing antisocial acts, thereby unconsciously punishing their parents. Among this group the most important one is the associational delinquent because his antisocial impulses are so often readily mobilized by his companions that he may become an actual offender. It is interesting to note that a momentary offender commits a crime often with great courage and power, but afterward feels exceedingly guilty and does not want to know about his crime. Because his Superego cannot condone his act, his Ego cannot accept it and therefore rejects it.

That this group of offenders are not difficult to handle, are not in any way dangerous, does not mean that they cannot be menacing because from this group can be developed other types of offenders, depending upon the personality make-up. The amount of antisocial character traits will decide to what degree the offender is a momentary one. This antisocial trait is present only transiently in this type of delinquent person. As soon as the situation which led into the crime has passed and the act has been committed, we may assume that this characteristic recedes and stays latent or dormant until the next situation arises, unless the individual in the meantime has learned to withstand his antisocial tendencies.

Among those offenders we find many children with behavior disorders caused by early emotional difficulties and reactions; for the latter reason they might be called reactive disorders. Of those behavior or reactive disorders, we can mention here habit disorders during which the child shows nail-biting and thumb-sucking, manifestations which arise particularly when parents quarrel and nag each other, thus neglecting the child. Usually appearing during the first years of a child's life, these conditions are oral in nature and indicate anxieties, a defensive reaction. When children are indulged to excess, or show similar reactions which continue throughout life, these manifestations can be said to be symptoms of an emotional disorder. In due time this may express itself in a mental or psychosomatic disturbance or in criminal activities.

The truant child who shows a conduct disorder can be included in this group of delinquents if the truancy is short lived.

2. *Neurotic offenders.* In this type, such as kleptomaniacs or fire-setters, criminal behavior has grown out of a neurotic condition. They may in addition show psychosomatic disturbances. Their criminal acts and their neurosis are almost as closely connected as the behavior and symptoms of the neurotic nonoffender. The paramount example of such a case is that of the kleptomaniac whose continued stealing is intimately connected with his whole personality make-up, in the same way as we see a neurotic individual with symptoms of phobia or other neurotic signs. In contrast to the neurotic person who finds himself so disturbed over his symptoms that he often realizes that he must have psychiatric help, the kleptomaniac or pyromaniac does not seek that help unless the court prevails upon him to do so.

Within the neurotic group, the emotionally fixated persons, we find those who are driven into antisocial acts by unconscious drives which they can neither understand nor control. Pyromaniacs do not always burn up people's houses out of feelings of hatred or revenge for those people; kleptomaniacs do not steal because they are hungry or in want. These people are sexually unsatisfied, usually because they have been either emotionally starved or overprotected as children and given to understand that any kind of sexual relations are unclean and harmful. At an early age they learned to repress their sexual desires, but their desires continued nonetheless and in time expressed themselves in other ways. And so it is that the pyromaniac frequently experiences a thrill when he sets a fire and a kleptomaniac finds sexual excitement in taking an article she does not need or even desire. These are unconscious sexual gratifications, and further examples of where crime originates—not within a person's malicious heart, but within his home, with those who may have loved him too much but understood him too little.

When we go more deeply into the phenomenon of kleptomaniacs, we find that the majority of them are women. As a matter of fact, when we think of a kleptomanic person, we think of a woman.

I think of Patty, an attractive, brilliant, twenty-five-year-old girl, who was arrested for shoplifting. When the police searched her home, they found closets full of stolen clothing which had obviously not been worn. No one understood why she stole, because she was extremely well dressed and had no apparent need for the clothes. When asked about it, she explained that the stealing gave her a thrill.

In the course of interviewing, I found that Patty was raised by wealthy but strict parents. She was not allowed to have dates and had only a few girl friends. For her college training she was sent out of town to an all-girls' school, where she became close friends with one of her roommates. During that time books disappeared from the college library, girls lost dresses and jewelry, but the thief was never found.

Patty had difficulty in securing credits for her degree, so just before her final examination, she left school and went to New York where she worked as a governess. After five days, however, she ran away with some jewels and lingerie.

Then she worked as a salesgirl in a department store, until one day she tossed a fur coat over her shoulders and started to walk out. One of the store detectives noticed her and took her to the office for questioning.

During our interviews I learned of her friendship with her college chum, which was of a sexual nature. She told me that at the moment of taking the clothing she felt excited, peculiarly relieved and satisfied. In other words, it was the *action* of stealing that gave her pleasure, not the stolen object. It was the thrill rather than the dress she sought. Fundamentally, her kleptomania was linked to her sexual desires which had been repressed throughout her life, distorting and destroying her sense of values.

When we look into the psychodynamics of such a kleptomaniac, we find she unconsciously wants to take what she has not been given. Since she strives for lost sexual gratification, it must in these cases be something related to the sexual sphere. Depending upon the stage at which the offender is fixated, the significance of the stolen object varies. If the woman is not too much emotionally disturbed, the male organ will be of importance to her. What she wants is what she does not have or has never been given, and the ultimate form of this is the penis. This unconscious desire manifests itself by taking what does not belong to her. This may explain the prevalence of kleptomania among women. She "takes the penis" as a revenge, reflecting in the deepest sense and unconsciously a penis envy. Such a woman therefore will suffer from castration fear. If, in addition, she develops a conflict between her Superego and Ego, then, little by little, she develops the idea that she has a "right" to steal. The usual result of this is that she feels guilty and therefore she has to steal so that she can be punished to make up for her guilt feelings.

Thus kleptomania and other forms of stealing are in many cases substitute or symbolic acts. So may be rape or robbery. Fire-setting too may be an expression of a sexual desire, but since every fire-setter becomes excited by the fire, it must be due to something

151

specific happening in the individual. In this connection, it is interesting to note that many fire-setters have been bedwetters. Noteworthy too is the fact that we find some bedwetters among firemen. If a fire-setter is analyzed, we usually find his pyromania to be tied up with urethral eroticism. In myths, legends or dreams, even in the Bible, we frequently find mentioned the combination of fire and water.

The pleasure in starting the fire becomes often a substitute for sexual elation, and the devastating power of the fire reflects the intensity of sexual desires. These fire-setters are extremely narcissistic, and like gamblers who suffer from impulse neuroses, force the fire to give them the love and affection they so sorely need. This narcissism can also go so far as to make them completely involved in themselves, resulting in the development of a psychosis.

Although the kleptomaniac is the prototype of the neurotic offender, we do find criminals suffering from other neuroses, although not so clear cut. Among thieves and embezzlers, for instance, and also among sexual offenders, robbers or murderers, is frequently found the passive dependent neurotic. He may have a most pleasant appearance and behave in a seemingly co-operative manner. He may seem to be anything but dissatisfied with his lot and the world in general. Rather than being tough and sure of himself, he may appear quite different and passive even to the extent of being soft and womanlike. Beneath this disarming exterior, however, may dwell a loathing that far exceeds that of the rough-and-ready boys, for it is a loathing that has been repressed through fear and therefore exaggerated in the process.

This passive offender is basically of an oral and dependent nature. He is used to receiving things rather than giving them. Thus he takes and consumes all he can. Nonetheless, he also resents this dependence upon others, for it is natural to want to stand on one's own feet. Thus a conflict is set up: he receives because he wants to, because he always has, and yet he resents his inability to stand alone and be the man he would like to be. This is the mechanism of dependence upon others and resentment of that dependence. A hatred of self may be set up which in turn involves others who, to this twisted mind, made him what he is.

The difficulty in assigning such a type to one particular group of offenders exists mainly because they show so many conflicting aspects of their personality traits. This difficulty increases when we come to the next group of delinquents.

3. These offenders fall into the category of persons who suffer from *unconscious guilt feelings*, either for something they did wrong when young or because of some hatred against someone in their family. Therefore they unconsciously want to be punished, a desire they fulfill by committing a crime for which they can be punished. The punishment they receive is not, to them, for the crime they have committed and for which society blames them, but for the unconscious desires, for which their strong Superego accuses them. As I have previously mentioned, such a desire to be punished is not only seen among criminals, but also in people suffering from a neurosis or a psychosis. Such a need to be punished is not, however, always unconscious; at times the offender may very well know it consciously. Here too we find psychosomatic disturbances involved.

Such offenders thus often betray themselves by leaving a clue for their detection. Therefore, when we hear about all the faulty acts of the criminal after he has committed his crime, the reason is that he wants to be detected. So much do they feel their guilt that by unconscious behavior they try to reveal it.

The noted case—Leopold and Loeb, who killed the Frank boy in Chicago—is a classic example. Leopold left his glasses at the scene of the crime, and they were one of the basic clues in the detection of the murder. (See *Crime and the Human Mind*, p. 163.) In this otherwise carefully planned crime, the murderers were caught through a trifling piece of evidence. Both thought that they were going to perform the "perfect crime," which does not exist very often.

Among the peculiar and faulty acts of this type of criminal is that he often revisits the scene of his deed, particularly if he is a kleptomaniac, fire-setter or a murderer. The reason, of course, is that he unconsciously wants to be found so he can be punished.

On the day after Christmas, in 1945, a rather comic scene was enacted in a midtown hotel in New York. However, it was not

153

without its tragic side. About midnight a holdup man entered the hotel and at pistol point ordered the manager and elevator operator, to get in the back and lie down on the floor, face down. Because it was Christmas, he took only seventy-nine dollars from the cash register.

Less than four hours later, he was back. Without a pistol, he again ordered the two men to get on the floor. About this time, however, a guest of the hotel walked in. Instead of complying with the holdup man's orders, he brought the man down with a flying tackle. The manager called the police while the thief was held.

When the detectives arrived, they discovered that the holdup man was an ex-convict. He had been released from a reformatory where he had served time for burglary and violation of parole. His record showed six arrests, starting at the age of thirteen. (New York *Times*, December 26, 1945.)

This man had such a strong sense of guilt that he had to return to the scene of his crime. The second time he entered the hotel, he did so without a gun in order to be sure that he would get caught and be punished.

It is a question whether we do not find guilt feelings in all types of offenders, with the exception of the genuine psychopath. The main point, though, is whether it is those guilt feelings which have been the prime mover in instigating the antisocial act. If this is the case, the offender may suffer from an obsessive compulsory neurosis or a psychosis to a varying degree. Sometimes this type of offender may be considered to be of a pseudo-obsessive compulsory type.

4. In this group we find those offenders who suffer from *character disorder*. They do not show neurotic symptoms as such, but their actions and behavior as a whole are substitutes for neurotic symptoms. The neurotic taint shows itself in the irrational behavior of the person himself. He can commit almost any type of crime. Most often we find these persons to be pathological liars, swindlers, marriage wreckers and nymphomaniacs, Don Juans, imposters, drug addicts and alcoholics, some types of homosexuals, rapists, and murderers, and some of those who commit pedophilia and incest. In all of them we find a certain developed antisocial character trait, more so than in the third group of offenders: they all "act out"

their desires or fantasies. Therefore, this group of criminals has been given different names. Wilhelm Reich called such a person "Der triebhafte Character" (Vienna, 1925) "Impulsive character"; Alexander called him the "neurotic character"; while psychiatrists in general and the lay public have called him the psychopathic personality.

After having investigated several hundred so-called "psychopathic persons," I have found that most of them can be classified and diagnosed in definite groups. Many individuals who are placed under that diagnosis are not psychopathic. They can be schizophrenic, neurotic or, as we have found to be the case, the majority suffer from a disturbance of the character and emotions which justify their being called neurotic. Hence, they suffer from a character disorder. Such a person has usually been raised in a family where there has been little or no supervision, little or no development of a Superego structure, little love or understanding. Sometimes there has been some one-sided discipline, at other times some overindulgence which has confused the youngster as to values. These types of people in varying degrees have some sort of conscience, but it is more externalized than internalized. They may fear the police not because they do something wrong against society, but because they might get caught. From early childhood they have learned to bribe their way, and if they don't get what they want, they use extortion, a way of life which finds its most distinguished form in the genuine psychopath.

Delinquent persons with a neurotic character disorder have never had occasion to form a relationship with anyone, and this lack of object relationship has made it difficult, if not impossible, for them to develop a Superego. Remembering all such offenders I have seen, one outstanding feature is that their parents, foster parents or other parental figures either did not have time to be with their offspring or did not care about it; that the child was switched from the one family situation to another; that there was no time for him to develop a relationship or to be able to identify himself with his parents. The result was numerous frustrations leading to a faulty formation of the Superego. Furthermore, these delinquent persons changed their living places frequently, with ensuing changes of schools and friends; their upbringing was inconsistent and they became ambivalent and dissatisfied. Because of their frustrations they felt it necessary to satisfy their instinctual demands at once and, therefore, submitted to them before they had been able to develop inhibitions based upon Superego development.

When such a delinquent feels remorse, it is in a detached way, coming rather late. His Superego is in a way isolated; because of his frustrations, he has learned that if he wants to get a thing, he has to take it at once, else it will be taken from him in the next minute. Some offenders have told me that often their father or mother gave them things and then took them back, or made promises of gifts which were never fulfilled. Soon they learned to take whatever came within their reach and keep hold of it. They always looked for emotional security, affection and attention which they never found.

This is possibly one of the characteristics of any type of this class offender, be he sexual, alcoholic or drug addict. What is so pathological about them is that they are driven almost by a compulsion to carry out their acts, leaving one with the impression that their impulses are instinctual in character. Belonging to them are the perversions which are sexual in nature. Pervert persons have the same sexual aim as children. Therefore, their sexual behavior is infantile instead of adult because their psychosexual development has either stopped or regressed. This is what we found in all of the 102 sex offenders we studied at Sing Sing. They were emotionally stunted. This does not mean that they all were suffering from a character disorder; I only mention it here in order to emphasize that it is a faulty emotional development that brings sex offenders into being unless they have an inborn or acquired mental deficiency or another organic mental condition.

It should be emphasized that sexually perverted persons have only one way of obtaining sexual enjoyment. Their energy is directed toward their partial instinct; but their sexual life is not disorganized as seen in children who are capable of almost any act. Among those people suffering from character disorder we find many homosexuals. The homosexual individual is one who has regressed to an infantile stage to obtain sexual gratification, thereby avoiding anxieties and fear which he would encounter were he able to have heterosexual relations. Besides biological and hormonal influences which may be of significance in the development of a person's sexual direction, some individuals may become homosexual because of confinement with men—in an army or in a prison—accidental homosexuality as it is called, a matter about which we will hear in the next chapter. In these perversions are frequently imbedded a sado-masochistic streak. If these people are sadistic, they are unconsciously struggling against their anxieties which may have been brought about by their feelings of castration. Often the perverse sadistic act has the nature of play.

Among these character disorders we find many offenders who become alcoholics. This is particularly the case when in addition to extreme frustrations there has been an exceedingly difficult family situation with pronounced family tension.

Since quite a few alcoholics suffer from a character disorder and since much has been written and agreed upon regarding the active role that alcohol plays in the part of crime, let us consider it specifically for a moment. So far little has been acknowledged about the frequently connecting link of sexual conflict. I do not mean to suggest that all who drink to excess are in a state of conflict regarding sex, for there are other conflicts that drive people to drink. But one thing is certain: when large amounts of alcohol are consumed, the origin of the difficulty lies within the sphere of the stages of the individual's growth. When crime enters the picture as well, there is an underlying passivity on the part of the alcoholic that he himself resents. He drinks in order to overcome it.

Excessive drinking has its beginnings in the latter, or cannibalistic, part of the oral period of the person's development. This naturally means that chronic alcoholics are for some reason emotionally fixated at this time in their lives. Add to that, then, an automatic resentment of the basic source of this fixation which, because she is the source of supply, is in most cases the mother, and you have at least in a man a foundation for the beginnings of homosexuality. By the time the early genital stage is reached, if there is no improvement in the mother's emotional attitude toward the

157

boy, he will turn from her and become enamored of his father. From then on, consciously or unconsciously, he will prefer men and basically dislike women.

When such an abnormal emotional state as this exists on an unconscious level, there is bound to be deep conflict with it. If this conflict is never expressed and the victim of it lives in a state of apparent passive acceptance, he may one day commit a crime to release his inner anxiety and tension. Those who commit crimes while in an alcoholic state do so because alcohol has made them aggressive enough; had they been overtly aggressive, they would not have needed the alcohol for courage to express their hostility.

We may see that when alcoholism accompanies crime, homosexuality often does too, though it is frequently latent.

In the same way that the alcoholic is looking for emotional security, in the deepest sense an oral longing, so do those individuals who are addicted to drugs. Most of these persons suffer from a character disorder. They not only need to be sexually satisfied but must achieve a particular gratification obtained only through drugs. By drug addict I do not mean the person who has to be given morphine or some similar drug to alleviate pain—but the man or woman who has come to depend upon it to such an extent that it overshadows all his activities. We may surmise that all addicts, be it morphine, heroin, alcohol or opium, react to the drug in a specific way. Through it they try to satisfy their oral drives which otherwise have been frustrated. Thus the drug addict is a problem of a personality structure, a point which must be kept in mind when it comes to his treatment.

In consuming the drug, the addict has in his mind some sort of fulfillment which he has not previously achieved. This desire for fulfillment is more pronounced than any other desire, the sexual one included. The addicts therefore regress to whatever stage they have been fixated upon. During that time they reduce what might possibly be left of their object relationship. That they do so indicates that they were never able to establish any relationships—and this is one of the main characteristics of those who suffer from a character disorder. They become, if possible, more egocentric than before, only interested in satisfying their own needs. They do not

158

care about people; if they do, it is only so far as they can serve as suppliers of the drug. Because of their extreme narcissism, and because the effect of the drug is felt almost like food or affection, they become impatient, intolerant and cannot stand frustrations, particularly in obtaining the drug. After each elation which gives them a narcissistic satisfaction, new pain sets in and they therefore must have another injection because the body has been conditioned to it, and the dosage must be increased. Finally the addict becomes so dependent upon the drug that everything else loses importance.

Like a little infant, he asks for it, wanting desperately to be satisfied. Thus he becomes in a psychological sense reduced to the status of a baby who can only take, but never give. He has reached an extreme level of passivity, which is also exemplified by the fact that the drug is given to him. During his development into a drug addict, he may commit antisocial acts which frequently have the nature of impulse actions.

Those people who show a distortion of their character are in general egotistic, defiant, lacking in responsibility and, by and large, without regard for others, clearly indicating their intention of standing alone. They might more correctly be described as falling alone and yet taking others with them, for all their lives seem to show an eternal bent for self-destruction invariably hurting those around them. They are an exasperating lot, too, for they often appear quite all right and have an unfailing capacity to ingratiate themselves. As is true with all sick persons, however, they can be spotted for what they are, for they seldom keep a job or sweetheart for any length of time; they must constantly feed their ego and their childish fancy with something new, for like an extremely young child, they are incapable of attachment.

Since the antisocial development of the character gives the degree of the character disorder, it is evident that in this group we can find types of varieties of personality structure within their character and their behavior. No wonder therefore that all these types, and others too, have been collected under the name of psychopathic personalities. This term has caused much confusion in the lay and the medical world. So much confusion in fact, that if they did not know what kind of a personality the person in question was, he was called a psychopath. People without education in the field are apt to use it to describe any deviation from the normal, and those who should know, use it both generally and specifically and often frankly admit that they do not really understand the term.

If there should be anyone who could be described as a "psychopath," we would expect to find him particularly among sexual offenders who have also been called "sexual psychopaths." When we investigated sex offenders at Sing Sing, we found that most of them had been labeled "psychopaths." But thorough examinations aided by psychological tests led us to the conclusion that this group of offenders were made up of different types of personalities showing various mental conditions such as neurosis, anxiety states, reactive alcoholism, paranoid conditions, psychosis and character disorders. Of these offenders about twenty-five showed a distinct disturbance of character prevailing in their mental make-up. For all these reasons, we discarded the terms "psychopath" and "sexual psychopath."

5. I personally have come to the conclusion that the only type of person who can accurately be called *psychopath* is the genuine one.

The genuine psychopath, a type that fortunately is extremely rare, is one who is neither psychotic nor mentally defective, who shows a marked absence of anxiety and guilt feelings, who is asocial and amoral, exceedingly narcissistic and impulsive, infantile, and lacking in ability to form real relationships with others. Because of his stunted emotional development, he shows a polymorph sexual behavior. He can have heterosexual relations, he can be homosexual, he can rape, perform fellatio or cunnilingus or show any other type of behavior in the sexual sphere. Since he has developed no Superego structure, he differs from the person with a character disorder who has developed some conscience; in the latter this process is less complete. The genuine psychopath differs from the psychotic individual in that the former's conflicts in its effects become externalized, while the latter's conflicts are internalized and stay that way.

The genuine psychopath is a person who has never been able to identify himself with anyone. His home life has been filled with frustrations, bitterness and quarreling: he has never learned to accept rules or standards. From an early age he has learned to live his own life more absolutely than the boy with a character disorder, a life completely according to his own emotions. He therefore is unreliable, unstable, demanding and egocentric. He will be a genuine psychopathic personality, just as amoral and uncivilized as when he came into the world. The difference will be the brain—oftentimes good in the psychopath—which he uses in order to get his way.

As do all socially unadjusted individuals, the genuine psychopath shows symptoms of his disease early in life. The trouble is that these symptoms are seldom recognized as such: the child is considered a brat, a young gangster; the man is thought of as a monster and an outlaw. The young genuine psychopath is extremely self-willed, often cruel and seldom truthful. He plays truant and commits petty thefts. When he plays truant it is because there is some condition with which he is dissatisfied and, having no conscience, he feels no remorse and, therefore, no anxiety. When he steals, it is an unconscious attempt to secure the affection and care that were denied him as a child. For money can be a symbol for love and an artificial expression of the security represented by love.

When the genuine psychopath with antisocial tendencies grows up, he is an exaggeration of his former self, and the things he does are exaggerations of his earlier unchecked activities. His emotional life is superficial and fundamentally cold; he can feel no real love. He is irresponsible and ungrateful, selfish and lacking in humility. He has not real purpose in life, no foresight, and spends his time satisfying his emotions of the moment, which are apt to fluctuate constantly. The genuine psychopath can be very gay and full of the joy of life one minute and covered with gloom the next. The mood of depression seldom lasts very long.

We can thank heaven that the type is rare because the offenses within the range of the genuine psychopath are without limits. They will steal, embezzle, forge checks and make brutal sexual attacks. They will commit profit murder for a sum as low as twenty-five dollars. They seldom commit suicide; they are much too narcissistic. They often characteristically take pride in their offenses against society, inasmuch as since childhood they have basically held everyone but themselves in contempt. When they are apprehended, they look upon their punishment as an injustice, which of course it is, but not quite in the way they think. They have no right to commit acts against society, but on the other hand, they can hardly be held responsible for these acts. They are sick; they are in need of care, not punishment.

Notwithstanding all of this, no genuine psychopath, once apprehended, should be allowed to roam the streets, for these people are capable of anything. They should be kept within walls and behind bars, and under these circumstances attended to as well as possible.

When Maurice stood before me for the first time, he had killed a man. He felt neither guilty nor sorry, and he regarded his prison term with the utter contempt of a man who feels completely justified in what he has done and disgusted only with the fact of having been caught.

Maurice's career of crime began early. A sick father, a negative type of mother and younger children in the family, who demanded and got the most attention, caused Maurice to feel himself without an anchor or ties of any kind. He was truant from school, beat up the neighborhood boys and stole candy from the corner store. When he was ten, his father died, and what little supervision he had had died too. Maurice began to steal from the cash register in the grocery where he worked after school. When this was discovered, Maurice was put into a child guidance clinic which was unable to effect any change in him. Soon afterward he was involved in shooting off the lock on a safe in a rich man's home, caught and sent to reform school. He was twelve when he went in and thirteen when he came out. His next offense was hitting a woman over the head and stealing her purse. He was put back into the reform school until he was sixteen. While in the reformatory, Maurice vacillated between being good and bad, interested in being released and indifferent about it. Almost immediately upon being released, he held up a store with the aid of other boys and took two hundred dollars. He fled, was caught, and put on probation and under psychiatric examination.

It did not take long for the psychiatrist to discover that this egocentric, narcissistic, amoral personality was a genuine psychopath, dangerous and irrepressible. His dreams were of movie stars, and he saw no reason why he should look for work; he was so good, the work should come to him. He could talk his way into or out of anything. He was that charming, that convincing, that good an actor.

After two sessions with the psychiatrist, Maurice gave up treatment altogether and took up gambling and white slavery instead. He was sent to a penitentiary for one year, during which time he married a girl he had impregnated. When he was released, he made no attempt to pick up his life with his bride but found new and different women, all of whom found him fascinating and filled with sex appeal. With his smooth attractive manner, he charmed both men and women. He became a salesman for a while, and within the various contacts he made, men loaned him money and women gave him themselves. Then one day a man played his own game with him: he lied and cheated and took Maurice's money. Maurice said nothing to him, but one evening he calmly shot him in the back.

Thus I met him, when he was thirty and appeared sixteen. Yet his eyes were those of an old man. His life had been one of waste and destruction, and now he had killed a man and was to pay for it with "not less than twenty years, nor more than his natural life."

This man was not insane, and had no plea for even temporary insanity. He was a genuine psychopath, without conscience or morals, remorse or guilt. He was completely incorrigible. As he had never known any emotional ties, it would be difficult, if not impossible, to effect one now. He would of necessity have to be kept locked up, for no one could be held responsible for him. That responsibility went back to many years ago, to a home without love for him and a family without thought of him as an individual. He became an individual in his own right, a "character," someone for others to discuss far into the night because of his odd behavior, someone to criticize, someone to love and to hate, a man without a soul because he could feel identity with nothing or no one.

Such waste will become more waste. He will sit in a prison, rotting day by day, supported by the people, hating himself and everyone. Mostly he will hate his parents, though perhaps unconsciously, for not giving him a better start. And well he might. They, in all innocence, put him where he is today.

This is the case of a genuine psychopath, whose traits are found in manifestations which sometimes appear on the surface to be neurotic. But while a neurotic person demonstrates his unsettled condition in the form of fear, anxiety, non-functioning, in contradictory behavior, the genuine psychopathic person indulges in antisocial behavior as a result of his basically hostile, undeveloped and untutored personality.

The genuine psychopathic type never developed a conscience, but began early in life to live in accordance with his emotions regardless of conditions, situation or others. Thus emotionally he remains an egotistical child. The neurotic developed a set of rules to follow and laws to obey, and then, at a certain stage of his development, the emotional machinery broke down. Emotionally he remained perhaps unconsciously in love with his mother, or disturbed about the abrupt way in which she weaned him, or interested in those of his own sex. Unconsciously, too, he resented this emotional fixation which was wrong, incestuous or immoral to him. So he developed feelings of guilt, or unworthiness. In time perhaps he found, also unconsciously, that he had to punish himself, to hurt himself, or even destroy himself. For these reasons he might commit a crime, a crime against himself, really, in order that he might be punished, not for the crime, but for his original sin.

6. In this last group belong *those individuals suffering from a psychosis* and where the crime is frequently contrary to the offender's usual behavior. The crime as such is not recognized by the offender, and he is legally called insane.

The schizophrenics are perhaps the most common of all psychotic offenders, as well as the most frequently found among the mentally diseased. Schizophrenics are both emotionally driven and emotionally fixated; yet their make-up is entirely different from that of the genuine psychopath and is only slightly similar to that of the neurotic. Besides being fixed in his emotions, the schizophrenic also withdraws emotionally at a certain age and from then on really lives within himself and only appears to live among others.

A schizoid condition begins early, and may be brought about by influences within the home. When a delicate and sensitive child is subjected to situations which hurt him, he may cringe and hide within himself and from then on may never let his feelings rise to the surface again. And so he becomes emotionally detached, whether he knows it or not. Though he may grow intellectually, his feelings will remain stifled, and the only way in which he will be able to express them is in an inner world of fantasy. The more the inner world grows, the less contact he will have with reality and the more out of contact he will become, until perhaps one day the withdrawal will be complete and this world will no longer exist for him.

Just as the genuine psychopath is completely primitive, the schizophrenic feels and shows no emotion insofar as the outside world is concerned. He finds it difficult to adjust himself to his environment because his ideas and ideals have no feelings back of them and, when he tries to make a decision, he is invariably in a state of conflict between these disconnected thoughts and inner emotions. Like the genuine psychopath, he has few friends, though for different reasons. The genuine psychopathic type appears to be warm and isn't; the schizophrenic tries to show warmth and cannot. The genuine psychopathic type is too biological; the schizophrenic is too austere and withdrawn from reality.

Because the schizophrenic is basically out of touch with the world, crime does not have the meaning for him that it does for, say, the neurotic person, who is in a state of conflict but nevertheless basically sane. A schizophrenic person lives in terms of words which act as a substitute for real people and objects to him, and through which he can justify any act whatever. Thus he may not work for months because he does not like to be with people; then, when he runs out of money he may steal or pawn his friend's watch. He will probably then tell himself or you that the man from whom he stole cheated on his income tax and deserved to be robbed, or that his friend's watch was just as much his as his friend's because they have known each other for such a long time; in any event he will not worry about these things, for he can always justify them with words that, though strange, are reasonably logic to him. He

165

may also kill and consider the act completely understandable. His instincts may have been aroused sufficiently for him to murder, say, his wife or sweetheart because she had been untrue to him. Questioned about it, he may simply say that she had done an evil thing and had to suffer for it. He may also state that he did it because he loved her, which will, of course, be another illustration of how little genuine meaning words have for him, as well as of the ambivalent and emotionally infantile person he is.

The mind is an unknown and uncertain quantity. We have accomplished and are accomplishing wonders daily with different forms of maladjustment, but now and then we are confronted with a disturbing and distressing condition which leaves nothing for us but to use our best judgment and then watch, hope and pray.

There is a young man on the loose today who is existing between two worlds and, frankly, we do not quite know what to do about it. This young man is an offender with a psychotic (schizophrenic) personality and will be known here as Bobby. His case is such a borderline one that almost any method of treatment is bound to be something of a risk. For the time being he is receiving a form of psychoanalytically oriented psychotherapy rather than psychoanalysis, as it is felt that just now it would be dangerous to break down his defenses. For the same reason we do not wish to attempt shock treatments. Whereas shock treatments are often of great value once a person has a psychosis, a person on the edge can go under altogether when subjected to anything drastic. We are at present therefore keeping this boy under control, nothing more.

Bobby stole a typewriter from the stationery shop which employed him three nights a week and which was his sole form of self-support. He then sold the typewriter for fifty-five dollars, with which he bought a pen and pencil set and several books and from which he kept a balance of seven dollars. His father put up bail for him when he was sentenced, and when the idea of mental examination was suggested, seemed highly in favor of it, as he had been having a difficult time of it with the boy for a good many years.

As a child, Bobby was spoiled by his mother because he was her favorite, and yet he was also the constant subject of her criticism. She wanted and expected perfection from him. Thus he learned no accepted mode of behavior and at the same time became extremely defensive. His father was stern and authoritative, and against him Bobby rebelled in silence. The consequent effect was that of a child withdrawn and secretive in his emotions yet belligerent and argumentative when approached on any subject that might reveal his insecurity. In the school he was a lone wolf and his marks were poor.

Bobby grew up with a burning desire to be important, to outdo others. He had little respect or concern for anyone but himself and lacked all apparent sensitivity. He would say anything and everything that came into his head and would stop at nothing to get his own way. Yet, although here was the surface picture of someone driven toward power and success, he would actually do very little to promote his own ends. Hours upon hours would be spent in daydreaming and reading, in a world apart from others. He disliked all forms of work, worked as little as possible and seldom held the same job for more than a week or two.

Bobby's dreams of being an important person were just that. The more he dreamed, the less he acted, until finally when his money ran out he would steal from his family and feel no guilt whatever about it.

He began to take money from his mother's purse when he was twelve. When scolded, his attitude was contemptuous and showed no signs of regret or of a desire to improve. He could justify anything and had no apparent comprehension of the difference between right and wrong or between truth and untruth.

Clothes, regular meals and sleep, friends—all of these were unimportant to Bobby. As he grew into a young man, he was looked upon by outsiders as an odd personality who could wound easily and yet was incredibly quick to take offense himself. He was more feared than liked, and people of depth and decency did not care to have him around.

Bobby is the victim of a psychotic make-up which makes him emotionally out of touch with this world. His thoughts and actions have no connection whatever with his feelings. The world of fantasy can be a very real one to a person as sick as Bobby, which is why there is no real distinction in his mind between that which is true and that which isn't. Bobby can decide he would like to have the most beautiful girl in the world for his own—although only in fantasy because he is incapable of transmitting love. In conversations thereafter he can so clearly describe her and her interest in him that after a while he will not only convince the person to whom he is talking, but himself as well. He might steal one hundred dollars from someone and then say that the amount was given to him by another person as an advance for some very important work and, in telling it, he will believe it.

A man who is this far gone would not need much to make the psychotic process complete. It is for this reason that psychotherapy on a superficial basis, in terms of guidance with a certain explanation of behavior motives, is recommended and put into effect, together with constant supervision. It is not at all infrequent that such a person will have what is technically referred to as a spontaneous remission. That is, he may himself effect an adjustment for a little while or perhaps for years. When this occurs, then it is sometimes advisable to suggest psychiatric treatment as a safeguard against the future. On the other hand, it is not always obligatory; the patient might possibly recover on his own.

Unpredictable and a constant challenge, the human mind, particularly the very sick one, keeps us constantly on our guard and often creates both awe and doubt within us. Bobby, no longer a menace because he is now under care, but still a problem nonetheless, may become well, may fold entirely, or he may stay as he is. We can at this point decide nothing about his future; we can only continue to do the very best we know how.

Many schizophrenics, be they offenders or not, are given psychiatric treatment and are improved. But Bobby's case is given as an example because it is fast becoming a very common one and, due to its uncertainty, we feel it emphasizes even more the necessity for good relations within the home during a child's growing years. Here too, education is necessary.

The schizophrenic offender shows an unsoundness of mind which appears to be related to his crime. If we follow the development of such persons, we find that often the early symptoms start with a loss of interest in their work and in their social activities. Even if they have a high intelligence, they often lack ambition and are unable to assume responsibility. They are infantile, as evidenced by the fact that they frequently like to play with children, reflecting their impoverished minds. Even if we do not find the symptoms which the layman believes are characteristic of the schizophrenic individual, there are other symptoms we must think of. When we examine these people more carefully, we find that their thinking is illogical, that their inhibitions are weakened and they therefore cannot control their Id impulses. Since their mental condition deprives them of their ability to modify their behavior, they are all emotionally rigid. Even if the psychosis is present in a mild form, it will influence their thinking and feeling and behavior.

In my experience there is not any type of a crime which cannot be committed by a psychotic person. The type of criminal act does not generally reflect what form of a psychosis the perpetrator suffers. Whether he suffers from an alcoholic psychosis or a syphilitic one or some other organic form, or whether he is a mental defective, will not alter his act. The psychotic person can murder, rape or rob; he can be homosexual or become a swindler. Or he can commit more harmless acts, such as passing false checks of small amounts or becoming an exhibitionist. A few years ago I remember that of twenty-five new delinquents we saw in one month, sixteen were suffering from schizophrenia. This does not mean that most offenders are schizophrenic; it only means that many delinquent persons do show this type of a psychosis, a matter we must be aware of.

The important point is that where there is a question of a crime which seems more senseless than usual—I will readily admit that all crimes, regardless, are senseless—and where it has been performed in a rather bizarre way, one may suspect that the culprit suffers from a deep-seated mental condition, possibly of a psychotic nature, most frequently a schizophrenic one.

One point more which ought to be mentioned is that a violent crime such as murder serves as a defense against the disintegrating effects of a psychosis upon the personality. It must be remembered that a schizophrenic person has within him strong emotions of rage, and we see that high degree of rage present in a man who commits murder or suicide. If a person slowly becomes schizophrenic, his Ego offers little resistance to the illness, and his personality is slowly taken over by it. If he tries to fight against the illness to ward it off, he will continue the fight as long as his Ego strength can stand it. When the psychosis finally breaks through, he either gives up the fight in resignation or he tries to make a last ditch stand in order to defend himself against it. That is the moment when he may kill, rape or set fires, or commit suicide, depending upon how pronounced are his delusions, social obligations or inhibitions.

A less frequently found psychotic offender is the manic-depressive, the man of moods. While in the manic stage of the psychosis, he is friendly and productive, cheerful and uninhibited. While in the depressive stage, he is gloomy, irritable, and without any feeling of hope. One phase follows the other without warning or even a set rhythm.

An offender suffering from a manic-depressive psychosis usually follows a pattern: he commits his offense while in a depressive state, which is brought on by guilt feelings as a result of repressed hatred; after the offense has been committed, he may be elated, or manic.

Beneath the surface in this type of psychotic offender, we find, as in all mental difficulties, a conflict. The natural instinctive strivings and desires have been checked by social traditions and ethical standards; the human being unconsciously rebels against being held back. For reasons unknown to him, he later strikes out against society in some way, and then, after he has done so, the release makes him happy and satisfied.

The manic-depressive lives in a stage of uncertainty, because he can never know when a mood will come upon him. He also never knows the reason for it, and usually resorts to explanations of a physical disturbance or disappointment or something of the kind.

Perhaps the fundamental difference between the manic-depressive psychosis and the schizophrenic psychosis lies in a depth of emotional expression, which is characteristic of the manic-depressive and non-existent in the schizophrenic. The schizophrenic also tends to be less in touch with reality, to be more episodic and bizarre. He is primarily influenced by the fantasies and sensations of his inner world. The manic-depressive is influenced more by emotional stimuli, such as feelings of inferiority and guilt.

The similarity between the two would seem to be a general disintegration of the personality. Whereas the schizophrenic is disconnected in his thoughts and feelings, the manic-depressive is disconnected in his moods and is therefore unpredictable in his attitude from one day to the next, or even from one hour to the next. Whereas a certain change in mood is found in all maladjustments, the range from the heights to the depths is most outstanding in the manic-depressive.

With the psychotic group of offenders must be counted those produced by alcoholism, syphilis or encephalitis or other organic conditions. Here too may be counted those psychotic disturbances which take place as a result of delirium, such as found in epilepsy, or under influence of drugs. We ought to add mental defectiveness if the intellectual endowment was the foundation for the criminal act.

This short summaric classification of offenders is based upon etiologic factors and upon the personality make-up of the delinquent. As any other classification, it has its shortcomings; but it still may serve as a guide to delineate the offender, and to determine what kind of psychiatric treatment he should have and from which he would best benefit. As our knowledge widens, this classification will change accordingly.

8

Sex and Murder

THE public reacts to sex criminals with disgust. This is mainly because they have broken a law which to most people is holy. Furthermore, the public feels that these sex offenders have sometimes emotionally mutilated their victims, if not physically mutilated or killed them. But it should never be forgotten that we deal with a certain type of offender, who, because of a distortion in his personality make-up, entered upon a crime which he himself in many instances could not help.

There is probably no other crime ever committed about which there has been so much bias, ignorance and general lack of understanding as this one. Among people who like to consider themselves both modern and tolerant, who often discuss sexual subjects openly and freely, we constantly find completely emotional reactions to the sex offender. They are branded as "fiends" and "sex maniacs," as persons utterly different and unworthy. Still, it is hardly pure speculation that some of the very men who sit in such high and holy judgment may commit virtual rape upon their wives and gain satisfaction from the pain they inflict. It was Freud who once said that in all sexual relationship there is,· in one degree or another, an element of sadism (pleasure derived through inflicting pain) and of masochism (pleasure received from such inflicted pain).

The first question we have to concern ourselves with is: Does there exist an offender who commits *only* sex crimes? This question is an important one, so important that it was one of the first prob-

173

lems we had to try to solve when we studied sex offenders at Sing Sing. We found that several among them had committed other types of crimes. One had even committed seventeen offenses of various types. Some of the men who had perpetrated rape or incest had also carried out thefts or robbery. One delinquent held up a woman with a toy pistol, then tied her but did not attack her sexually, or he followed a woman into her apartment and then tied her without otherwise touching her. But always he took some money from his victims so that, according to his own explanation, the police and the courts would believe he had been burglarizing or robbing them. What he himself did not know was that he took the money from them since he had to "take" something he had not received. Remembering also that, psychiatrically speaking, robbery is a symbolic expression of rape, many of the offenders' crimes were in a symbolic way an expression of their sexual drive.

Possibly the only type of sexual offender who basically keeps on with the same sexual manifestation is the homosexual and exhibitionist. But even this is not always true. In particular it has been asserted that a man who commits exhibitionism does this only. However, we have a few cases where a man started out with exhibitionism and then about ten years later was convicted for rape.

In 1950 we made a survey of about eighteen hundred inmates at Sing Sing prison to ascertain how many of them had committed in reality sexual offenses. The result was that about 25 per cent of them had committed sexual crimes, while according to the legal definitions and convictions only 10 per cent had been sentenced for sex crimes.

Furthermore, of the 102 sex offenders who were given thorough psychiatric-psychological examinations by a psychiatric social worker and a psychologist, and whose cases were discussed in a staff meeting, it was found that forty-four of them had perpetrated crimes other than sex offenses. Sixteen of the 102 had committed sex crimes previous to those for which they had most recently been sentenced; in all, fifty-six of them had been previously sentenced. These numbers indicate that sex offenders repeat their crimes, a fact which is in contrast to some previous claims. Realizing the nature of sexual behavior in general, and judging from the

174

numbers given, there is no doubt that the sex offender is a repeater. In our cases there was a repetition in their behavior which took on the nature of a compulsion. Only twenty out of 102 sex offenders had not committed a previous crime. Twenty-two of the 102 had committed both sex and other offenses previously. (For assistance in my work, I am indebted to one of my associates, Ruth Brinckman.)

The findings indicated that all sex offenders in our study were emotionally distorted; that many of them committed their crimes because of an almost compulsive drive, and often under the influence of alcohol; that all of them were rather under-sexed than over-sexed; that those who sought out children, the "sex fiend" in particular, were emotionally immature or had never or rarely had either successful or unsuccessful sexual relations with adult women.

Most striking was the emotionally and physically insecure childhood experienced by all of our cases. Many of these men had no stable parental figures, as they had been passed from mother to grandparents, to aunts and uncles, while fathers were in and out of the home, or mothers deserted. Many mothers remarried and stepfathers had been cruel and abusive to those men as children. Their own parents had been strict, dominating, sometimes cruelly abusive. Often we found a strict father and an overprotective mother or the other way around. This overprotectiveness is less a sign of love than of the need to dominate the child and keep it as a love object. The physical insecurity of these offenders' early lives was particularly noteworthy. Often there was no place geographically which they could steadily call home. This means that also there was no older person, either man or woman, with whom they could establish a good relationship and feel secure in being loved and accepted. Institutionalization, such as experiences in orphanages or in correctional institutions, also played a part in these men's lack of ability to identify with a parental figure. No wonder that they were confused in their sexual role, since they had such poor experiences both with men and with women.

This disturbed childhood was also reflected in their attendance and in their behavior at school. About 60 per cent of them had played truant or had become disciplinary problems in other ways

175

and/or showed gross emotional maladjustment which neither the parents nor the school could handle. From their erratic truancy or somewhat insignificant aggressiveness many of them developed behavior disorders which led them more and more from the rules of society culminating in a crime.

It is important here to make an essential distinction about the classification of the sexual offenders. They are usually called "sexual psychopaths." The overwhelming presence of mental conditions through which they can be recognized and classified has shown in our cases that the term "sexual psychopath" is a myth. When this type of offender is studied sufficiently, every investigator will see that there is no such entity. As a matter of fact, our investigations clearly indicate that these sexual offenders comprise a group of people who suffer from different types of mental disorders and social maladjustments, all having, however, a common manifestation—sexual deviation. But these deviations can be also found in other types of offenders, particularly in kleptomaniacs and firesetters as well as in embezzlers, murderers, and so forth. Many of the offenders, too, show a great deal of sadism and brutality in their personality make-up. Although some of them had been "model children," still they harbor many aggressions which have only temporarily been subdued and which can be released when they are provoked.

I quote from our report: "It is interesting that fourteen of these 102 sex criminals were at one time considered model children, and at least 32 others seemed to be good boys. Actually this behavior was a defense mechanism; they were submissive through fear of asserting themselves. The offenses they later committed expressed their long-suppressed resentment and rebellion against the authority of parents to whom they had no satisfactory emotional relationship. One of these offenders brutally raped and sodomized an older woman. As a child he had been extremely well-behaved and always dressed like 'a little angel.' "

It is also interesting to note how many sex offenders were considered "sissies" or "mother's boys" as youngsters. Often their parents or other relatives worked them very hard or gave them family responsibilities far beyond their capabilities. In any event, they got

176

very little out of being "good." We found that when these boys became adolescent, many of them underwent a real change. That means that the good boys became bad boys, that they began to go with gangs and to be tough. This seems to have been the only way in which they could break away from the family and from their earlier patterns.

It is not surprising to find that most of these sex offenders have had a severe conflict of authority. They hate and fear authoritative figures; they want to get even. They feel resentment toward anyone who has power over them. What is more surprising is the great proportion whose underlying personality structure is dependent and passive. Over this passivity have been laid traits which conceal the extent to which these men are seeking something which they have never had, satisfactory human relationships in which love would play a part. The normal development of conscience and an acceptance of the social code has been greatly interfered with by the lack of acceptable parental figures in their early lives. While many men can hold the tendencies which will get them in trouble with the law in check when sober, when they have had too much to drink, impulsive behavior occurs. This can and does get them into trouble.

Of great interest is the fact that many of these sex offenders cling to work as a safeguard. They try to protect themselves against their own impulses by sticking to their job in a compulsive way. If there was ever truth in the rule that work keeps a man out of mischief, it certainly is applicable in the case of the sex offender.

Every sex offender we examined was found to be emotionally disturbed, but such an emotional disturbance is not characteristic of sex offenders alone. We cannot find any decisive dividing line between sex offenders and other law breakers. In all offenders, be they sexual or non-sexual ones, two outstanding factors were found: early emotional deprivation and a resulting hostility, resentment and hatred. The sex offenders we studied did not suffer from one single type of mental condition. The same basic emotional disturbances with different manifestations are found in robbers, thieves and murderers.

Furthermore, many of the men who have raped were brought up

177

by sadistic mothers who made the boys fearful and insecure of the other sex and from whom they received the impression that a woman had to be taken by force. When such a man married, he chose a wife who in many instances turned out to be as sadistic as his mother had been, a fact we discerned when we examined her psychiatric-psychologically.

In our research we have found that the way a man or a woman chooses his partner is not at all accidental. Deep psychological unconscious motivations are at work here. While we have for a long time said that we should try to understand the parents of the offender, there has up to now not been any research concerning the psychology of the wife of the sex offender. This is more regrettable when we remember that in many cases he is not returned to his parents but to his wife, and it is this home environment which is of such importance for an emotional rehabilitation. We therefore also made a thorough study of the personality of the offender's wife whenever that was feasible. In addition to psychiatric examination, the study was undertaken by means of psychometric tests, Rorschach tests, and other detective techniques. One of my associates, Rose Palm, Ph.D., has been devoting much time to this particular aspect. Although the number of wives examined is not many, still certain definite findings stand out.

"The consistency in the psychological pattern of these women proved amazing. They appeared almost identical on most points. First of all, it is important to know that none of these women, though they all married severely disturbed individuals, was of inferior intelligence. Their intelligence rated as average or even above the average. Another interesting factor is that all stayed with their husbands in spite of cruelty and proven unfaithfulness. While some of them were temporarily separated or ran away on occasion, they always returned to their husbands, even against the advice of parents or friends. It is evident that there was in the relationship an element of strong attraction. During the many years of the offenders' incarceration, the wives all remained faithful and waited for their husbands' homecoming.

"This may not seem amazing when one realizes that on the surface all of these women showed masochistic trends. At first glance

178

the picture would appear simple: the sex criminal needs an object for his pent-up sexual aggression and chooses a submissive partner. Underneath, however, the situation proved far more complicated.

"Through treatment of sex offenders, it has become clear to us that their offense usually constitutes an act of revenge and rebellion against their rejecting and threatening mother-figure who does not respond to their dependency needs. The most striking finding now in these eight psychograms was that these wives, without exception, showed under the mask of submissiveness outspoken sadistic traits. They all showed a latent masculine orientation and a need to compete with men. Underneath, they all showed a need to dominate and to sexually defeat and castrate their partners. They appeared to be rejecting and frigid. They threatened the sex offenders in their most vulnerable spot, their doubts about their masculinity. The result is apparent through a neurotic choice: these men found themselves back in the same psychosexual situation in which they had been since childhood—threatened and castrated by an overpowering female figure. The wife unconsciously repeated what the mother had done. She drove the offender into attempts to prove himself in different ways, and without realizing it, stimulated the various forms of sex offenses."

One interesting instance is that of one inmate who was arrested for entering the apartment of a young married woman during the night while she was sleeping. He hit her on the head and later had sexual intercourse with her. In an attempt to describe the motivation for his crime, this offender said that "the idea was to force my will upon a woman—violently."

This wish on his part may become understandable in the light of the personality structure of his mother. In our study, objective test results on the mother showed her to be a rigid person, greatly lacking in emotional responsiveness. Her test pattern indicated that she was sexually maladjusted, unwilling to accept a female and motherly role. The offender obviously was trying to break out of his role of submissiveness to a domineering mother.

It is especially interesting that this offender's relationship with his wife was an almost complete duplicate of that with his mother. He unconsciously chose a mate of the same pattern as his mother, with the consequence that his neurotic choice aggravated his problems by the accumulation of more pent-up rebellion and the inability to release his aggression directly.

Like the mother, the wife of this inmate was described as self-assertive and aggressive. Her record too showed strong sexual frustration and a denial of her femininity. Like the mother, she showed masculine attitudes and a need to compete with men.

It goes without saying that this man's failure to compete successfully with the two masculine women who were so intimately connected with his life contributed to his seeking to solve his problems by an antisocial act.

As was found in our previous research among other types of delinquent persons, here also we found a great deal of emotional impulsivity which individuals have difficulty controlling.

In general, it can be said that there is always an attraction between man and woman, be it biological or psychological. This attraction possibly comes more to the fore when an offense of a sexual nature takes place. As a matter of fact, this conscious or unconscious attraction not only on the part of the man toward the woman but also on the part of the woman toward the man may be in many instances responsible for the man's sexual attack.

We do not find this seduction limited only to sexual offenses, but to many other crimes too. Many women swindlers or "con" men seem to be able, because of a certain seductive ability which basically is sexual in nature, to cheat seemingly honest people out of their money. When we examine these victims, we find that they, too, had seduced or intrigued the swindler into continuing the money game. Bribing and extortion are two devices which are found both in the swindler and his victim, in the aggressor and his victim. They are two counterparts in the same way that sadism and masochism are present in the attacker and his victim. The same relationship we find in many murder cases where homosexuality is involved.

In particular, we find the mechanism of seduction operating between son and mother or between father and daughter, both forms leading to incest. It is a question whether or not the aggressor always is seeking for his sexual aggressions a person who once was close to him, be it in heterosexual or homosexual relationship. Deep psychological mechanisms are at play here, most of them unconscious. Therefore, the persons involved are horrified when the real motivations come to light, and deny vehemently what might have been in their minds.

Unconsciously, a woman would like to be taken by force. In literature, such a theft as that of the bride in "Peer Gynt" for instance is quite a common phenomenon, and is undoubtedly instigated by the unconscious wish of the woman to be raped. Frequently we find this seductive inclination in small girls, in their being flirtatious, seeking out rather dangerous or unusual spots where they can be picked up, or exposing themselves more or less deliberately to sexual attacks.

Here it must be recalled that just as a child has his parents as objects to imitate when young, he has them before him as someone physically desirable too. A child is aware of sexual sensations at an extremely tender age. There is on occasion a reversal of the usual roles: a girl will at times identify herself with her father and therefore desire her mother, in which case she will probably become a lesbian or, if not, at least very frustrated sexually as she grows older. The same can be true with a boy: he may identify himself with his mother and desire his father. A reversal of this kind will give rise to homosexual activities, also punishable by law, and also created by lack of understanding, properly controlled attention and, perhaps, a mutual sexual attraction between parent and child.

The usual situation, however, is rather the positive one of opposite sexual attraction. When, as sometimes happens, there is an incidence of a brother and sister becoming sexually involved, this is only an unconscious punishment of, or revenge upon, the parent. A boy may think to himself: "You see, Mother, I have a girl, I don't need you, you who have rejected me for my father. . . . I too am a man, not a mere child." And a girl would reason in the same vein about her father.

This, then, is the beginning of sex in the child's mind. When that mind, or rather the emotional outlook of that child, is not developed, or is subject to shock, the child will become unconsciously fixated at this stage.

181

Of course, this unconscious attraction between man and woman is not the sole motivation for the sexual attack upon a woman or, for that matter, upon a man. One other basic reason for a man seeking out another person in a sexually abnormal way is that the attacker is not emotionally grown up. This lack, unless it is mental defectiveness, is invariably emotional. When there has been an interruption in the transition from infancy to adolescence, to childhood, to adulthood, the effect is fear. Fear is the one basic emotion of which we are all capable, the one trap into which anyone can fall if he does not keep his wits about him. This fear may in given cases make a man afraid of women of his own age or of men as old as he is. As a child every one of us is more or less unconsciously living in a fear of being abandoned by our mother every time she goes away or puts us down.

The thought of incest is deplorable to everyone of social conscience. It is when this attraction, within civilized surroundings, develops to the exclusion of those outside the family group that it is abnormal, and it is then that the aspect of a basic fear is so much a part of the picture. When the attraction is this extreme, it means that there is timidity and insecurity insofar as going outside the blood ties are concerned. And a man who has had strong incestuous desires for his mother will undoubtedly have the same kind of feelings for his daughter; his wife will be a virtual stranger to him.

This is perhaps sickening, but more important, it is sick, particularly inasmuch as incestuous desires are, more often than not, unrealized, unrecognized, and simply the foundation upon which are built many peculiar patterns of behavior.

Some years ago I had a young lady in treatment exactly one hour when it became clear that it would be necessary for me to see her father. Ann had stolen a considerable sum of money, and it was immediately apparent from what she said that her father was making so many demands on her that he had unknowingly twisted her entire life unmercifully, all under the label of love. It was love, yes, but it was more than parental love; it was unconscious sexual interest as well. Ann's father objected to her frequent visits to the library because they took her away from him and also gave her a form of independence. What he sincerely believed, and told her, was that she should be putting the energy expended in this pursuit of knowledge into the natural feminine one of homemaking: an unconscious desire on his part for her to be and act out the role of his wife.

Mr. K. objected to every young man that called on Ann; none was good enough for her. Ann rebelled against this and ceased having them come to see her; instead she went to their house. When in time she found that she was to become the mother of an illegitimate child, she expected to be disowned. Instead, her father said he wanted to adopt the child, thereby illustrating his unconscious desire to have a child by Ann himself. And Ann, who had unknowingly become pregnant primarily through a desire to obtain revenge against her domineering father, felt that she had been tricked by his reaction. So she turned to theft, which did manage to humiliate him. Upon interviewing this man it was soon evident that he had also been sexually attached to his mother, just as unconsciously as he was to his daughter, and when his mother died, he simply transferred his biological desires to another feminine member of the family.

When we examined sex offenders who had committed incest, we found a strong anal sadistic trait in them. In our interviews, they spoke as if they wanted to frustrate the chances of marriage for their daughters. They wondered "if their daughters would explain to the men they were going to marry, that they are not virgins, and whether they would tell them that it was their fathers who put them in this condition." Apparently, they wanted to keep the daughters for themselves. It was also quite interesting to note that all these inmates kept away from other women, which might indicate that they could not be potent with them.

I recall a case wherein a young man actually attacked and experienced intercourse with his mother, telling her as he did so that he could not marry her and would therefore have to have her this way.

Upon being questioned about this in jail, where he would spend at least the rest of his twenties, he said he could not understand what came over him. What came over him was a mobilization of a sexual fixation upon his mother, started at a very early age. The offender forced his mother to go with him to the cellar where his father used to beat him, and then he raped her. He associated his early torture with guilt feelings about his desires for his mother.

In this case our examinations showed that the mother had exerted a seductive influence upon the boy. This was brought out by the extremity of her guilt feelings at having had sexual relations with her son; also her previous history indicated it.

This was a case of incestuous rape. Experienced officers of correctional institutions and detective agencies have frequently stated that there usually is no such thing as rape. In many cases this is true; from all the evidence available, there seems to be an unconscious desire on the part of the victim to be attacked. But no mother would admit even to herself that she had had sexual desires for her son, although she could very easily have had them. And it is here that the logical question naturally arises: if those mothers and fathers who have neurotic children were sexually adjusted themselves, that is, completely and thoroughly advanced beyond the stage of sexual blood ties, would not their children also become adjusted? We know that tension within families brings upon all kinds of maladjustments, but it also stands to reason that, just as we do not go on loving a person who does not care for us, if the person we are interested in sexually shows no conscious or unconscious interest in us, ours will eventually fade out too.

An often unrealized point about any kind of incest, rape—either statutory or forcible, to use legal terms—or rape with murder, is that each and every one of these sexual crimes is fundamentally tied up with the Oedipus or Electra complex.

Perhaps the most clear-cut illustration of the natural incestuous tendencies in man is to be found in the high incidence of incest among illiterate people. There are certain sections of these United States wherein the practice is so accepted that it is never questioned, any more than eating or talking is questioned.

In less civilized times, the father, according to custom, would have physical relations with his daughter before he gave her away. In pornographic literature, the personalities practicing sexual activities of various kinds are very often related, usually father and daughter, or brother and sister. This is illustrative too, considering the educational level such reading matter usually reaches.

When rape occurs, it is, no matter who the victim, an unconscious attack upon the parent. Civilization rules that there is to be no sexual contact between parent and child, thus a child suppresses his desires and later takes his resentment for this suppression out on someone else, while in the very depths of his mind he carries a picture of his mother and an ingrained loathing for her hold upon him. When murder follows the rape, the psychological conditions are the same, but the hostility is greater, and thus the offender gives way to his baser instincts of release from hostility, satisfaction of sexual desires, and murder.

When we examined persons who had been convicted of rape, usually a large discrepancy in age was found between the rapist and the woman raped, she either being much younger or much older. Rapists seemed to avoid women of their own age as sex partners. We found that those who did rape women their own age were basically more obsessive than the others. When, for instance, they were working, they did a conscientious job and were very obsessive about it, but it seemed that suddenly their obsessive tendencies lessened or even disappeared for a short time, while they committed a crime with apparent little sense of guilt. In this way, they differed from the obsessive compulsory neurotic persons we saw in the clinics, who if they had committed an antisocial act of which they themselves disapproved, suffered from a high degree of guilt feelings. Many of the offenders who had committed rape or incest did not actually regret their crime, although some did, but mostly they regretted the consequences of having been apprehended and convicted. This indicates that they did not think they did anything wrong. The only wrong thing in their eyes, was that they had been caught. This personality trait we also found in the case of Alex (described on page 28) whose wrongdoings also depended upon whether or not he was going to be discovered. The faulty Superego development here and in the cases of the rapists is the reason why they started to regret their crime only when they were convicted. Many of these offenders had definite traits of an antisocial character; their upbringing had been inconsistent and they had constantly been alternately neglected or overprotected.

As to their psychodynamics, it may be assumed that these obsessive compulsory offenders had some type of temporary release of their Superego during which time their crime was committed. This particular aspect might be what is antisocial about them, which is not a definite neurotic sign. That is what is pathological about them.

What can be readily surmised is the great disproportion between the rapist's impulses and his control of them. From the psychological testing we were able to find that the men who had attempted and completed actual rape showed the greatest disproportion between their impulses and the control of such impulses. Those men who used violence had a weaker motor control than in the cases where there had been voluntary co-operation on the part of the girl. The man who only attempted to rape, but did not complete it, showed only a small disproportion between his emotions and its motor control.

The rapists we examined at our project were attracted only to certain types of women, and *only* toward them could they be potent. Also, it was quite extraordinary to see that these types of delinquent persons are not promiscuous by the common definition of the word because they constantly seek out the same woman or girl.

Homosexuality being a sexual relationship between members of the same sex was previously called "sexual inversion" and is extremely common. It has been estimated that from 30 to 40 per cent of the male population has once or more in a lifetime had a homosexual experience. Kinsey, of the University of Indiana, who had gone through data for more than 12,000 case histories in the nine years preceding publication of his book, *Sexual Behavior in the Human Male*, has estimated that a major portion of the male population has had some homosexual experience between adolescence and old age. The social and psychopathological significance is tremendous in view of such figures. Dr. Kinsey believes that if homosexual experience were to be the criterion on which to isolate people from the rest of the community, about one third of the male population would be included. If all individuals who were homosexual were to be institutionalized, they would have to segregate 30 per cent of the population. Dr. Kinsey goes on to say that the homosexual person has been a significant part of human sexual activity ever since the dawn of history, primarily because homosexuality is an expression of capacities that are basic in the human animal.

Frequently, we find male homosexuals in those who have been unusually fixated on a man. With the consequent regression, they select men who in one way or another remind them of their original object. Often though, many of these homosexual men have a longing for women. Frequently, they have been fixated to their mother, a fixation which is extremely pronounced. Homosexuals very often talk about their mothers in a devoted way which cannot but impress everyone, a matter every psychiatrist has experienced.

The more a boy identifies himself with his mother, the more he will develop into a homosexual. Such an identification, however, depends to a large extent upon the person with whom they have experienced most frustrations and disappointments. We therefore often find people who are inclined to become homosexual in those families where the father was rather weak, or where there was no father figure at all. These men had a mother around them constantly with the result that they became frustrated in certain definite matters. Of course, this does not preclude the possibility that there are children who do become homosexuals even if they have had no mother. If a boy is brought up by male members of his family, he may have an inclination to develop toward homosexuality, a matter Freud pointed out when he thought that the prevalence of male homosexuality in old Greece might be caused by male slaves who raised the children.

Often homosexual men are masculine-looking, which is an over-compensation. More frequently homosexuals seem to be feminine, soft-spoken, seductive. It is quite significant to see how isolated homosexual persons are. As a matter of fact, this isolation is a manifestation we have found in all types of sexual offenders examined. Since these homosexual leanings are something the individual fears and thus tries to repress, and since homosexuality is not accepted in our present-day society, this particular phenomenon has to lead its own life "sub rosa." Frequently, we find homosexuality as a motivation in many actions which are not easily understood by the lay public. In one celebrated criminal case in which the accused was found guilty, there possibly was present between the two men involved some homosexual leanings which never were brought out in court and which possibly had been fatal in their relationship.

Even exhibitionism and pedophilia, or sexual interest in children, can be traced back to an emotional stunting centering around the parents. When a man exhibits himself, he is unknowingly demonstrating to his mother that he is a man, for such activity can almost invariably be found to have originated at least in the mind when the mother rejected her son in some way, or made him feel weak or inferior.

Both exhibitionism and pedophilia are manifestations of deep feelings of passivity. When a man is abnormally interested in small children, it only means that unconsciously he is trying to establish a feeling of potency and of superiority. On a more surface level, the cause of pedophilia is a self-identification with small children: the offender unconsciously has always been a child, and he is here associating with his equals.

With exhibitionism, the more obvious explanation is a narcissistic nature: a man who shows himself apparently loves himself. Yet in many instances the cause for exhibitionism is a man saying unconsciously to his mother, "I will show you what I have and you show me what you have." The offender is afraid of being castrated and in order to deny it, he has to show his male organ. Unconsciously, he wants the onlookers to react to it, or he may unconsciously be saying to them, "I show you my penis so that you can be afraid of me."

All the cases of exhibitionism we have seen have been dependent persons who were brought up by a rather domineering and overprotective mother. These offenders have frequently been mentally defective, but very often have also suffered from a neurosis. It has been surprising to note how many exhibitionists have been psychotic.

Intimately connected with this exhibitionism is voyeurism. Those with this condition have had early experiences which have raised anxieties and feelings of castration. Those scoptophilic individuals little by little develop a constantly increasing need for looking at their objects and this may at times take on a form of sadism. This voyeurism is a form of passivity; the practitioner does not act, but looks only. In this way, as Fenichel states: "Peeping may from the beginning be a substitute for sadistic acting." (*The Psychoanalytic Theory of Neurosis,* p. 348).

Coprophilia is a condition in which a person becomes sexually excited with his excretory organs. Closely connected with this is an individual's interest in using obscene language and collecting pornographic literature. Here is undoubtedly a combination of sadistic, exhibitionistic and coprophilic tendencies.

Clinically speaking, when sadism plays a part in sexual desire and gratification, it is because of the initial introduction the person had, as a child, in matters pertaining to sex. When a child is threatened with punishment if he indulges in sexual activities, he becomes conditioned to pain and fear in connection with sex. A neurotic condition then sets in whereby the person cannot experience orgasm, or complete sexual satisfaction, without pain or fear. These more than less unconscious emotions are, therefore, considered the punishment that has to be paid in advance for sexual pleasure. Then too, inasmuch as children react to interference in their sexual life with resentment and anger, these attitudes can also become combined with the sexual life, so that when the person grows up, he must inflict pain upon his partner in order to fulfill the prerequisite necessary to obtain orgasm. Thus not only do sadism and masochism work together in a relationship—that is, a sadistic person requires a masochistic person with whom to work out his neurotic emotional needs—but sadism and masochism are also inevitably intertwined, and a person does not have the one without some of the other as well.

The need to inflict cruelty and the need to experience it are often extended outside the sexual sphere. But then too, all sexual desires are often expressed in other ways or, to use the technical term, displaced onto other forms of behavior, as mentioned previously.

It is impossible to go into all aspects of sexual behavior that should be known by everyone, but a few points have to be mentioned. We have found through individual and group study that

189

the amount of sadism and masochism expressed by individuals has a direct relation to the amount of pain and fear to which they were subjected as children.

It can be said that unless a woman has been approached psychologically before physical contact is established, she will be in a less advantageous position. Unfortunately, many men and women because of their own ignorance or narrow-mindedness about sexual life are incompetent adequately to judge sexual relations. Yet many of the very same people are called upon to judge other people. They are inclined to consider any sexual activity as perverse unless it fits into their own pattern of behavior. So particular has mankind been about sexual life, that it has always had special laws dealing with it, especially establishing a penal code for sexual conduct.

One reason why the individual encounters so many difficulties in his sexual life is that, normally, another person of the opposite sex is necessary for sexual outlet. If a man, for instance, is hungry, he can find food and be satisfied, but to find a partner for the purpose of sexual intercourse may not be so easy. This is not so much because the other person is unavailable as because of his own personality make-up. He may be afraid of women, resent or hate them, or he may be too attached to his parents, all of which arouses guilt feelings in him, thereby consciously or unconsciously inhibiting him.

In order to designate sexual behavior as a satisfying experience, orgasm and emotional satisfaction must accompany sexual relations. The means through which this can be accomplished are varied. However, the one pattern as determined by anatomy and physiology and which is most frequently employed, genital to genital relations, is considered to be the standard method. (But this does not mean that all other methods are abnormal; it means simply that these patterns of behavior are "modified." If we use such a word we may be able to rid ourselves of the word "perversion," which connotes moral judgment.) When a deviated manifestation of sexual behavior takes place, it occurs because of an increased desire for additional stimulus. When we examine such deviationists, we most frequently do not find any pathology of the body. Their inability to perform the sexual act is caused by conscious or unconscious inhibitions. When the individual cannot perform in the standard way, he resorts to a modification and that brings him emotional satisfaction.

There are many variations of this modified pattern of sexual relations. The accompanying manifestations such as sadism and masochism are well known; what may not be known is whether these two manifestations are as natural and normal a part of sexual life as they have been claimed to be. Our basic problem is: How does it happen that pain, which means not only suffering pain but also inflicting pain upon others, not only is incorporated into bringing about sexual satisfaction, but becomes a condition through which sexual satisfaction can be obtained. If it is true that sexual relations should be the highest form of human life, then why should there be any pain in natural sexual life?

Through clinical experience, we have learned that when a child is told by a parent to stay away from sexual activities and is threatened with punishment, he may become conditioned to pain connected with sex. It is very easy to understand that such an individual, loaded with feelings of guilt and anxieties and fearful of punishment, cannot experience orgastic satisfaction without first experiencing torment and fear of being punished. Within the life of every child brought up in such a way there is bound to come a time when pain is considered as punishment or payment in advance for his sexual pleasures. Very frequently this situation is complicated by the fact that many individuals react to interference in the sexual life through spite and defiance and with anger. Thereby, anger and rage can also become combined with the sexual life so that as an adult he can inflict pain upon his partner thus fulfilling the prerequisite necessary to obtain orgasm.

Much of sexual behavior then is intermingled with pain, a condition which is acquired. We see the same thing happening when a woman experiences pain in giving birth. This may also have something to do with a fear of punishment because she has done something forbidden. This leads to one important conclusion: that much of the pain and fear which accompany sexual behavior is an acquired condition which may be alleviated if educational and psychiatric measures are taken. The mechanisms underlying sexual behavior are mostly unconscious and therefore difficult to change unless probed. Those who experience pain, anxieties and fears in their sexual life will show to a great extent the same symptoms in other spheres of their life, which indicates that they have not grown up emotionally.

An important question is: Why do sex offenders take it out on little children? It is because men who are emotionally ill are also emotionally immature and basically feel themselves to be children. This is also true, to a varying degree, of those men who commit virtual rape upon their wives and then condemn the "sex maniac."

The great number of sex crimes speak their own language. It has been estimated that in New York State alone about 600 sex offenses, including prostitution, are committed every day. According to the Federal Bureau of Investigation's crime report, 16,380 rapes were estimated to have taken place in 1949 in the United States, while in 1950 the figure had risen to 16,580. There has been an increase of violent sexual crimes but possibly this increase is not more than could be expected in view of war conditions which to some extent have destroyed family life and separated husband from wife. It is interesting to see that in England the number of sex crimes has increased from 5,000 in 1938 to more than 13,000 in 1950. Other crimes of violence have similarly increased from 2,700 to 6,200 in the same period.

Frequently we hear about "waves" of sex crimes, but these waves are very often the outcome of the way the press handles special cases. The daily press has given the sex crime in general much attention, but it is only fair to say that the problem is far greater and more complex than people usually suppose. It must be noted that persons who are convicted of sex crimes are only a small part of those sex offenders who appear in the police records.

When in 1950 we prepared our report to Governor Dewey on sex offenders, we had this particular problem in mind. Statistics for the State of New York show that during 1949 we had 24,760 arrests of offenders for major crimes, all of whom were verified through fingerprints. Of these 1,338 were charged with rape and 708 with other sex offenses, particularly sodomy and carnal abuse of children. Let it be said here that in statistics it is impossible to distinguish between crime of rape in the first degree and in the second degree. The first involves use of force, the second is with a girl under the age of eighteen even if she might be willing. These offenses are quite different in a psychological way, and that point is not understood by lawmakers because the law does not distinguish between them as sharply as it should. Many cases of rape are in the second category, sometimes not worse than a love affair between a boy and a girl. (*Report on Study of 102 Sex Offenders at Sing Sing Prison*, p. 11).

Viewed in another light, if all American men were apprehended and committed for their illegal sexual acts, about 95 per cent of them would be sent to jail. The other 5 per cent would be left to support and guard them and, with the remaining women (about whom at this writing there are no such statistics) carry on the world's work.

Such is the relationship between that which we, in an effort to preserve society, have established for ourselves in the way of rules and regulations, and that which is inherent in our basic natures. It has been said that we are two people, that which we would be and that which we are in spite of ourselves. Man is the highest form of animal, but only the highest form, and he cannot divorce himself from his biological inclinations. He is also a spiritual being and an idealist. So he has a fight on his hands, satisfying both of his selves. He can only win it by acknowledging and understanding both.

Murder somehow holds a special thrill for a great many people. It is shocking and daring, for it involves a thorough overstepping of the boundaries of society. Many a law-abiding citizen would like to overstep, but never dares; only in his dreams, fantasies or wishes may he be bold enough to kill. Yet it is hardly uncommon; an average of twenty murders a day are committed in the United States alone. Seven thousand and twenty homicides were known to have taken place here in 1950, and in 1946 the Federal Bureau of Investigation reported that 400 murders occurred in New York State and that New York City had 346 of them. This same year only 41 homicides occurred in New Jersey, and in 1950, 63 murders took place there, according to information from the Department of Institutions and Agencies, Trenton, while in New York

City during the same year 733 murders, manslaughters or other homicides occurred, according to Commissioner Thomas F. Murphy's report of June, 1950. The great increase here from 1946 is because of the recent overhauling of police customs in recording crimes and is probably not owing to any appreciable increase in crime itself in the City of New York.

Murder carries with it the mystery of death and violent death. But there is another side to this vast interest, a deeper side, one not readily admitted. Murder is the extreme and final illustration in active form of the hatred that may be present deep within the human being against someone or something, or, more often, against several persons and many situations.

When we tighten up with resentment and mutter unattractive words under our breath, we feel slighted or wronged or unfairly treated; we are giving in, if only verbally or mentally, to an intrinsic antisocial force within us which puts us first and others second. When the sensation of being put under is permitted to continue for a long time, with no release, no expression, murder may occur, for many are capable of it.

More often, however, murder arises from deeper causes that are unknown to us, for we have all learned well the rules of society expressed in the commandment, "Thou shalt not kill." This regard for other humans is so carefully imprinted on our minds at an early age that the situation of the moment would have to be very great indeed, and to have existed intrinsically for an incredibly long time, for us to give in to it.

Murder is most often brought about by completely unconscious motivation, which in many instances has its emotional roots in childhood.

Murder may be committed in a psychosis as a result of unconscious motives, but a man who kills is not necessarily insane by any means. He may be neurotic, or a mental defective, or have a character disorder. He is almost never, however, a victim of pure circumstance. We, with the help of our mothers and fathers when we are little, for the most part create our own circumstances.

A psychotic man may kill his wife whom he believes is going to leave him, and he may be convinced that this is his reason for killing her. Deep within his mind, however, he unconsciously may be identifying his wife with his mother, who left him when he was a child. In such a case, the desire to kill may be dormant for years and then be activated by similar circumstances.

Another man may kill a woman in a fit of jealousy because he thinks he loves her. Actually it may be that in his insecurity he feels possessive about her and, when she shows attention to someone else, he loses his self-esteem. Killing her restores his own opinion of himself; he feels that he is potent, that he still is the master.

We find still another deviation in triangle murder situations. A young man will often kill the woman in the case because of the injury she has done to his pride, but an older man usually kills the rival, particularly if the rival is a younger person. An older man in such a case may unconsciously feel sexually inadequate, and therefore inferior, to the other man.

Occasionally a murder is committed for no apparent reason. The unconscious reason may be an identification of the victim with the offender's father or mother. Seeing someone with the same general appearance, or hearing a voice that is similar may bring to the fore the instinctive desire to kill that one's father might have aroused, and which was kept under control by the well-learned lesson of "Honor thy parent."

I shall never forget the first time Angelo came to see me; here was a man who had killed his wife and had attempted to kill her lover.

The name this man gave me was an alias. His real name was a long, strange one of many syllables, and he was forever fidgeting for fear one of his wife's relatives would shoot him in the back. There is an accepted rule in Sicily, where he was born, that if a person is murdered, the relatives of the victim have a right to slay the murderer. This fact complicated the case, making it difficult for me to decide if he was the victim of a persecution complex or in very real danger. It finally became clear that it was a combination of the two conditions, plus the fact that he was apparently attempting to prove insanity and thus free himself of the charge against him.

Angelo stabbed his wife in the heart because she had been unfaithful to him, and then tried to kill her lover, too. Angelo did not

know it, but his wife symbolized his mother, who had had an affair with a man other than his father right before his eyes when he
was a child. At that time Angelo thought his mother was behaving badly, not in relation to his father, but in relation to him, for he
was strongly attached to her and remained so all through his growing years and during his marriage years as well. When Angelo witnessed infidelity again, all of his early suppressed aggression came forward; a woman lost her life; a man, her lover, lost his foot where the
knife fell the second time; and a son lost his birthright to freedom,
forever to be known and tagged as the son of a murderer.

Angelo had a deep underlying schizophrenia, which took a little
time in revealing itself, for he was, of all things, trying to prove he
was psychotic in order to escape his sentence. He couldn't have
been more insane; all he succeeded in doing by his antics was to de-
lay any kind of certain conclusion. He was finally put on probation
and under psychiatric care.

While on probation Angelo went job hunting, but he found that
he wasn't very well suited for anything. In resuming his old work
as a waiter, he was in constant conflict with those around him. This
was in 1945 at a time when help was scarce, so his employer kept
him on. But in late 1946 when waiters started to be more plentiful, the restaurant owner told him that he would have to behave
politely toward the customers. Angelo, who still had to fight his
hostile attitude, had difficulty in getting along with the patrons
because they too demanded politeness of their waiter. When an incident took place during which Angelo insulted a customer, the
manager had to let him go.

Angelo became then a night clerk in a hotel. But here too his disposition was all wrong for the job: he insulted the guests, antagon-
ized the night manager to such an extent that he was asked to
leave. The next day he came and saw me, and I was rather exasper-
ated about his behavior. Angelo himself was very unhappy and
promised me that he was going to behave next time he got a job.
However, I was not satisfied with his promises because I felt that
he would have to have a job where he could utilize in one form or
another his aggressive tendencies. I then asked him whether he
wouldn't like to become a butcher. Angelo looked up happily and

answered, "That's it!" He left the office, got himself a job as a butcher and has been able to get along happily ever since. He takes out, on chopping up raw meat, the frustrated aggression he feels against his wife's lover. Having been able to sublimate his murderous impulses, he has since been quite content.

I recall another wife murder that occurred some years ago. It will live long in my memory because of its brutality and also because of the tremendous stir it created among men and woman alike.

A man of Greek God beauty, Eric, stabbed his wife fifteen times with a butcher knife, and then forthwith went dining and dancing with her best friend, Lola. He was apprehended the following morning while considerately feeding the birds in the park and feigned utter surprise at the news. He admitted that he knew Lola, had always loathed his wife and had on several occasions voiced the wish that she were dead. But he insisted he was innocent and as an alibi, claimed that he had been at a concert at the time of his wife's death and even produced the stubs.

Investigation, questionings and psychiatric examinations produced quite another story. Eric had indeed been to a concert, but he had become bored with it and had left early. He then went to see his wife, learned that she had cut him off from the allowance she had been giving him, his sole source of support, and in a fury he killed her. His going out with her best friend immediately afterward was caused by complicated reasons. One, to escape the anxiety produced by such an incident, it is quite common for an offender to engage in some kind of entertainment or other seemingly cold-blooded activity; Eric was here no exception. Two, he had a great contempt for women, all of whom, including his wife, represented his mother to him. Thus he took a malicious delight in telling Lola, a friend of his wife, that his wife had on many occasions, including this one, asked him to take her out. He knew full well how she would feel when she learned that his wife was already dead. And, of course, he attempted to place the blame on Lola for his wife's murder.

Eric was a parasitic individual who had never done a day's work in his life. He suffered from an extreme type of a character disorder with pronounced homosexual tendencies. Before his marriage, his comfortable income stemmed almost entirely from his sexual activities with men of means. He felt no qualms about describing these acts in detail, and his assumption appeared to be that his appeal and ability along these lines were well worth any reward he received.

While Eric described his lurid scenes of made-up men in feminine boudoirs, men with earrings and ankle bracelets and perfume, waiting for him to visit them in their beds, women sent him notes and checks and presents. He had killed his wife and didn't care, yet women were still pursuing him. Those women who found Eric fascinating were sexually frustrated and unconsciously convinced that his unrefined, uncivilized behavior was a sign of sexual potency. He was also handsome and daring and unattainable to women—a devastating combination, inasmuch as it was a direct challenge: only one could win out, and each woman thought she was the one. Poor deluded creatures. . . . By a strange paradox too, he also brought out the maternal instincts in women. He was helpless, needed looking after, needed their support, which was one reason why he did not need to work. The women paid a high price to spend a night with him—up to five hundred dollars, which was the ceiling price.

This man unconsciously wanted revenge for the insults he had suffered in early childhood from his mother. This was strongly repressed in him because in all my examinations he never even gave a hint that he was trying to get at his mother. His father was a weak character, given to alcohol at times, who possibly had little, if any, influence at all upon his son. Eric could not identify himself with his father although he may have tried to do so. Instead, he became attached to his mother and this unusual constellation of a family situation, coupled with the emotional tension between his parents, brought out Eric's basically antisocial character development. He could not develop any concepts of conscience; he could not develop any attitudes of what was "mine or thine," and could not feel like a real man. For that reason he took part in all sorts of sports, trying to develop his body, the result of which was that he appeared as a well-built, six-foot-tall athlete with brawny shoulders, good-looking—an eye catcher. Men fell for him, but so did women. He finally ended up by selling himself, becoming a male prostitute from which he derived a great deal of pleasure. His narcissism was gratified when he was able to manipulate both sexes according to his own feelings.

Only once did I see that he felt badly that he had killed his wife although he tried to deny it. At that moment he had tears in his eyes and lamented that he had brought disgrace to his mother. The last time I saw him, he asked me how long a time he was going to get. I answered that I was not a judge so I could not say. But when he repeated the question and I ventured, "Maybe thirty-five years"—since he had been found guilty of second-degree murder— he laughed it off and said, "I will not get more than seven."

The next day the judge gave him thirty-five years. I had not spoken with the judge and, even if I had, it might not have changed his attitude. This man was sent to prison, which, by the way, is a gentle irony, inasmuch as he would be quite an influence in a place where there is no sexual outlet of any kind. He should have been put under psychiatric treatment, not just thrown in with other sick men who were also being punished. But more about this later.

Here again, we have a pure and simple product of an unfortunate home situation, of a weak father and an egocentric mother who had little interest in her home or family and, therefore, made no effort to bring up her child properly. Eric lived completely as he pleased, in his own world, but developed a tremendous facility and a need for comfort and affection from others, and yet could maintain no affection ties himself. In his peculiar untutored thinking, he also made no distinction in his mind between work, play and affectional relations. He was, as many women thought, a brute, but he was a perverted one, thus making the tragedy somehow complete.

It is part of the same tragedy we see happening in any murder. When a man kills, it is safe to say that he has wanted to kill for a long time. He may not have been consciously aware of it, but this hostility and hatred has been within him. Depending upon his personality traits and their relative quantity, his aggressions turn outward or inward: a homicide or a suicide may take place. Senseless though a murder may appear to anyone, to the killer himself it has a meaning even if the meaning is symbolic. If a profit motive such as found among gangsters is not present, murder is frequently the killing of a substitute when the real object is not at hand.

It is surprising to see the high homicidal rate in the United States. It has been estimated that a murder takes place almost every hour. In England the homicide rate is much lower. In England in 1949, murder known to the police per million of population was 3.1, while in 1948 it was 3.9. In 1945, just after the war was over, the rate was 5.1. (Information taken from *Criminal Statistics, England and Wales,* 1949, Table E, p. 17. Courtesy of Dr. Gruenhut, England.) This means that while in England the rate per murder has been one in 300,000 of the population, we in America have one murder in about every 16,000, or between fifteen to twenty times as high. In Sweden 11 murders were committed in 1913, while 6 were committed in 1941, and 2 in 1947. In the two other Scandinavian countries, Norway and Denmark, the rate is as low as in Sweden.

It is difficult to estimate accurately the rate of homicide or any other type of crime committed. However, whatever the figures, the rate of crime in general and the homicidal rate in particular is high here. Beside the psychological factors which are related to the individual's aggressions, there are some sociological factors here which have to be taken into consideration. In addition to the previously mentioned competition among people, we also should make note of the early frontier life in America which, judging from the prevalence of guns available practically for everyone, has still left its impression. The United States has been considered the foremost land of private enterprise and this attitude has by now become rather ingrained and has made itself felt in all expressions of life, including homicidal attacks. If we consider, for instance, that Australia is also very much like a frontier country and, except for natural resources, was developed in the same way as America was, by immigration, etc., it is surprising to find that the homicidal rate there is so low as compared with the United States.

In Australia, in 1946, there were 53 homicides carried out by males and 37 carried out by females, altogether 90. The population in Australia, in 1946, was 7,517,981 according to official yearbook of the Government of Australia (Commonwealth Bureau of Census

200

Statistics). This means that there was one murder for each 80,000 inhabitants.

One explanation may be that the competition here is much stronger than in Australia and that emotional tension prevails possibly to a higher degree in the families than there. Also, the population of Australia was, in 1950, only 8,185,539 spread over a vast continent, while here we have people crowded in cities which number from two to seven million inhabitants. In some localities here there are so many people around one has to go a long distance in order to get away from them. Think only of the great masses of people in the subways or on the highways or on the beaches. Without being aware of it, the individual may feel fenced in, overpowered. Under pressure of so little elbow room, there may be a general higher inclination to become hostile, aggressive and hateful than in a country where there is plentiful space.

Although these factors may be considered extraneous, they are of a certain importance, because they have in many instances given the background of the murder scenes. These sociological factors are part of the stage for what could be called a typical American murder where gangsterism is involved.

We will here try to illustrate how such murders come about as part of racketeering. "Murder Incorporated," a gang of racketeers staffed with many professional murderers, operated in the nineteen thirties in Brooklyn. The information given here is partly through the Senate Crime Investigating Committee headed by Kefauver, and other sources.

The interesting point was that homicide originally was not the purpose of "Murder Incorporated." They started out in liquor, in prostitution and gambling, branching out into control of unions, became owners of night clubs, during which time murder was incorporated as a "legitimate" way to handle competitors or people who were considered troublesome. "Murder Incorporated" was among the criminals called "The Combination" in Brooklyn. They organized an association of criminals who branched out to Detroit, Chicago, San Francisco. While Benjamin ("Bugsy") Siegel, later killed, was dictator on the West Coast, Charles ("Lucky") Luciano, later deported to Italy, and Louis ("Lepke")

Buchalter, later electrocuted in Sing Sing, operated in New York. According to the New York *Times*, April 1, 1951, and to the Kefauver Crime Investigating Committee, the leaders of "Murder Incorporated," were Joe Adonis, Abe ("Kid Twist") Reles, who died by falling from a window in 1941, and Albert Anastasia.

It has been estimated that in the years between 1931 and 1940, "Murder Incorporated" killed 63 men in the New York area alone, and that a greater number than that were murdered by gangs in Detroit, Chicago and San Francisco. The individuals killed were people who the gangsters feared would become informers and tell upon them or competitors who were in the way of the gang. Among their greatest undertakings was extorting money from longshoremen. The means these gangsters used to get rid of the union officials or other enemies were infamous. Persons were killed with ice picks, buried alive in sand or even burned alive. One gangster was thrown into the river with his feet encased in cement. That the gangsters murdered other gangsters did not prevent them from killing law-abiding citizens too.

The breakup of this gang came in about 1941 when Reles, faced with a gangster who was going to tell on him, promised to tell on the gang if he himself were given leniency. Several theories exist as to his death, but even when Reles was kept in custody, watched by six policemen, either he fell to his death or was killed. It has been thought that Reles may have been killed in order to eliminate the State of New York's case against Anastasia.

Important as these persons are for the prosecutor and for the public in understanding how such a gang could come into operation, possibly more important is the psychological make-up of these gangsters. We can say, of course, that they were antisocial, highly egocentric, impulsive characters, on the whole possessing personality traits which reflected their hostility and hatred and led them to kill. Homicide is the highest form of aggression, which may lead to murder or assault regardless of whether highways are jammed or apartments are overcrowded.

It is a pity that these gangsters who were a menace to the United States have never been psychiatrically examined. It is a pity that the Senate Investigating Crime Committee or other bodies

202

of investigation have not themselves approached the problem by suggesting that these criminals be psychiatrically and psychologically examined. If they were, one would be surprised to find the amount of mental pathology present in them.

9

Prisons and Imprisonment

SHOW me a man who, in undertaking to work in a prison, is at all times unaffected by the job, and I will show you a man as completely without a soul as the most hardened racketeer in the country.

When I reported to work in my first prison assignment in the States, the first unforgettable scene I encountered was that of a row of five men facing a wall in utter silence. Upon making inquiries about this extraordinary sight, I was told that they were prisoners who had just arrived and were waiting to be officially admitted. But no one could tell me why they stood, in a row, silently facing a wall.

Apparently, rules and regulations become so much a habit that no one questions them. The men who work in prisons have simply decided in a practical way to do a job that has to be done and in the process have pushed out all emotion in order that they might go on with that job.

When we made our laws and built our prisons, we took into account certain facts of what man may and may not do. A man was convicted of a crime, had to be punished, and for that reason the prison was established. However, the way we went about it was colored by the way we felt prisoners should be dealt with. Firstly, we built our prisons as far removed as possible from cities, and we devised systems and conditions that were to exist behind the brick

205

walls. Many of these conditions were, of course, a precaution against dangerous offenders. In earlier times we were not much concerned with what went on within the man's heart; unfortunately in many places that is true even now, for to many people's thinking, these men have no hearts—if they did, they could not be criminals.

Imprisonment comes after a fair trial and is supported by us, the tax payers. Within prisons men and women are fed, clothed and kept clean. They now even entertained and permitted privileges. Undoubtedly there are many of us who think their way of life is too good for their sort. But their sort is the same as your sort or my sort. The makings may have differed, and the environs, and the opportunities. Otherwise they are human beings, individuals, just as we are.

Only those who have been incarcerated in a prison are able to realize what it means to be deprived of freedom. To have to get up in the morning at a certain time, have meals at a certain time, go to bed at a certain time, is a thing the average citizen does every day. But he can, if he chooses, stay home from work or, take his family out for dinner one evening, or go to a movie. That the prisoner cannot do, and that is the difference. He is confined for a specific time to one place, to one cell, to one walk, to one sort of people, to one life: incarceration. Therefore, always uppermost in his mind is: "When can I get paroled?"

If I seem to be harshly sitting in judgment on society, I do not really mean to, for it has taken me a number of years to correlate what I think and feel, to make a solid effort to get it on paper and then into print for the public to read and, I hope, act upon. I know well that the large majority of my readers have never even been in a prison, and, like the prisoners, we can hardly be condemned for that which we do not know about. I speak of society as being responsible in terms of the future, not the past. But the future is quickly catching up with us, for prison is failing now as it has always failed, and crimes are mounting all the time. The modern improvements, movies, baseball games, the everlasting cleanliness are marvelous in themselves, but they are not enough. What is wrong is that we are facing the issue upside down.

I do not know how long it was before I was aware of the apathy among many prison workers. Their attitude was not wholly assumed for defense against their deeper feelings. These men were underpaid, very badly underpaid. They were often unqualified for their jobs. Some of them were illiterates who were unemployable elsewhere. They were either poorly instructed or not instructed at all concerning attitude or behavior, except insofar as keeping the prisoners in line was concerned. With many guards who had had no opportunity to assert themselves elsewhere, this was an excellent chance, and they delighted in blowing their whistles or in telling the men what to do. Nearly all of them appeared completely unconcerned about all things and truly uninspired. I often found myself wondering who were the most unhappy and dissatisfied, the prisoners or the employees.

Were the matter of employment handled right in the beginning, prison work would, first of all, be considered a highly specialized and worth-while job; a job in which the whole future of the country is at stake, a job through which one can have a hand in the delicate and challenging business of remaking broken and dispirited men and women. It would be considered a prestige position, one with a future, one in itself covered with glory—not a catchall for anyone who wanders in unable to find employment elsewhere.

There are, of course, those few commendable citizens who, in spite of all the basic shortcomings of prisons still think they can help and who work there even though they could obtain infinitely better paid positions elsewhere. To those persons I hereby apologize for the above, make it clear that the category is by no means all-inclusive, and admit to deep admiration with a slight edge of pity because of the handicaps under which they work at the present time.

This last group almost invariably includes doctors and psychiatrists, for whom there is a crying need in the outside world but who recognize the greater need beyond the cold stone walls.

Some time ago I read a book called *I Am a Fugitive from a Georgia Chain Gang*. The book had quite an effect on me because of the brutal conditions it described under which men were treated as animals rather than human beings. Yet even so, it would be difficult to imagine anyone subjecting a dumb beast to the labor, beatings and filth under which those prisoners were forced to exist. It was extremely heartening to learn that upon publication of the book, although the author was still at large, an investigation of this chain gang was launched and the worst conditions ordered cleaned up. When the fugitive was finally apprehended some years later in California, he was granted a pardon and set free.

This story illustrates the progress, steady improvement, and great heart that make up so much of American life, and it also gives me hope for the future of the large inhuman institutions known as prisons. For ours has been an error in judgment, not mercy. If it were mercy alone, there would not be the continued consolidated effort toward entertainment and decency of living quarters for prisoners. We have simply used the wrong starting point.

We know that crime is not perpetrated solely because of external situations. We know that it is far more the result of twists in personality, or, in other words, emotional factors. It therefore stands to reason that we cannot tackle the problem of correcting criminalistic tendencies within individuals unless we consider first the individual. We have thus far concentrated upon better external conditions in prisons for the prisoners en masse. This is rather like trying to remove temptation from the potential offender while carefully forgetting the broken or unhappy home with family tension that made him susceptible to temptation in the first place.

An alcoholic drinks to cover up his fears and anxieties, but when the binge is over and the hangover has subsided, he is right back where he was: nothing has been accomplished and the problem is, if anything, worse. When a man commits a crime, he most often does not know why he committed it. He frequently has an excellent reason to offer which he will consider satisfactory, for he has reasoned it out that way. But there is no surface circumstantial logic acceptable for crime, any more than there is for alcoholism. With both conditions, the person is compelled into his behavior by unconscious drives that are in no way apparent to him. Already conditioned into a certain set pattern of feeling and acting at a certain age, he continues with it without knowing why, just as a dog that has been at the front in war will cringe when he hears a gunshot or firecrackers exploding.

Take a man who has committed a crime and put him in prison, and all you do is suspend him. You very seldom change him or teach him or rehabilitate him. Most of the time you do not even punish him. He is in his own eyes simply caught: he must stay in prison a certain time and, if possible, get out sooner than he is supposed to. When he gets out, he will sometimes be the same man he was when he went in, a little older, a little more bitter and perhaps a little wiser in a thinking way. But his thinking did not get him into trouble—his feelings did.

When you talk with an imprisoned man, he will tell you that he is never going to get in trouble again, that from now on he is going to go straight. He is at the moment so overwhelmed with his imprisonment that he is willing to say anything in order to get out. His feelings dominate his thinking. As soon as he is released from prison and is on his own, he often forgets what he said while he was there. A short while ago I spoke with an offender who had committed a serious crime and who finally was going to be paroled. In my last interview with him, he overwhelmed me with his earnest protestations that he would never come back here because he had now learned his lesson. He talked with so much vigor and so much insistence that he could have convinced anyone of his beliefs. Three months later he was returned to prison as a parole violator. I spoke to him when he was back in prison. He was a little ashamed but had apparently forgotten what he had told me the day before he left prison. I reminded him of it. He looked down and said, "I couldn't help myself."

That is just the reason why so many prisoners fail when they come out. They cannot help themselves because they themselves do not understand what is going on in their minds. Thus, many of them commit new crimes as soon as they have been paroled. It has been found that of those paroled in New York State in 1934, 52.1 per cent were returned to prison within a period of five years. And 42.6 per cent of those paroled in 1941 became parole violators during the following five-year period. (*Federal*

Probation Quarterly, March 1949, p. 41.) We can note here some improvement.

When we consider offenders who have been sentenced in Federal courts, James V. Bennett, Director of the Federal Bureau of Prisons, states that for the country as a whole approximately 60 per cent of all the men who pass out of the gates of the prison return again within a period of five years. In some states this percentage of repeaters is less, in other states greater. (*Federal Probation Quarterly*, March, 1949, p. 19.)

In what sort of condition are those inmates when they leave prison? Most of them leave prison psychologically unchanged. If there is a change, it is more often for the worse than for the better. Bennett has stated that only 30 per cent of all men and women in American prisons experience any reconstructive activity while they are in prison. He goes on to say, "Prisons everywhere are inadequately equipped, staffed by poorly paid, dissatisfied and superannuated personnel working long hours. Their programs have been skeletonized to the point where rehabilitative forces are all but stifled."

Although there has been some decrease in the number of parolees being returned to prisons, still the high number of recidivists who every year commit new crimes and are again imprisoned indicates that our system on that particular point has failed. It is correct that punishment in many cases is a deterrent against committing crimes. And as long as human nature is so frail, we will have to have policemen and we will have to have prisons. But our system will have to be arranged in another way.

We send all kinds of offenders to one and the same prison. Robbers, embezzlers, exhibitionists, kleptomaniacs, murderers, and a score of other types of criminal are kept in the same place and get the same handling. There is no individual dealing with inmates in the prison except in the extreme case of an offender who becomes insane and is sent to the hospital for the criminally insane; or of the troublemaker who therefore has to be put into isolation. The great majority of inmates stay in prison without being given much individual attention.

To incarcerate all kinds of criminals in the same institution is the same as sending patients suffering from peptic ulcer, fractured legs, brain tumors, tuberculosis, cancer and infantile paralysis to the same ward in a hospital to be treated by one and the same doctor. We don't do that today with people suffering from sickness. But that is just what we do with prisoners. Also, patients in hospitals receive treatment while prisoners, practically speaking, get none.

The word imprisonment in itself connotes punishment. Yet let us consider the irony here. Present-day prisons have everything from classified employment to education, from excellent food to varied recreation. To all appearances, they do everything within their means to keep the inmates happy. But with a little imagination and depth of humanity, the so-called punishment or segregation from society could be effected and at the same time the men and women themselves could be kept contented while being mended and made into worth-while future citizens.

Before we can begin to consider what would be right, first let us consider fully what is wrong, and start from there. Only then can we try to build a new institution.

Psychologically, I think that the best initial step would be to abolish the word "prison." By dictionary definition a prison is a public building for the confinement of criminals. Practically speaking, a prison is a place where we house offenders, keep them in custody so they can be out of circulation, away from law-abiding citizens. But all delinquents are more or less emotionally disturbed. In them is a sickness and a human tendency toward revolt when injustice has been felt, at whatever age.

Who are those people who sit in prison? They consist of various individuals, old, young, some talkative, others silent. Some try to cover up their anxieties and make the best of a bad situation. Others are emotionally upset and quite disturbed. But all are deeply depressed within themselves. Some are in prison for the first time, others for the fifth or tenth time. Many are like those friendly fellows you see every day in the street; only a few are threatening. In my experience at psychiatric clinics and correctional institutions, I have only been threatened once and that was in a psychiatric hospital.

211

Of all the inmates in a prison, there are only about 20 per cent who can be considered dangerous and who therefore need to be kept in maximum security prisons. All the rest could be kept in places without walls or bars. But in order to keep 20 to 25 per cent of the offenders in prison, we also have to keep another average 75 to 80 per cent there. For this 75 to 80 per cent, we should establish rehabilitation centers to which they would be sent not in terms of years but in terms of how ill they are.

This would mean that they would be given no time span for confinement, for this is meaningless. Those confined to these centers would be given to understand that they have need of and will receive treatment, individually. The genuine psychopath would, of course, have to be treated not only individually but as a special case, for his is the extreme one, and unfortunately not hopeful for recovery. He should thus be kept closely guarded and, if he is considered dangerous, behind bars. The bars, however, would mean nothing more than protection of society in general. They would be put up in the same spirit that they are at the windows of psychiatric institutions: thus there would be no question of punishment.

There has been much discussion about the best method of dealing with the incorrigible monster, this genuine psychopath of which we speak. Men of exceptional brains and ability have suggested that we take their lives, that we destroy them lest they destroy us.

What is such a method but a pure admission of defeat, just as we admitted defeat when, with all our special endowments, we decided who the war criminals were and thenceforth did away with them? Sometimes I wonder who actually won the war, or the peace, when I consider that to secure our safety we found it necessary to kill a large number of very sick men. We forgot, because we chose to forget, the conditions that created their inhumanity and lust for power. And in our forgetting we also made it clear that in our opinion any country that wins a war inherits the right to kill off any of its enemy's so-called guilty leaders—as though anyone who actively participates in war could be free of guilt.

If we were to resort to such barbaric tactics as killing the incorrigibles, would it be possible to free ourselves of our own guilt? And is it really possible that we consider ourselves entirely within our rights when we put to eternal sleep a man who has killed another? An eye for an eye, a tooth for a tooth—have we progressed no further that this in our involved civilization?

There is a term for people who speak as I am speaking. Soft school, they call it. I do not belong to any such school of thought, but rather am interested in the hard inescapable facts. War does not stop war, and killing does not stop murder. We must get at the source, for the more we undertake retaliation, the more we are all guilty, until one day we will all be hardened, all removed from the fundamentals that should make for good, clean, decent living. Six lines from Oscar Wilde's "Ballad of Reading Gaol" have haunted me for years:

> But there were those amongst us all
> Who walked with downcast head,
> And knew that, had each got his due
> They should have died instead:
> He had but killed a thing that lived,
> Whilst they had killed the dead.

In summing up my whole attitude concerning punishment and retaliation, perhaps I might best say what I have always believed: Beware of the man of complete unquestionable virtue, the upstanding self-righteous citizen, who for all creatures of weakness has one general attitude: "Give 'em hell." This is the man who dreams of sleeping with the voluptuous maiden on the corner while carefully reassuring his wife she is the only woman, who envies his devil-may-care business partner at the same time that he reaches for the bi-carbonate of soda and who, when hearing or reading of someone's making or winning a lot of money sneers and secretly wishes it had been himself. Many of these are the villains who make our laws, and we are the suckers who live by them, knowing no better. For they sound so good, or at least we think they must, even if we don't know what they say—for they are the law.

Those who would kill others for their misdeeds want and have not the courage to undertake murder themselves. This, of course, does not apply to those who advise capital punishment from a humanitarian standpoint (although it is sometimes difficult to believe they have no unconscious motivations), those who have faced the issues and the human sadness involved. With those people I merely disagree, and toward them I feel no animosity. For we all are human enough to arrive at wrong conclusions, and it is with the people who see things wrongly but with a heart that one can bargain; not those who are at all times coldly and impersonally correct.

These excellent examples of solid citizenry are also twisted, so twisted in fact that if they did not keep themselves in complete control constantly they could at any time exchange places with the murderers, the rapists, the thieves, whom they hold in such utter contempt. Sometimes, though, they slip up.

Prisons are such an easy way out for us. We do not have to associate with them; we but maintain them, and this we do painlessly, or in any event ignorantly, for it is never pointed out to us just how many dollars of income tax goes toward keeping men from their freedom. We do not have to witness any of the old-time cruelties, and we are thereby kept free from stain or the sensation of participation. When a man is released and ends up turning to crime all over again, we calmly say that they will never be able to do anything with him, that they should never have let him out.

They never really tried to do anything with him, and when they let him out they did so to a society that is completely hostile to the "jailbird." Most of the time when he tries to go straight, we won't let him because we won't give him a job, or at least not a decent one. So, in his indignation, he turns to crime again, to live and to strike back.

There are others who are worse upon release than when they went in because of the influence of men who have learned the hardest way that although crime may not pay, going straight once you have served a term pays almost nothing at all. Now and then we find employers who appear to be magnanimous in employing ex-convicts and giving them their chance, but by pure conditioned reflex many of these employers watch the men very carefully and may even be suspicious of them. They fear former criminals. Human sensitivity is much too delicate to ignore such reactions and they hardly make for good working conditions. The slips, errors, mistakes in judgment therefore occur, and the ex-convict out of a job is once more an ex-convict with negligible resources.

I have not been able to find any estimate of how much it costs society to maintain a prison. We therefore went through the cases of nine offenders who had been in trouble with the law before; they had either been in a reformatory, in a prison, on probation or on parole for varying lengths of time. We looked carefully into their life histories and we tried to find out how much society (that means the taxpayer, you and I) has paid until now for those offenders. All in all, we came to the astonishing result that nine offenders had cost the State of New York about $75,000. That means over $8,000 each. If we apply this cost, for instance, to the 1,800 criminals who are kept at Sing Sing, we come to the result that these prisoners so far have cost the state, at a conservative estimate, ten million dollars. In this figure is not counted the price of law enforcement, probation and parole. It costs the State of New York about one million dollars each year to maintain Sing Sing prison alone.

What does the state get in return for its money? Certainly not healthy individuals. The prison stay dulls the inmate in many cases, makes him lose initiative and courage and puts him into a depressive mood where there is little hope. Judging from the high numbers of recidivists, our system of correction and rehabilitation has failed. This is no reflection upon the personnel working in a prison. Rather it is a reflection on all of us who make up society. It has been my fortune to work with many prison officials who have basically been good. I remember Commissioner Lyons of the Department of Correction who believed in rehabilitating prisoners and who held out so much hope for psychiatric help for them. The unfortunate thing is this, though: As long as we have the basic principles of prison system still existing, there is little that can be done. Prisons should be only for those criminals who are considered dangerous and those who for the time being are considered untreatable.

Psychologically, it is true that many offenders seek punishment through their crimes, and therefore one might argue that they must be imprisoned because they actually need it and even unconsciously want it. But imprisonment seldom washes away their feelings of guilt, which are far too deep for them to understand anyway. The imprisoned felt guilty before they committed a crime and therefore had to be punished. If that punishment is effected, there is bound to come to mind eventually the guilt for the crime that was used as a device to seek the first punishment. The cycle thus would never end. In the event that a term of imprisonment could rid a man of his feelings of guilt, he would never escape the feeling of being punished anyway, for the world, in spite of the laws that say it does, does not recognize a term of imprisonment as a debt paid to society, a slate wiped clean. By our attitude, behavior and outlook, we say: "Once a criminal, always a criminal, never to be trusted, never to be permitted to live. Stamp him out, for he is a treacherous thing."

We also encounter the situation of a prisoner having served a term, feeling that he has paid for his crime and therefore believing he can go out and commit another. Having paid for his old crime, he does not see any reason why he should not be permitted to commit a new one. In other words, the fact that we permit a prisoner to pay for his crime gives him a license to commit a new crime. Having served his prison sentence for the first crime, he feels he has squared himself with society and his conscience is eased.

Of course, this argument which the prisoner has within himself and with which he tries to explain away subsequent crimes is a fallacy, but it shows how we give the criminal new means to repeat crime.

It should also be pointed out that if there were no punishment, crime would be so frequent that there would be no end to it. This is true in any case.

The natural human inclination is to think that men in prison are guilty men. With rare exceptions, they are, technically speaking, but so are many, many more. Roughly speaking, out of 1,000 who commit crime, 500 are reported to the police; the other cases are considered insignificant or are let go because of mitigating circumstances. Petty thefts, prostitution, and transportation of liquor into a dry state are often not reported; either the people in-

216

volved do not care enough, or the police on the case consider it unimportant.

Of the 500 cases reported, perhaps 250 offenders are caught. Of the others, the accused successfully deny the charges, skip town or are freed through political connections.

About 150 of these 250 go to court: for the other 100, restitution is made or the charges are dropped. Perhaps 100 of the 150 are sentenced: the other 50 have alibis that stand up and therefore they cannot be sentenced. This leaves, out of 1,000 crimes committed, possibly 100 or fewer that receive sentences—and that number would be undoubtedly less were it not for insurance companies continually pressing charges which might otherwise be dropped.

Thus we see that the men who are sent to prison are sometimes simply the unlucky ones, or those not clever enough to escape the law. Sometimes we succeed in catching criminals who should be behind the bars. They represent only a small minority of offenders and of crimes committed, and this goes for those among your society as well as any other. For what is the essential difference between the man who rather proudly swipes carbon paper or pencils from the office in which he works and the man who steals bread so that his children may eat? One is more intellectually disposed perhaps and can laugh off what should be the pangs of his conscience; the other is terrified for fear he will be caught because he knows the bread does not rightfully belong to him.

What is the essential difference between the man who experiences illicit relations with a woman and the man who enjoys homosexual activities? Neither is acting under the protection of the law or the approving eye of society. Yet the first man, if caught, does not become imprisoned even though he might impregnate the woman and bring an illegitimate child into the world. The second man, if discovered, is imprisoned despite the fact that his partner may have enjoyed the relationship, plus the all-important aspect that homosexuality is a distinct sickness sometimes curable, but only by treatment and never by punishment.

If we can say then that criminals differ from other people in degree, so can we say that one crime differs from another only in degree, and that none of us is as innocent as we would like to think. We are as honest or dishonest, and as agreeable or belligerent, as our consciences and our early training will permit. With most of us when we do a wicked thing, the suffering in our mind far surpasses any outside punishment that might be inflicted upon us. When this is not so, someone other than the wrongdoer has been at fault. It is up to us to find out where these things began, and to re-start these people out in the world from there. When we cannot do so, then it is up to us to keep them, for they are our monsters, of our own making no less than Frankenstein's monster was of his. If we are so specially endowed and self-righteous as to decide the fate of a man who has erred, then we can surely be no less noble in admitting and taking the responsibility for our own errors of stupidity, education and lack of understanding.

Another devastating aspect of prisons is the politics that run them. Of course if we do away with prisons, we should thereby automatically do away with the politics too. But unfortunately, as we know, such idealistic conditions are seldom automatic.

When I undertook my first prison work here, one party was in power in government and in the prison as well. The former fact I knew; the latter I did not. I was therefore somewhat taken aback when an acquaintance said to me, "You must belong to the prevailing party." When I told him I had no idea of what he was talking about, he asked me how I ever managed to get in, and carefully explained to me that almost everyone he knew who worked in the prison got his job through pull.

I am still trying to figure out which is worse: this, or those who worked there because their ability, education, and initiative could secure jobs for them nowhere else. I am inclined to think that those who get in through their political connections are the ones to be the most concerned about, for they were as basically dishonest as any inmate of the institution. All of which naturally means that the whole foundation was built upon dishonesty, making a beautiful paradox when we consider who were the men chosen to look after the offenders of society.

Let us not forget the reports about prisons and the fact that they were on occasion issued at election time, though they seldom gave the full story. Omissions that whitewashed conditions resulted in an acceptable and even encouraging picture that fooled the people, unlike the planned deceptions that the prisoners inside the prison tried and were caught at.

Within a prison we frequently find corruption. Very often brutalities occur which never come to the public ears; those brutalities, however, must take place because here is a system which is based upon force and discipline. Force reaps force, whatever form it takes. Therefore we also find—and not infrequently—murder and suicide among the inmates. Frequently a prison break takes place. About these details the public is informed, which again might indicate that we try to show to the world how bad those people are who break out of prison. Some of them are dangerous, that is true, and should never be out of prison; but most of them could be outside.

Because of the confinement the inmates experience, the prison is the perfect place for rumors which reflect the insecurity and anxiety every prisoner feels. In these rumors are mixed their dreams and wishes. They live in their own world, isolated from the real one. For that reason also they have created their own prison jargon. Since they feel threatened by law and are afraid and anxious, they do not dare to use common words and have invented their own verbal expressions. I have in front of me a list of such words.*

If freedom were the only thing a prisoner lost when he entered prison, it would probably not be so bad, even though losing freedom is sometimes more than a person can bear. Added to this is a loss of prestige, status; there is a feeling on the part of the prisoner that he has been rejected, put away for a long time. All of this is intended by society, although it may be unconsciously.

But in addition all possibilities for a normal sexual outlet for the prisoner are eliminated. This, despite the known fact that physical contact with members of the opposite sex is as natural and fundamental a function as eating and drinking. For that reason, all sorts of sexual activities such as masturbation and homosexuality take place. Since prisoners have been deprived of sexual gratifica-

* A glossary of prison jargon will be found in the appendix.

tion in the accepted manner, they have had to resort to the unacceptable way. If you ask a prisoner what he is most concerned about, he will answer, parole and sex. Naturally, the average citizen outside the prison feels the same since very often the thought of freedom and sex enters his mind. That men inside and outside of prison frequently tell sexy jokes expresses their own impotence and frustrations.

The fact that prisoners resort to masturbation and homosexuality does not necessarily mean, as some are inclined to think, that these practices change one's sexual habits for life. One's course in this connection is usually established at an early age. Still, an extended period of abnormal sexual outlets will not contribute to emotional adjustment. On the contrary, an inmate may develop a distorted sexual drive which was formed in prison.

It is a question of whether or not the prisoners should be given permission to receive their wives or common law wives for a night or at least a few hours. It has been reported that in Mexico some such arrangement has been carried out. It must be emphasized that the prisoners do not have any warm human contact while incarcerated except for the homosexual ones which often are of an abrupt nature. It is important for inmates to experience emotional security, at least for some short-lived moments, which might further their emotional well-being.

Think for a moment about this purely emotional side of prisoners' lives, of their wives and loved ones, and what it all must mean. What an empty and demoralizing existence it obviously is, for instance, for the "rock widows" to make their permitted visits to the prisons (for which, mind you, they originally must be fingerprinted), and then return to their silent homes to await the next timed visit. In between they can write a certain number of letters, for which they can receive a certain number of answers, all of which are read and censored. As for the future, the happy day when their men will come home, there is the hunted, unsure and unpardoned way of life to haunt them until they shall perhaps both die in the poorhouse, at our expense, and at our hands. And their children—what can they be, considering all we know of family tension?

As for those within the walls, how can they be sure what their wives or sweethearts are doing, that at any time they won't give up in disgust and perhaps write what was known in the army as a "Dear John letter"? If such a letter were to come, consider how powerless they, like the men in the army, would be to do anything about it.

The dreams which the prisoners have while incarcerated are significant in that they reflect their fantasies and wishes. Frequently they dream about being on the outside with their loved ones. Sometimes they dream they are being chased, cornered, or fenced in. The dream of being chased invariably means a homosexual flight from another inmate. This reveals, of course, the homosexual tendencies in the man concerned.

Some inmates dream about falling, or standing on an edge and losing their balance, and then they wake up screaming. One inmate told me that in the prison he constantly dreamed he was falling and that he never had such dreams before he was imprisoned. It was interesting to note that in his associations this inmate said his life had been crumbling, that his life was on the decline and that he was afraid of losing everything he had.

Sometimes prisoners have dreams in which they play the role of a hero who is returned to his home town with flags flying and bands playing. At other times they long for a good meal and dream that they are taken off by car to a restaurant where they can have steak and ice cream, hot coffee and pie. Hearing about dreams of this sort makes one feel full of pity. In our daily routine we take so many things for granted, while thirty miles from us live people who are forgotten by the average man.

Frequently, inmates dream that they are separated from their wives or children. Often the recurrent dream is: "I couldn't get to my wife; the crowd was keeping me away from her. I was trying to get to her but couldn't reach her!" Or "I saw my mother on the other side of the street but couldn't cross the street. When I looked at the other side again, she was gone." This inmate was one of many who before he came to Sing Sing did not dream at all. When he was separated from his family, he started to dream, or more correctly, he began to remember his dreams. Inmates have told me that during the night one can hear prisoners talk in their sleep, moan, scream in fright, or call for their mothers. All these dreams reflect their unconscious state of mind, their tenseness and anxieties. These dreams mirror the unconscious but, nevertheless, the most real part of themselves.

Prison life encourages the inmates' dependency. The simple fact is that we pay to maintain men in an unwholesome atmosphere in which only a few are re-educated and rehabilitated. What we really do is develop people who become passive and dependent upon the state. While it can truthfully be argued that a few of the prisoners are being trained or given some experience in a trade, our system allows the far greater majority to become passive and dependent.

It is good that prisoners are paid for the work they do. Some receive three cents a day, some five, and those in skilled industries receive as much as fifty-five, plus rations. This money is kept for them, or they make arrangements for at least part of it to be sent home. Those who today complain bitterly that they cannot exist on wages of a dollar an hour will most likely be impressed by this, and then be careful to follow up the reaction with the fact that prisoners are supported, and why therefore should they be paid at all. The question is, why should they be supported? Once again, under existing circumstances nothing else is feasible, for their occupations have little connection with the outside world and are often concerned with the running of the prison itself.

If offenders had to work for the food they eat and the places they sleep, together with food and shelter for their families, we in turn would be building instead of breaking those already very near the breaking point. If delinquent persons had to participate in the world's work in order to live, they would do so; they do their work now, uninspired as it is, and for as little all-round purpose as it happens to be.

It is a known fact that inmates, although they may spend their entire term of imprisonment thinking about ways of getting out and perhaps even scheming about illegal methods of doing so, once they have reached the point of release invariably have a certain reluctance to leave. It is the same kind of thing that happened with so many men in the army: they had been sheltered for so long that the idea of going out into the world and shifting for themselves, when the time actually came, seemed too much of a challenge. That is why many men re-enlist. For this very reason prisoners may unconsciously get themselves caught in more crime, in order that they may comfortably become little children again and not have to shift for themselves.

Those of you who are always shouting that the prisoners are only getting what is coming to them, and becoming indignant because we have to pay for their very existence—this should strike a bell with you. Indeed, why should you support these people who have sinned so badly? Why don't you do something about it? See to it that they have to support themselves. Why should society support them?

As for you others, who can see the humane side, think of the possibilities here. A community, self-supporting, of many sick people under treatment. Those who do their work well would get paid and live accordingly. Those who do their work badly or halfheartedly would get paid less but still live well. It is the sort of rehabilitation to put spirit back into a man, give him something to live for and to look forward to.

As for all the cries that may now arise to the effect that they had their chance and failed, so why should they come through now —I can only say that I do not believe they have ever really had that chance.

I think it should be obligatory for every citizen to visit a prison at least twice in his lifetime, at least so long as prisons exist. It would, I think, be impossible for anyone of sensitivity, or even mere sensibility, to feel detached from such an experience, to feel it unnecessary that *something* should be done.

And yet unfortunately there does exist the attitude that criminals in prison are getting what is coming to them. A bright young college man I talked with recently expressed such an opinion to me. It is this attitude we must methodically break down, by new teachings, new systems; by looking at the facts, not the figures; at the men, not the customs.

One little break from the gloom that surrounds me after a visit from the place impersonally known as prison, is remembrance of the warm full-hearted co-operation that is accorded me from the clerks and officials there. I often sense their own unexpressed indignity over the prevailing conditions and over-all punitive methods still employed. Somehow I have the feeling that they know I am with them in spirit, and with the inmates as well, and that I am trying to do something about an unhealthy, unhappy and outdated setup. I always have the assuring impression that they sincerely want to help.

I keep talking about myself, as though I were a single special crusader with reactions quite different from those of other people. Nothing could be farther from the truth. A good part of what I am saying about what I feel has been said in one way or another before. I give all my personal experience in the hope of conveying it to my reader, because essentially this is what I know and know best; and the stronger I can make it, while sticking strictly within the confines of truth, the better I will like it.

Our first impressions are often the strongest ones, and even now my original prison experience comes back to me. I at times find myself inclined to ruminate over the incongruity of a series of events and circumstances about which unfortunately all too few are even aware, and I ask myself how confused can we be before things begin to clarify.

I remember from Diagnostic Depot, Illinois State Penitentiary in Joliet, how impressed I was when I saw that the prisoners were served roast beef and ice cream, food almost unknown in prisons in the country from which I had come. This kind of menu was not uncommon at the prison here, and was given to inmates and prison personnel alike. Though nourishment of the spirit was denied, the prisoners' stomachs were certainly not denied.

I remember too that I often witnessed the sight of five or six men standing facing a wall without a word. Only on these occasions they were not waiting to be admitted: they were being punished for some infraction of the rules. . . .

This desire of wanting to punish is deeply ingrained in many of us. It reminds me of something I said in a lecture a couple of years ago: "The evil for which we punish others is of the same substance as the evil in our own thinking and feeling."

If we intend to improve society, we have to find a better way of helping those unfortunate individuals who have committed crimes. Prisons are unworthy of a society which calls itself enlightened. We owe it to most of the men inside there, to their families and their loved ones, and to ourselves, to undo the wrong things.

It is time that we now let right be done.

10

Treatment and Rehabilitation

W HILE the previous chapter indicates our failure in our dealing with delinquents, I am glad I can now write about a basic
constructive part of our fight against crime—treatment and rehabilitation. Not all offenders can be rehabilitated. Just as we have
people who will die of cancer or tuberculosis every day, or others
suffering from an incurable psychosis or a neurosis, so also we will
have delinquents who are beyond psychiatric help, whatever
method is used. But the majority of them can be helped if only we
have enough psychiatric facilities.

The reasons why people are still reluctant to believe that delinquent persons can be cured are twofold. First, many have believed
(and this includes those who should know better, physicians and
lawyers, for instance) that the criminal was born that way and cannot be changed. That is an error. Only in a very small percentage of
cases—offenders who are found to be constitutionally that way, or
who have acquired a disease such as encephalitis—can we speak of a
"born criminal" or an incurable one. Aside from this small percentage, every man who becomes a transgressor has developed delinquency because of environmental forces.

The second reason why so many have viewed psychiatric treatment for offenders with suspicion and disgust is because they feel
that prisoners should be punished, not "coddled." They do not
know that the task of the psychiatrist is to make the patient un-

227

derstand with his feelings that he has to be realistic, that he has to view life, painful though it may be, according to facts, not according to his wishes and desires—and act accordingly. To treat a patient in such a way that he can grow emotionally is not coddling. During his process of learning, which is of long duration, usually from two to four or five years, the patient gains emotional insight; it is only this type of insight which is important. The patient can very rarely be advised what to do unless his choice is something which definitely will harm his life. During psychiatric treatment, whether it follows traditional psychoanalysis or a modified form of it, the patient's unconscious material is mobilized, brought up into his conscious, so that he can learn to deal with those impulses which were heretofore repressed.

In general, it can be said that psychiatric treatment tries to free the individual from his symptoms so that he can adjust to his own demands and those of society. It requires, therefore, that a patient be able to reduce his personality abnormalities, be they aggressions, inhibitions or fears, to the minimum, so that he can adequately function.

The aim of our treatment is to settle permanently the conflicts between the instinct, the Ego and the Superego. We try to bring the forces from the Id into the realm of the Ego so that they become influenced by other parts of the Ego. We usually are able to bring about at least a modification of these conflicts. The decisive factor of the real problem of mental health is the dynamic interrelationship between the Id, Ego and Superego.

From a general point of view, we know that results of the treatment depend upon the constitutional strength of instinct and of the possibility of modifying the Ego.

. It may be said that when the causes of a neurosis are traumatic, we know that psychoanalysis has a better prognosis. With many offenders, particularly sexual ones, however, there is not one predominant traumatic event. In all our cases of the latter type there have been several traumatic events, spread over a whole life span through infancy, late infancy, early childhood, late childhood, adolescence. One of the most strenuous treatment situations arises when the offender's instinctual drives are constitutionally strong, making it difficult to alter the Ego. In this case, his Ego is distorted or crippled. It is usually the instincts which are responsible for the alteration of the Ego. As in all cases, including the neurotic or psychotic ones, it is the struggle between instinct and Ego which decides the outcome of whether or not the person will be able to function adequately.

Treatment of delinquents has as its aim changing their antisocial attitude into a constructive one. In psychiatric treatment of an offender, which is a re-education, the purpose is to effect a growth of his feelings so that an integration between them and his intelligence can take place. Once this has been accomplished, the desire to commit another crime will cease, inasmuch as the patient will then be aware of his motives in each instance.

As we know, the patient should come for treatment voluntarily because psychotherapy cannot be simply applied. If he refuses treatment, as happens often with the offender, the psychiatrist is helpless.

A prerequisite for every type of treatment is that the delinquent person be given a psychiatric-psychological and a medical examination before treatment is instituted. In addition, we also should have at hand the evaluation of the psychologist and the result of the psychiatric social worker's examination. Where teamwork is involved, a good procedure to follow is the one we use in our research: to discuss at a staff meeting the personality structure, diagnosis, type of treatment and prognosis of each case, whether the delinquent be a child, adolescent or adult.

As to treatment in the prison, I made in 1948 the following observations: "The principle of imprisonment collides with the principle of psychiatry which is the treatment of people under freedom and responsibility, except where the patients are psychotic. As long as imprisonment seems to be a necessary evil for handling offenders, any psychiatric treatment within a prison must be seriously impeded. In many cases, the psychiatrist is able to relieve tension and anxiety in the prisoner by simple psychotherapy, but in most instances the therapist is confronted by conscious and unconscious resistance to treatment, which is far more pronounced than in treatment outside a prison." (*Evaluation of the Treat-*

ment of Criminals, pp. 58, 59.) Since this statement was written, we have started treatment of offenders, including sex offenders, in Sing Sing Prison, and of paroled persons at Psychiatric Institute, New York City.

In our treatment, we have used a modified form of psychoanalytically oriented psychotherapy with interpretations and follow-up questions and group therapy. In cases where it was indicated, no interpretations were given in order not to weaken the personality of the delinquent, his Ego. This was particularly true in cases which we suspected had a predominant psychotic core.

Among some of our cases we have found definite improvement which is expressed in lessened anxieties and less pronounced antisocial aggressions. Those findings also have been verified by psychological tests. In many cases, it may be assumed that there will not be any repetition of offenses or a repetition of any other pathological actions.

One point we are rather concerned about is that as the psychotherapy progresses, we may not achieve further changes in the individual's personality even if treatment is continued. In such a case we have to evaluate the effect of the traumatic events, the constitutional strengths of the instincts and the modification of the Ego. If, for instance, the delinquent's instincts are very strong and cannot be counteracted by his Ego, and if he is suffering from the influence of traumas or precipitating events which his Ego cannot overcome, then the prognosis must be considered guarded. We must recall that the stronger the constitutional instincts are, the easier will the trauma lead to a fixation, a matter which happens frequently in many chronic offenders.

We cannot here go into the usual psychotherapy of prisoners which is undertaken daily by the prison psychiatrist and which is a form of mental hygiene. That involves dealing with inmates suffering from mild depressions or anxieties or phobias, all of which can be overcome with a few psychotherapeutic sessions, unless they are symptoms of underlying pathology. What I am more concerned about is treatment of offenders who show deep-seated mental disorders. The offender's imprisonment is not a normal situation, and therefore confinement almost counteracts the influence of psychotherapy. Also, psychiatric treatment within a prison is seriously hampered by the fact that the inmate cannot act under freedom and responsibility while being confined. Then, too, the inmate is afraid of revealing anything about himself that might be used against him, although he is always reassured about the confidential nature of that which is revealed to the psychiatrist.

Furthermore, the attitude of the prison's personnel is often an obstacle to successful psychotherapy. Although some of the guards are helpful, others disapprove of psychotherapy and frequently make it difficult for the prisoner to keep his appointment with the psychiatrist. Also, since the inmate associates constantly with other inmates with whom he identifies himself, this raises another barrier against treatment. In our work here we have had great help from the psychiatric social worker, Sidney Connell.

It is a prerequisite here as in every other type of psychotherapy to establish an emotional tie, a transference situation, between the patient and the psychotherapist. If not, the therapy will not be successful. The transference situation in a prison is difficult to keep on an even level. In addition to the inmate's original aggressions and hostilities, he has resentment and hostile feelings superimposed upon him, brought about through the artificial environment of the prison. This is particularly true in cases where the delinquent does not take any blame for his crime, and considers himself innocent. These added emotional elements make it harder to give treatment in the prison than in the free community.

It should be noted that the treatment of the delinquent depends upon his ability to identify himself with the psychiatrist. Because of the offender's inability to identify himself with his parents, authorities or the law, he has already developed an emotional attitude from his home environment which is built around his Superego. He has fortified his Superego and is therefore defensive, which makes it difficult, if not impossible, to penetrate it.

We have not always been successful in dealing with criminals not only because of the barrier established by the law but also because our diagnostic methods and therapeutic procedures are inadequate. Treatment of offenders in general and of sex delinquents in particular is thus, practically speaking, a new development.

Previous treatment of delinquents in prisons has not been successful. Alexander and Healy (*Roots of Crime*, p. 304, 1935) treated eleven prisoners in the course of six or eight months with limited success. From my own material which contained only a few cases until 1948, I felt that there was little or no chance in changing these inmates because of their strong defensive and suspicious feelings. Only later did I realize that these cases cannot be treated by the classical method of psychoanalysis. A neutral attitude on the part of the analyst toward offenders in general will in most instances have an unsuccessful result on the patient. In view of our present treatment, I have since come to the conclusion that the prisoners I previously treated were not sufficiently prepared for this treatment.

We can differentiate between two types of psychiatric treatment, be it inside or outside the prison. The symptomatic treatment is directed more at the mental hygiene of the prisoner, while the basic treatment aims at changing the individual's antisocial forces into constructive ones. I might here interject the question whether it is possible to effect a complete, one hundred per cent cure in a psychological sense. Since we all have antisocial tendencies, the question of cure will be how to check these inclinations and transfer them into constructive, useful channels.

For diagnostic, prognostic and practical purposes, it is necessary to group the various offenders. When we made our study of 102 sex offenders, we divided them into four categories:

A. Those offenders who are violent and untreatable at present.
B. Those who are untreatable at present.
C. Those who are treatable in a mental hospital.
D. Those who are treatable in an out-patient clinic of a mental hospital.

This division has been very helpful to us and can be extended to all types of offenders.

One case comes vividly to mind:

This was a nineteen-year-old boy, Martin, who was sentenced for robbing a young girl. This was not the first crime which he had committed, for in 1944 he had been arrested for the first time at the age of sixteen. At that time he used to tie up women, and while doing so would have an erection though never an ejaculation.

Upon further investigation much was revealed about his home life. His father was aggressive, hostile and dominating. His mother, although a frustrated woman who frequently submitted to her husband, was able to control the situation at least to some extent. Her relationship with her son had always been very close. As a youth the boy considered himself a woman hater and was too shy to ask a girl for a date. Psychological tests performed on Martin indicated that he was disturbed in his contacts with reality.

Martin had always been a good student. He was particularly interested in mathematics and science. However, when he started his criminal activities, he was no longer interested in school and his marks dropped because apparently he was then involved in his need to deal with his increasing sexual urges.

The boy's early traumatic experiences marked the childhood development of his personality structure. He had a punitive father who restricted his sexual activities by telling him, for instance, that every time he had an ejaculation it meant loss of a pint of blood; he also punished him severely for masturbation. Martin showed a marked rebelliousness toward all authoritative figures, became extremely inhibited in all social and sexual activity and markedly hostile toward people because he felt that his inhibitions were imposed upon him from authority without justice.

The feeling that his life was interfered with unjustifiably made him also extremely suspicious of others. He constantly feared rejection. The major precipitating event in Martin's entire social behavior toward women was the onset of puberty. The immediate precipitating event appears to have been his graduation from high school, which symbolized for him the release from control by arbitrary authorities.

When we looked into Martin's psychodynamics, we saw that he showed marked hostility toward the punitive and restrictive father who denied him all sexual gratification. Unresolved oedipal severing was quite clear. On the other hand, he also showed pronounced hostility toward his mother who he felt should have preferred him over the father. Because of this apparent rejection

233

by the mother, Martin came to feel extremely inadequate and, therefore, very sensitive to any defects within himself. He did not believe that he could win love by offering what he could to a woman and so felt that he could only gain sexual gratification by force. Because of his sexual incestuous drive, he had marked guilt feelings and was therefore ready to accept his father's teachings that masturbation and other sexual activities lead to serious injury. He constantly feared that his rebelliousness and sexuality would carry through his conscious control, which by the way, was also indicated by the Rorschach test. When he finally graduated from high school, which to him meant freedom from control of authority, he began to tie up girls which seemed to him to be the only way to get sexual gratification. In tying up the girl, he was frustrating himself but he also made the girl helpless, or as it is technically called, castrated her. At the same time he also castrated himself. This process of tying the girl was basically a wish to tie his own mother. In an unconscious sense he was saying: "Look, mother, I am tying you up. I don't want you, but you are not going to get me either."

Psychiatric treatment, which was that of a modified psychoanalysis, was started with him in 1948. In the beginning he was depressed, and continually repeated, "Mother is the same way." Gradually, he talked about himself, the pimples on his face, masturbation, and the frequent threats by his father that he would become insane if he continued to masturbate. In the following sessions, he talked about suicide, about hanging himself. At the age of ten or eleven, he had almost hanged himself. "I had a rope, and I was fooling around to see what it felt like." Suicidal tendencies appeared again later on. Therefore, a possible transfer to a mental hospital was discussed.

At that time, psychotherapy was taken over by another psychotherapist, Nathan Roth, M.D., of New York City, who deserves much credit for the time he treated him. Martin mentioned that he once had gone into five apartments, in one of which he found a pistol that he began to use to hold up women. He would tie them up by the hands or by the hands and feet, and leave them. In the Middle West he once tied up a woman and walked her outside of

234

town, where they spent the night on the side of a hill. He was very tired and fell asleep. In the morning he walked the woman back to town and released her. He had the feeling that the whole thing seemed "crazy" and in order to have some rational motive, he took some money from the victims' pocketbooks.

The following month in treatment, Martin appeared somewhat withdrawn. He said that he mistrusted anyone connected with the state and spoke very harshly about authority. The only times he liked authority was when he himself was the authority. Such a mistrust indicates how difficult such a case is to treat in prison. His resistance also showed up in the following hours when he mentioned that he was afraid of revealing himself to people; he said he was afraid to talk to people because they would hold him in contempt or find him ridiculous. His next question was how this could be related to his tying up women. It was pointed out to him that he wanted attention of women, but he feared he could not win it and hold it; therefore he decided that he would force women to stay with him by using his power. The following therapeutic sessions brought out the fact that he never carried out orders because he then would have to give up a pleasure. This pleasure was, as Martin himself said, masturbation. At that time he was told that his feeling so frustrated in prison and so deprived of his sexual life was based on being rejected by others. He began to make real progress in gaining insight. He admitted he was a spoiled brat, that he felt the whole world should treat him as he wanted his parents to treat him, that when he was not gratified, he used devices, one of which was to sulk to make people feel guilty at the way that they treated him.

This led to the subject of his behavior with women. When he could not get complete love from women, he sulked and remained away from them, thereby revealing his anger at them. By tying women up he could force them to give him what he wanted. He always felt strong self-contempt for it. The reason why he had not made any sexual attack upon women was because of revenge, something which he at first did not understand. When he walked away from the women, he was denying them the satisfaction of their own wishes, thereby revealing his complete contempt for them.

235

The reason he wanted to feel unjustly treated was that he wanted people to feel that they should give him everything he wanted.

When it was pointed out to Martin that he had not been able to remember any dreams, he said that he had had many nightmares. In one dream he was standing between two buildings talking very freely to another person. Since his associations were sparse, it was pointed out to him that he is engaged in an activity with which he is not accustomed. Asked what the two buildings might mean, he mentioned the legs of a woman. Later on in the hour, since the question of parole had come up, it was suggested that he possibly was trying to convince a member of the Parole Board that he was suitable for release.

At that time Martin was eligible for parole and, of course, was preoccupied with the Parole Board meeting. He was given one more year and felt, therefore, dejected and frustrated. Shortly thereafter he had a dream that he was on a platform and that the view was obstructed. The dream indicated that there were many obstacles in his way. At that time Martin was also very busy with the suggested new laws pertaining to sex offenders about which he had read in the newspapers. He could not stand being in prison very much longer.

One half year later, his psychotherapist resigned, and I took over the treatment. The change caused some concern, but he pulled through very well. He began to dream of being out of prison. However, he dreamed one time that the guards were opening the doors of the cells and when they came to his door, they passed it. He started to scream, and woke up. This dream indicated some fear on his part, that he might be passed over, and that he still felt unjustly treated.

During the two years of analysis, the patient learned how to submit to authority and to understand the motives of his attacks upon women. Along with that went a solution of his feelings of inadequacy and inferiority. His personality make-up improved considerably. Psychological retesting at that time also showed that he had a more conscious control of his motor impulses than previously.

At the time when he had been given notice that he was to be paroled, I asked him in the prison to write down what he felt and thought. He wrote me the following: "Frankly, I feel kind of happy and tired. Happy because I will soon be going home and a turning point in my life has been reached where I believe the future years will be much more pleasant and happy than the past ones, and tired because for a long number of years I have been waging quite a battle to understand and conquer the deficiencies and fears which for too many years became an integral part of my personality and led to much unhappiness and ultimately to jail. I am very grateful. . . . I feel myself quite sure that by continuing the process of self-understanding when I return to a normal physical environment (that is, when I get out of jail) that I will be able to lead a happy life and in some small way be useful in this world."

This man was paroled a few months later and has been out since. He has been in psychotherapy on an out-patient basis out of town and according to my information, he is getting along well. He has a job, goes out with friends and with girls. At the time of this writing it is, of course, too early to say whether or not treatment has been completely successful. But so far so good.

In conclusion it may be said that Martin suffered from a severe compulsive-obsessive neurosis intermingled with traits of a schizoid coloring. The original Rorschach test showed him to be extremely narcissistic and infantile, but our current psychiatric and psychological tests revealed that he has lost many of his inhibitions, that he is in closer contact with reality and that now he has a better and a sounder appreciation of himself.

We have had in treatment for about a year a twenty-five-year-old man who has been in prison for thefts. He sought treatment in prison because he had heard about our research and that some had improved under it. His family history was drab, his alcoholic father having left his mother when he was only a young child. He attended high school but quit after one year so he could take a job in a shoe factory. Once in a while he used to drink and when after one such spree he did not show up for work in the morning, he was fired. He then got another job in an office. One day alone in the office, he noticed a large sum of money lying in the open drawer. He took the money and left the office, never to return again. The following day he was apprehended and arraigned in court where it was discovered that he had had previous arrests for similar thefts. He was convicted and sent to prison.

In the psychotherapeutic sessions he was at first somewhat hostile, but in the course of a month he developed an emotional relationship with the psychotherapist. He was able for the first time in his life to talk freely with someone and felt much relieved as he discussed his problems. For the first time he no longer felt rejected because he understood that the therapist had an interest in him. Slowly the patient began to gain emotional insight into himself which resulted in a personality change. His resentment against his father lessened and he became interested in trying to make good where he previously had failed. Through the treatment he became more emotionally secure and felt able to stand on his own feet.

Another case was that of a twenty-eight-year-old man who, while intoxicated, brutally raped and sodomized an older woman and took her money. He then gave her his name and address, accompanied her to a subway and handed her ten cents for fare. This man has very strong needs for aggression, and a conviction that human relations cannot be regulated on a level of equality, but that one person must dominate the other. This philosophy was consistently practiced by his mother. Another conviction of his is the expectation of severe punishment after every misdeed.

His mother influenced him much more than his father. His relationship with his father was frictionless on the whole, but only because it was superficial and distant. His greatest conflicts were created by his mother. This would in part explain the fact that he criminally attacked a woman and that she was much older than he.

This man's history and personality make-up disclose that unconsciously he is always seeking his mother's love. Therefore, he suspects rivals everywhere. As illustration, he tried to make an appointment with his victim, and at the end he treated her as a man who was trying to please a lady.

Perhaps the most important motive for the crime was a strong desire to humiliate his mother (through displacement) by committing a crime. However, despite his desire for revenge for the way she treated him, he basically feels submissive to his mother, feels she will win in the long run, and therefore he expects punishment. With punishment expected, there was no point in taking precautions. He has been considered violent and untreatable, and yet, both for research purposes and the benefit of the community, efforts are being made to help him work through his psychological problems. We also have seen both his mother and wife quite extensively in an attempt to effect a workable relationship between them and with the inmate in order to relieve external pressures from him since he still suffers greatly from internal pressures. The Church, Alcoholics Anonymous, and our contact with this man all represent sources of strength and hope which he needs desperately. He has strong obsessive-compulsive and sadistic traits and, beneath an apparent neurosis, it seems that some underlying pathology may exist. The way he, for instance, speaks of God controlling the Parole Board and his swings of mood give an indication of a deep maladjustment.

Some valuable progress was made with this man, so far as insight and mobilization of guilt were concerned. On one occasion, he was hit by another inmate to which he did not react except to say, "Thanks." He was pleased to hear that any other reaction would have made matters worse for him. His psychological retest of 1950 showed some distinct improvements over that of 1949. He revealed less rigidity and aggressiveness, as well as more hope for the future. The sado-masochistic tendency seems to have weakened.

This man was later paroled, and we suggested that he should not return to his mother or wife but live by himself. Unfortunately, this plan could not be carried out because of housing conditions, and he therefore remained with his family. In the course of a month's time he began to drink, became insulting toward his wife, started to beat her and stayed out nights. We used to see him once a week as an after-care, but he soon discontinued his visits. One day we were informed that he had been arrested again for beating his wife, and he was returned to prison as a parole violator. His treatment was continued as long as possible.

It seems that his case was a failure, but this is not completely true. While he previously had raped a woman whom he did not know, this time he beat his wife. Incredible though it sounds, this can be interpreted as progress because by now he has at least localized his aggressions, directing them against his wife while he previously directed them against any woman. It is difficult, however, to make anything more than a guarded prognosis in this case, inasmuch as the man still shows paranoid trends and interests in power as the main basis of regulating human interrelationships.

Another form of psychotherapy is group therapy. This we started in Sing Sing in 1949. We have had four groups of offenders in group therapy. Two groups consist of sex offenders while other two groups contain both sex and non-sex offenders. One of my associates, Arnold Abrams, Ph.D., has been very active in this type of treatment.

In the beginning of the group therapy, the men complained about the prison and its conditions. After this negative period subsided, they began to concentrate on themselves and their own problems. The group therapy aims at having the inmates express emotions and orienting them socially. One such inmate had a long history with the law to the extent that his whole attitude toward society was distinctly warped. As a result of almost a year of group therapy, he abandoned his resentment and hostility against society and the Parole Board, realizing that this hostility was a repetition of earlier experiences against authority. He has shown considerable insight and has become convinced of the benefits of group therapy, which he has expressed without hesitation. He has even gone to the extent of requesting that the Parole Board permit him to stay on in prison for another six months. Although this request may sound as if it has masochistic traits, yet he himself feels that he still needs treatment.

On the whole, we may say that group therapy has in many instances had a wholesome effect upon the inmates treated. In group therapy an "acting out" of the conflict takes place. "Acting out" is basic in this type of treatment and may give important clues to unconscious material. Nathan W. Ackerman, M.D., states that individual psychoanalysis works from the inside outward while group psychotherapy works from the outside inward. ("Psychoanalysis and Group Psychotherapy," *Group Psychotherapy*, 3:204-215, 1950.)

In all treatment including group therapy, we have to be aware of the fact that when a prisoner says he wants help, he may not have a genuine desire for it. Sometimes the prisoner wants to ingratiate himself with the psychiatrist in order to obtain a good report which eventually can be presented to the Parole Board. Furthermore, in prison the offender cannot pay for his treatment, a matter which also may encourage his "secondary neurotic gains." It is a healthy idea that the patient should pay a part of the fee for his psychiatric treatment.

Psychiatric treatment in prisons is not enough. When the inmate is paroled, his treatment has to be continued. We have established after-care treatment for parolees at the New York State Psychiatric Institute where they are treated once or twice a week.

In this connection I want to mention the case of a forty-year-old man who had served four years in prison for carnal abuse of a child. While in prison, he received psychiatric treatment during which it was revealed that he had always had a deep fear of women. In particular, he distrusted his mother who had been too busy for him. He never developed an adult or a close relationship with any woman and therefore started to seek out children. In psychotherapy he became aware of his basic tendency to drive women away from him.

When he was paroled, the treatment continued. At that time it turned out that he had a tendency to become involved with his daughters which was only averted through psychotherapy, which gave him a great deal of insight. The psychotherapist had all the time worked closely with the parole officer in order to avoid any recurrence of his previous behavior.

Since he started therapy, he has been able to give up drinking completely and is getting along quite well. It is now almost two years since he was paroled and the prognosis for his adjustment is considered good.

Another twenty-seven-year-old inmate whom we had treated in prison had been convicted of having made advances to a young woman in her apartment. She screamed and bit him, and he escaped by the window. He was diagnosed as having an obsessive-compulsive neurosis and has since his parole received psychoanalytical psychotherapy once a week. He has maintained himself successfully on a socially acceptable level, has gained insight and progressed in both planning ability and self-control. His chronic alcoholism is under control since we placed him on charcoal treatment in conjunction with his psychiatric treatment.

I mention these as examples of success cases. We do also have cases where we have failed. The difference between paroling a delinquent to the community with or without psychiatric treatment is that when he has psychotherapy, there is a possibility of changing his emotional attitude. His aggressions are then lessened, his emotional insight is increased, his hostilities are weakened, and he is better able to cope with his situation because he more clearly understands his actions and the actions of others. Without psychiatric treatment an offender will not be able to gain as much insight into himself, although of course once in a while we can see an improvement in him. The danger for the parolee when he returns to his community lies in the fact that he is unprepared for his new life. The first six months to a year out of prison is the most important period in his readjustment, and he must therefore be watched closely. We have seen psychotherapy be of invaluable assistance to him because at that time he feels lonesome or depressed and in such a mood is apt to commit antisocial acts. It is therefore of significant help that he can talk over his problems with his psychiatrist.

When an offender commits a crime—and this cannot be stressed enough—it is to satisfy his own feelings or desires. But he does not know it because he is unaware of his emotional needs. Since he is unconscious of his feelings, it is of no avail to say to the delinquent, "Don't commit any more crime." That would be just the same as saying to a blind man: "Don't cross the street on the red light." There is, however, one big difference. Though the blind man cannot actually see the danger of traffic, you have with a logical argument persuaded him not to walk out in the street. Even if he would have a strong desire to do so, he will not because he understands he cannot see the danger.

But you cannot use the same logic to a delinquent person because he does not realize his emotional necessity for committing a crime. He is emotionally blind and, therefore, cannot understand it.

While treatment of offenders within the prison is, notwithstanding some good results, most difficult and discouraging because of the disadvantageous atmosphere in which the psychiatrist works, treatment of offenders outside the prison should be more effectual. Unfortunately, this is not so. At the present time there are few organized institutions for the psychiatric treatment of juvenile or adult delinquents, such as for instance Community Services, the Jewish Board of Guardians and Catholic Charities and a few other agencies in New York City. It is interesting to note that the rate of juvenile delinquency in the Jewish population within the last fifteen years has decreased from well over 20 per cent to under 7 per cent of the total number of children's court cases in New York City. (See "After 50 Years: An Agency Looks Ahead," *The Jewish Social Service Quarterly*, December, 1944.)

In treatment of juvenile delinquents, it must be noted that the sooner the boy is treated, the better the outlook. If it can be done within a week after the crime has been committed, many headaches are avoided. Furthermore, prior to the initial interview, it is also advantageous to visit the school and talk with the teacher and in the first interview it is important that both the delinquent and his parents be present. I have found that authority can be used in a constructive way when juvenile delinquents are prepared for treatment. However, such authority can be used only when the therapist takes a proper emotional attitude. This attitude is largely based upon a correct diagnosis. ("Preparation of Juvenile Delinquents for Treatment," *The American Journal of Orthopsychiatry*, Vol. XVII, No. 2, p. 150.)

In evaluating any improvement or cure in an offender, we must remember that we have those cases which show a spontaneous remission of symptoms. Not only do we find this in patients suffering from mental disorders but also from delinquency. Very often young delinquents, after having been given a suspended sentence once or twice, have disappeared from the court record and later on have seemed to have adjusted without further trouble.

I quote from my paper previously mentioned: "In treating offenders one must keep in mind that the principle upon which the offender can be changed and re-educated is based upon his social experience and his reaction to it. This social experience is the basic stimulus for the individual's re-education. This social experience

243

makes him either a normally adjusted person or a neurotic or psychotic person; hence it forms him into whatever he becomes."

Probation is also treatment. I would like to quote from the case of a young man who committed several thefts from a department store for which he received a suspended sentence and was recommended to us for psychiatric treatment. When he began therapy with us, he was resistant and hostile, felt victimized and lost. After a short period of treatment he became amiable and comparatively composed, gained some insight into his habit of blaming others for his misfortunes. His greatest change, however, has been a more subtle one: his Ego strength and self-assurance increased. After eight months of treatment people told him that he had changed very much. Whereas he formerly found himself involved and emotional over small things, he can now control himself and to some extent also the situation. His physical symptoms have improved, and he has taken a better attitude toward his business associates. It is interesting that though his crime was not a sexual one, his whole main conflict lies within the sexual area.

When we start to see a delinquent on probation it frequently happens that he shows so much resistance to treatment that he does not appear for the interviews. Some stop coming after they have felt some relief and are then admonished by their probation officer to come for treatment. If this is the case, we usually are not optimistic about the outcome since the correct emotional attitude toward it is lacking.

One of the patients on whom psychoanalysis was used was a twenty-one-year-old man who had been arrested for stealing while drunk. He was emotionally blocked and unable to function, suffering from an obsessive-compulsory neurosis. The Rorschach Test showed hostility against women, homosexual inclinations, depression and feelings of unworthiness. He had a great fear of impotence and felt guilty toward his mother. At first he gave the impression of living a normal family life, but when we started to examine the family, we were quite surprised to see the pathology present. His mother was psychotic, his father was an obsessive-compulsory man, very rigid and self-centered. He even showed suspicious and paranoid traits. The patient explained his father's make-up by saying, "My father is physically or mentally too old for my mother."

The patient's mother showed a psychosis of a mixed type beneath which we could ascertain a compulsive and hysterical trait. She suffered from severe depressions, had suicidal thoughts, was childish and egocentric. The Rorschach report stated, "She has little interest in people, is not really a social-minded person. There are traits of coldness and hardness. She has very poor rational control over herself, is confused and unrealistic and her wishful thinking verges on the delusionary." The Rorschach record, furthermore, showed that she was extremely sexually frustrated, a matter which is readily understood in the light of the psychogram of the father.

The offender himself was the third of four brothers and sisters. His oldest brother, who had been twice married, showed traits of being rigid, stereotyped and inflexible. He was self-centered, and extremely blocked and self-conscious in regard to sex. Like his father he showed sadistic tendencies. The patient was greatly intimidated by this older brother who liked to show off his knowledge. I quote from a paper, "Family Role in Diagnosis and Treatment of Offenders," by Rose Palm and myself, printed in *The Journal of Nervous and Mental Disease*, Vol. 112, No. 4, Oct., 1950:

"From the point of view of family dynamics it is very interesting to note that the paternal rigidity and the maternal negativism on sexual matters had created homosexual tendencies and enuretic trends in both brothers, both revealing fear of their father. . . . His older sister showed emotional poverty and blocking and a personality pattern very similar to that of the father. . . . Emotionally she functions, at least at the surface, in a blocked and empty way. Although well organized, she has very little originality or creative drive. She is somewhat narcissistic, has little interest in other people, and actually may be a little suspicious. Under the surface of emptiness and blocking, she shows certain obsessive fears and tendencies, mainly in connection with sexual conflicts."

The patient's younger sister was the most receptive and warm of the three women in his environment. But she too was very unstable and too egocentric and childish to be a real companion to her

245

brother when they grew up. She revealed marked obsessional tendencies, was conflicted about pregnancy and children, but there was present in her an element of underlying pathology of a schizoid type.

So rather than growing up in a "normal family," this offender had been raised in a family where the members were cold, had a tendency toward cruelty or sadism, lacked genuine warmth and showed obsessive fears and paranoid traits. He had always dealt with a mother who was moody and unstable and to whom he could never adjust. It was this frustration about his mother, leading to hostility and the reaction against his abnormal home life, which was a basic constituent in his criminal behavior. Not only did he have to work through his emotional problem with regard to his mother but also that concerning his brother, a fact which was repeatedly brought out in analysis.

In the analysis he changed considerably. He seemed to overcome his fright, his hostile feelings against his mother decreased and he also became aware of the fact that his stealing was an expression of a desire to punish his mother. Unconscious material, particularly about his childhood, was brought up and he could now see matters from a more realistic viewpoint. He was able to stay away from drinking and from criminal activities, manifestations which possibly were linked up with his homosexual tendencies.

This case in particular shows the necessity for careful psychiatric examination of the offender and the utilization of psychological tests including projective ones such as the Rorschach Test. It also shows the necessity of treating not only the offender but also the family in order to change the home atmosphere.

In order to evaluate progress or change of the personality, we have in our treatment utilized psychological methods which have been a great help to us. One of my associates, Zygmunt Piotrowski, Ph.D., in conjunction with the other psychologists on my staff, has been most helpful in finding criteria for the change, improvement or worsening seen in the offender through treatment. Unfortunately, it is not known exactly which minute changes may be found from the Rorschach examination. We know only certain minute changes which are pertinent. The one among them which seems to bear the most obvious relation to increase of self-control is the decrease of the difference between the number of color responses and the number of light shading responses. Repeated examinations of patients undergoing psychotherapy (including patients treated with deep, prolonged and intensive psychoanalysis) has shown that the smaller the difference between the light shading and the color responses—other conditions being equal—the better and easier is the adjustment made by the patient to the environment in which he lives.

In cases treated at Sing Sing and in cases of parolees we have made the same observation: that is, that the difference between these two types of Rorschach responses decreases gradually with the clinically observed improvement of the men who have had psychotherapy.

It is said that the greater the subjective discomfort of the patient, the greater is the desire to improve, other conditions being equal. The Rorschach method is particularly sensitive to the measurement of subjectively experienced anxiety. The Rorschach Test which is most closely related to acute anxiety, manifested in overt motor behavior, is the very uneven pace at which responses to the ink blots are produced. With psychotherapy this sign of anxiety disappeared from the repeated Rorschach records.

In general, the greater the similarity of the offender's Rorschach records to that of a normal person or a mild neurotic with hysterical features, the better were the therapeutic results. It is possible to construct an ideal Rorschach record. The inmates who improved as a result of therapy have come closer to the ideal record on reexaminations.

On the whole, Rorschach records of offenders who had committed their crimes in a state of intoxication showed a much greater deviation from the ideal normal personality structure than men who had committed their offenses in a sober state. Consequently, they were not as good therapeutic risks—other conditions being equal—as those who refrained from offensive behavior in their drunken state and committed their antisocial acts only

247

when sober. Expressing it in different words, we might say that men who commit their crimes when they are drunk have a longer road to travel to reach a near-normal level.

It is interesting to see that through psychological testing we were able to find, for instance, that a man who had attempted and completed actual rape showed the greatest disproportion between his impulses and their control. Those men who used violence had a weaker motor control than in cases where there had been voluntary co-operation on the part of the girl. The man who only attempted to rape, but did not complete it, showed but a small disproportion between his emotions and its motor control.

Frequently we meet an offender who has been rejected by his family, which makes psychiatric treatment difficult. The delinquent in such a case has to maintain himself in his new environment, and the psychotherapist has to initiate an emotional tie with him. Although it is a basic principle that one should try to establish a transference situation with only one person in psychotherapy, in the case of a genuine psychopath or a schizoid person with whom it is difficult to maintain transference, the offender can be seen by the psychiatrist and by the psychiatric social worker alternatively. He can thereby work out his ambi-/or polyvalent attitudes. Some delinquents, or for that matter, many neurotic individuals, need not only a father but a mother as well so we have to make an attempt to give them these necessary substitutes.

The genuine psychopathic personality presents one of the greatest problems of society. Since he shows consistent resistance during psychotherapy, I interpret resistance to him whenever possible. Psychoanalytic treatment is extremely arduous because transference with this kind of person is so difficult to achieve. Inasmuch as he has never experienced any kind of emotional tie with anyone in the past, it stands to reason that it would be unnatural for him to establish such a tie with a psychiatrist. It can be done with effort but the tie must be constantly renewed; there is nothing lasting or dependable within this type of personality make-up.

As a general rule it may be said that versatile treatment is necessary for the offender and that before any treatment is started we have to explore four factors so that we can decide how suitable the offender is for therapy:

1) The degree of rapport which the offender shows with the psychotherapy.
2) The Ego strength of the personality.
3) The constructive traits or "strength of will" shown by the offender toward recovery.
4) The ability of the offender to identify himself with the psychiatrist.

All these elements are basically present in the delinquent's social experiences and reactions. In order to be successful in treatment and in order to change his emotional attitude, it is necessary that the psychiatrist have the co-operation of the family. This is essential since it is the offender's hostile attitude which is mainly responsible for his antisocial traits. We know from previous experience that the transference situation is important in the treatment of a mental patient and it is equally important in the person who is delinquent. Emotions present in him are mobilized during the psychiatric treatment with the psychoanalyst. This whole transference mechanism must be known by the psychotherapist. By analyzing the transference, we always find that the delinquent's early life has been disturbed either by overprotection or by deprivation of affection and attention.

If the delinquent person also shows neurotic manifestations but with criminalistic tendencies more or less prevailing, I start out behaving as a good parent. In the course of treatment, my attitude changes. If the child, adolescent or adult has recently been taken to court, I do not question him about his offense. I try to assure him that he can tell me only what he wants as I realize discussing the offense may be painful to him. At that time the delinquent is willing to talk. When he understands he can tell me what he pleases, he will drop his defensive attitude. Frequently we have used group therapy in connection with individual therapy. It seems that these two types of treatment complement each other.

249

Over the years, I have treated in all about two thousand children and adults who have been emotionally disturbed and who have carried out delinquent activities, and sometimes their family members as well. Many of these cases have been seen two or three times a week, over periods lasting from six to eighteen months, others for shorter periods. If the delinquent was a child the success of the treatment depended in addition to the four previously mentioned factors, upon the kind of co-operation we received from his parents.

Use of drugs, "truth serum" as it has been called, has been advocated by several investigators. Yet there are some misgivings about it. We have tried to use it on patients who did not show much sign of transference. During the narcosynthesis a transference was established, but as soon as the effect of the sodium amytal had gone, the transference disappeared. At the same time we found that many delinquents deliberately fabricate symptoms while in narcosynthesis. Calling the drug a "truth serum" indicates that the person under its effect would tell the truth. This is not so. Many patients can withhold information and many also tell lies. We have found this particularly to be the case of those offenders who suffer from a character disorder. Furthermore, several persons are also suggestible to questions asked by the psychiatrist. Narcosynthesis should be used only when the offender voluntarily agrees to it after he has been made aware that he might reveal things which he really would not like to have revealed. Often we have used narcosynthesis in order to be able to clarify the diagnosis, particularly to differentiate between a neurosis and a psychosis. In these cases it has been a great help.

Some other aspects of the sex offender come to mind. The lay public's attitude toward him is that of punishment at any cost. In the course of time several procedures have been utilized in order to combat sex offenses. One was castration. Although some seem to have found a theoretical basis for its use, it still seems to be a rather controversial procedure. Laws about castration have been in force in Scandinavia since 1929, and the personal reports I received from those countries seem to indicate that there are some promising results. When I talked with Dr. Sturup, Director of the Institute for Psychopaths at Herstedvester, Copenhagen, he told me that of the 120 sexual offenders who had been admitted to his hospital, 80 had been castrated. It was surprising to learn that only two of them have since committed new sexual offenses.

Dr. C. C. Hawke from the State School of Mental Defectives at Winfield, Kansas, issued a report on about 300 mostly mentally defective sex offenders who had been castrated. He feels that the remedy for the confirmed sex criminal is castration, which they have used since 1894. As a general viewpoint concerning the effect of castration, I want to state that loss of sexual potency in a man does not necessarily mean that he may not attack anyone sexually. Sexual offenders are, as a matter of fact, more or less sexually impotent, be it physically or psychologically or both.

So far there have been very few reports about change of sexual behavior after lobotomy. Drs. Julius Levine and Harold Albert (*Journal of Nervous and Mental Disease*, pp. 113:332-341, April, 1951) report that they interviewed forty patients after lobotomy in order to determine changes in their sexual behavior. In four patients the operation could be said to have been in some way responsible for involving them in social difficulties. One patient had been a sexual psychopath before he became psychotic, and became promiscuous after the operation. It seems that the patient's fantasy life was impoverished after lobotomy, becoming less frequent and less vivid. Relatives reported that the patient's moral and social attitudes before the operation were about the same as after the lobotomy, although at the same time there seemed to be a lessening of guilt and modesty in association with sexual activity.

It should also be mentioned that in England, Golla and Hodge started treatment of the sex offender with hormones. Although only a few cases have been described and these reacted well under treatment with estadiol, a later report indicated that the results cannot be considered durable. In our own project at Sing Sing, we have treated eighty-seven sex offenders such as rapists, homosexuals, exhibitionists, and persons convicted of carnal abuses and incest. Of those, sixteen were paroled; four have been returned within half a year for parole violation. One of these four men has later been released after having served his full maximum sentence

251

and received upon his own request continued treatment on an out-patient basis. We have had some cases where there was a definite change for the better in the personality make-up, a change also reflected in the psychological tests. If more appropriate facilities were available for psychiatric treatment of prisoners, possibly better results would follow. Manfred S. Guttmacher, M.D., in his book (*Sex Offenses*, 1951, p. 112) mentions that Dr. Conn gave treatment to twenty-three male sex offenders. He saw them in one-half hour interims once a week from one-half year to a year. He used a treatment termed "hypnosynthesis." Police records confirm Dr. Conn's optimistic viewpoint in that almost all of them have not reverted to their earlier sexual crimes. Except for one case, no follow-up studies of these offenders seem to have been made.

Although we have found psychiatric treatment to be worth while in many cases, it is too early to evaluate our results. Our study of the sex offender has shown that the problem is a broad mental hygiene problem, related to the individual's emotional as well as educational aspect. We found that many of these cases are so extreme that they could only land in prison. A final solution will possibly take place when educational measures are taken on a large scale.

We have found that many of the sex offenders are predisposed to violence and therefore should be taken out of circulation. For that reason, and since we know that many of these offenders repeat their crimes and are a menace to women and children, I suggested that such an offender should be psychiatrically examined and given psychological tests before being sentenced by the court. If he were found to be dangerous and suffering from a deep-seated mental disorder which did not indicate a psychosis or mental defectiveness, he could be sentenced from one day to life and transferred to a prison for psychiatric treatment. If he were found to be alcoholic or senile or more of a nuisance than a threat to public safety, then he should be sent to a farm colony. In case he showed a mental disorder, but was not psychotic or mentally defective, he should be treated in a mental hospital; or if he did not reveal a mental condition that necessitated hospitalization, he should be given psychiatric treatment as an out-patient in a hospital. In our report we stated further:

"We recommend legislation providing that when any offender be convicted of rape or sodomy involving the use of force or violence, or against small children, or convicted of felonious assault involving a sexual purpose, the Court after psychiatric examination of such offender may sentence such offender to serve an indeterminate sentence having a minimum of one day and a maximum of the duration of his natural life. . . .

"We recommend further that, whenever an offender shall be sentenced to such a term of from one day to life, the law shall impose upon the Department of Mental Hygiene, the Department of Correction and the Board of Parole the solemn duty of giving his case prompt and intensive study, to be followed where feasible by therapeutic treatment, to the end that such offender may be rehabilitated and released whenever it may appear that he is a good risk on parole. When serving under this form of sentence, it should be required that a prisoner receive thorough psychiatric examination not less than once every two years, and consideration by the Parole Board." (*Report on Study of 102 Sex Offenders at Sing Sing Prison* as Submitted to Governor Thomas E. Dewey, p. 44 and p. 45, March, 1950.)

The reason for such a law is that by instituting a one day to life sentence for a sex offender who, in the opinion of the psychiatrists would be a menace, we felt that society would be protected as well as the individual. This law provides for the rehabilitation, treatment and release of offenders who usually suffer from some form of mental or emotional abnormality and at the same time provides for continued attention to those who clearly are still a danger to society. It was the opinion of the commission that such a law "will be administered with due regard for the rights and welfare for the offenders as well as for society."

This law was approved unanimously by the Legislature in March, 1950, and signed by Governor Thomas E. Dewey. In these cases, as in all others, the Parole Board has the final word.

Up to this time there are about fifty sex offenders in the New

253

York State Prisons who have been sentenced according to the new law from one day to life. Some of them, who are in Sing Sing prison, are thoroughly examined and each one is considered carefully as to treatment, possibility and outlook.

The success of such a law requires the largest possible psychiatric facilities in order to implement it. It was originally suggested by the commission that an institute for criminal behavior be established where most of these and other cases could be treated, where psychiatric personnel could be trained and where further research on delinquents, including sex offenders, could take place. Unfortunately, these proposals were scrapped, which may seriously hamper the success of the law. Yet, within the limitations under which we are working, this is one of the first times that any state in the union has tried to deal realistically with the problem of sex offenders. This law is a revolutionary step, and other states—Michigan, Illinois, Massachusetts, and Indiana—have similar laws under consideration. Florida has already enacted a similar law. The State of New Jersey, in 1949–50, made a legal sociological survey of sex offenders, directed by Dr. Paul Tappan, of New York City. The State of California is now in the process of making a study of sex offenders, directed by Karl Bowman, M.D., of San Francisco.

But laws in themselves cannot solve any problem of criminal behavior, nor can prisons solve antisocial conduct. I once had a man, Edward, who had embezzled over $35,000 and was brought into court. As I was able to unfold the story, he had taken this money because of a woman. He bought her clothes, jewels and furs, although he was never intimate with her. Something was wrong here, something twisted. In my interviews with him it turned out that this woman had acted the role of mother to Edward in an effort to compensate for her own guilt feelings. Edward in turn wanted and encouraged her mothering because he had never had it when he needed it; his younger brother had received it all. Edward's father had been stern and strict, causing Edward to be obedient but resentful in a quiet, passive way.

The foundation of his family was on the surface built on ethics and proper conduct. But any discussion on sex was strictly taboo, and many wholesome boyhood pursuits were forbidden in the undying effort to make a gentleman of Edward. The home atmosphere was one of confinement which created tension with insecurity and fear, particularly in that he was denied the affection that his younger brother received.

The early memories stayed with Edward, even when he was convinced they were no longer important or even a part of his life. He married, but the marriage did not give him the warmth he needed. After the age of forty he met the other woman and began to embezzle company funds, used, in effect, to thank her for her kindness and the feeling of emotional security she created within him. Also, deep within him, was a desire to strike back at his father, which he did by becoming a transgressor.

Insofar as Edward himself was concerned, he took the money both for the feeling of power and security that went with it and in order that he might punish himself for the hostility and consequent guilt he felt about his parents.

Edward was never intimate with the woman because unconsciously he felt that she represented his mother. He might have liked to be intimate with her for this very reason but did not dare. For the woman's part, she was innocent of the larceny; she thought the money was Edward's own. Insofar as her being aware of his marriage and family was concerned, rightly or wrongly she undoubtedly rationalized that his wife had failed him, whereas she had not, and that since she could not have the security of marriage, she could at least conscientiously accept a substitute.

When I finally became aware of all the facts in the case, I recommended in my report that Edward be placed on probation and put under psychiatric treatment, rather than sent to prison. I shall never forget the day when the judge questioned me: "Can you guarantee that if this man is given treatment he will get well?"

"No," I told him, "I cannot guarantee that he will get well. But I will guarantee you this: if he is sent to prison, he will become a hardened offender."

The judge said nothing. Edward was not imprisoned; instead he was given a suspended sentence upon the condition that he pay back the amount of money he took, and that he undergo psychiatric treatment. Today, some years later, he is back at his old job

255

and happily living with his wife and children. His debts are paid both to the firm and to himself and he is, he tells me, in his many letters to me for the first time a genuinely happy man. In a letter I recently received he told me that he never understood himself before or why he was so miserable.

I think I hardly need say that Edward's case has given me confidence in what can be done with delinquents, and hope for the future status of prisons and the punishment that they automatically imply.

11

Mental Health and Schools

I CANNOT stress too much that what basically stimulates us in our life are the experiences we have in our infancy and childhood, in our family and in our community. If therefore, we are going to re-educate an individual suffering from emotional maladjustments with or without delinquency, we must build upon the principle that his social experience is the primary stimulation for the re-education. At the same time we must remember that the person's social experience works through the medium of his mental, emotional and spiritual make-up.

It is impossible to go into all the situations which may exist in the home of a maladjusted child. In general, there is no stock answer to any problem, be it that of a child, adult, or for that matter of any situation. If we think we have an answer for any and every given situation, it means that we do not know the answer. I can therefore only try to outline a few examples of how to deal with maladjusted behavior of children. Truancy is not only a matter for the school to take note of, but also for the parent to investigate. Composite factors produce truancy; it may be due to poor scholastic standing, fear of teachers and authority resulting in shyness and timidity, jealousy of children who are more advanced or better dressed, inability to get along with "cliques or groups," or lack of parents' interest in their children's schooling. The parents have to look into themselves and try to evaluate their own situation, particularly with regard to their feelings toward their children and toward themselves. It must be remembered that when a child starts to rebel, to lie or steal or shows on the whole undue hostility, it may be due to a distorted family setup.

Peter was a curly-haired, blue-eyed ten-year-old who got along very well until he went into the fifth grade. For no apparent reason he began to stay away from school. His mother discovered it when she left the house one day and saw Peter standing in front of a theater. When she talked with the teacher, she found that Peter had been out of school for two or three days. Up to this time his grades had been very good and he seemed to get along well with the other children, so his mother had a talk with him one afternoon. She found that he was bored with school because he was through with his exercises long before his classmates. She told him that she would see if she could have him advanced and Peter promised to be good.

Shortly afterward, she noticed that money was missing from her purse. When she asked Peter about it, he said he had taken it to go to a movie. At that point the mother became frightened, and I was consulted. I found that both parents were working and that Peter was taken care of by a maid when he came home from school. After having talked with Peter and discussed the matter with the teacher, I advised the mother to try to come home earlier in the afternoon so that she would be there when he returned from school. The mother, who felt guilty about neglecting the child, followed the advice. Peter upon my request was given an intelligence and a performance test, with the result that he was advanced to the next grade. From that time on, he gave no further trouble.

The truant child is very often a rejected one, and so we say that his staying away from school is an expression of a conduct disorder. The same is true of a child who lies, steals, sets fires and shows general destructive tendencies. This type of behavior may develop when a child is two years old and take other forms later on. As he grows older, for instance, he may have an inclination to be persistently absent from work, just in the same way as he was absent from school.

When we remember that six hundred children are illegally absent from New York City schools every day (according to *Children Absent from School*, Citizen's Committee on Children of New York City, Inc., 1949) either on the grounds of truancy, or because the child is kept home by the parent unlawfully, or because the child is working with the parents' approval but without working permit, or because they have not even registered the child in school, it is evident what kind of problem this poses for the school. What is needed in any school system is understanding of what goes on in the truant child. This means that teachers, the attendance officer and child-guidance clinics must become aware of the emotional difficulties of the youngster before a rational handling of him can be started.

Let it be said here that a comprehensive plan for the school system must be worked out in order to handle properly all problems of emotional maladjustment in children. Within this scope we must include all types of cases of truancy. Such a program will have to build and expand upon existing services. If they are not there, they have to be created. I have particularly in mind the child-guidance and mental-hygiene clinics which, though understaffed, have tried to help out in a situation which has been too overwhelming for them. Beside lack of personnel, there has been lack of a goal in their work. And even if the goal has been thought out, there still has not been any evaluation of the work of the child-guidance clinics and how it can be improved. (While this is being written a survey is being undertaken of the Bureau of Child Guidance in New York City.)

Our four years' research showed that it is an impossible task to give treatment only to the child; his parents too, or at least one of them, the strategically important member, must be consulted and taken under treatment. In short, instead of having child-guidance clinics, we should have child-parent-guidance clinics. Not only do we have to deal with problem children but also with problem parents. They need guidance and help, often more so than the child. Child-guidance clinics were originally established in 1922 as a social agency in order to help the child who showed emotional or behavior disorders. The first demonstration clinic was established in

259

St. Louis, Missouri, and later headed for some years by Frank O'Brien, M.D., now Associate Superintendent in the New York school system. The idea since that time has spread throughout most the country; where no clinics are established, traveling child-guidance clinics are available (See George S. Stevenson and Geddes Smith, *Child Guidance Clinics: A Quarter Century of Development*, New York, Commonwealth Fund, 1934).

From July 1, 1950, to June 30, 1951, the Bureau of Child Guidance in New York handled 16,879 children (including old cases which were reopened) between the ages of two to nineteen years old. Of the old cases 64.7 per cent were boys, the rest girls. The largest percentage of this age group were those eight years old. Of the boys, the most frequent age groups of referral to the clinic were, in the order of the ages, eight, seven, nine and ten years. Of the girls, the order of the age groups were eight, nine, seven, ten. Two thirds of the children were referred from elementary schools and one third from high schools, either by their teachers, principals, or parents.

During the same year the Social Service of the Bureau of Child Guidance in New York city had 44,796 contacts, the psychological staff made 33,968 contacts, 11,147 of which were psychological examinations while the psychiatrists made 7,319 contacts, and the number of pediatric service contacts was 1,070. (Information received from the Bureau of Child Guidance, New York City.) Contacts here refer not to the number of children seen, but to the number of weekly interviews the child may have had during the year.

All this work was carried out by a small professional staff which numbered usually only 195 members. In addition, the Bureau of Child Guidance acted as a consultation service for teachers and was also active in carrying out the educational program by trying to introduce principles of mental hygiene in the community. Many of the children treated have improved, but no statistics are available.

It can be said in general that child-guidance clinics not only have to take care of emotionally maladjusted children but also to participate in the education of mental health in their communities. The clinics have to assist children and their parents; they have to help teachers and agencies dealing with children and they have to aid probation officers and judges. The National Mental Health Act which came into being in 1946 has made federal funds available for the expansion of the child-guidance clinics. Although there is a shortage of trained personnel, the funds should be a stimulus to finding more persons interested in this type of work.

Important as the work of the child-guidance clinic is for the child and the parent, its work also has to be expanded to the classroom. Beside its educational aim, the school may be considered an important agency for prevention of mental maladjustment with or without delinquent behavior. The reason for this is that many schools deal by and large with all children from the time they are at nursery age, about three years old. One of the functions of the schools is to be concerned with the development of emotionally and physically healthy children. Only on such basis can an integrated personality and social responsibility be developed. Only if the school can participate in such a program, will it be able to develop individuals with integrity and thus prevent mental illness and delinquent behavior.

I cannot stress too much how important it is to be aware of the factors which go into the making of a healthy personality. In our quest for such an answer, we have through necessity delved instead into the person with an emotionally disturbed mind and have found a great many insights. This knowledge we have tried to apply to the healthy personality. It is now time that we try to find the criteria which go into the making of the healthy personality, a problem with which the Mid-Century White House Conference on Children and Youth was concerned. This point, of course, is closely connected with the problem of normality which we have raised previously.

As mentioned before, no one is born bad, he is made that way. That means that babies are all right. As long as they are babies, they are not yet bad; they get that way when put in touch with their environment. It is not enough only to respect the child as an individual, but we must know him as a person and understand him in terms of himself and the ties he knits with his family, community and society, his emotional relationships. Furthermore, the child goes through a process of physical, emotional and mental growth during which he learns to achieve a goal. The struggle to achieve this aim persists throughout his life and is a true reflection of his personality. The development of a child is thus a continuing process, high-lighted by certain times of crisis. Such a crisis can be linked to his biological development, or to stresses or strains he experiences throughout infancy, childhood or adolescence. We have tried to find out what age is the most difficult one, but my feeling is that there is no way of judging that. We can only say that experiences in childhood are the most important ones for healthy development. Dr. Rene Spitz has stated that the first half year is the most significant one, while Dr. Erik H. Erikson (*Childhood and Society*, 1950) states that the second half year of the child's life is the most significant one; that is the time when the child develops trust, as Dr. Erikson calls it. One might add that an equally important period of a child's life is his negative period when he is around two years old.

In trying to define what constitutes a healthy personality, we may say that an individual who has a healthy personality participates actively in life by giving of his surplus and still having something left over for himself. In contrast to what people in general might believe, health does not mean only absence of sickness. Health means individual and social functioning without illness; it also means being able at the same time to give and still have left resources for new accomplishments. The child can learn this if he takes cognizance of his environment in a realistic way. He has to learn to grow emotionally and to act realistically and he can do so only in a social reality.

It is this social reality the school has to provide. Therefore, the task of the school is not only to teach subjects, but to teach children. And to teach children in such a way that they have a feeling of achievement so that their school attendance can be happy. This seems self-evident, yet I have seen many school administrators more concerned about the school program than the children. Schools will have to take individual differences of children into consideration, a difficult matter because of large classes, in several communities. Specialists to help children in preventing problems of maladjustment will have to be engaged on a larger scale than heretofore, and school counselors to be fitted into the school system will have to be trained. For this job we should be able to find teachers who could be trained in social work and education.

In passing, let me say that some may believe mentioning the schools is outside the domain of this book. I hope that I have made myself so clear that it should be almost superfluous to give my reason for including such a point here. Mental maladjustment and delinquent behavior is the consequence of what an individual feels and sometimes thinks and acts because of his personality make-up. His individuality is molded through his home and his social institutions, of which one of the most important is the school.

I believe there should be less emphasis upon intelligence tests and more stress laid upon a child's aptitudes and emotions. A child should be tested periodically with regard to his interests, encouraged in them, and at the same time watched so that his hostilities may be curbed and the altruistic side of his nature encouraged.

Children need to have knowledge all around them in such a way that they may absorb it. If they are made to feel that learning is obligatory, school is sometimes a burden, whereas it should be a source of enjoyment.

In addition to factual information of pertinent subjects, the school must give children moral and spiritual values. It is noteworthy that the American Association of Better School Administration in *The Nation's Schools*, September, 1951, stated in the Educational Policies Commission: "The public schools should teach objectively about religion without advocating or teaching any religious creed. The schools should be hospitable to all religions but partial to none." The report states further: "The public schools reflect the religious diversity and tolerance that have helped to make our nation strong. A common education consistent with the American concept of freedom of religion must be based, not on the inculcation of any religious creed but rather on a decent respect for all religious opinions. Such an education must be derived, not from some synthetic patchwork of many religious views but rather from moral and spiritual values shared by members of all religious faiths. . . ."

Important as it is to have an emotional balance in the family, it is also important to have it in the school system. The schools want to create children with rounded personalities; a well-integrated personality has to have a certain basis, therefore it is necessary that schools acquire definite or basic values as their goals.

What are those values? I have previously mentioned that one of the values so prevalent here in the United States is the search for success, so often regardless of the means. While the word success should connote life and the joy of life, we know that men have died for success, both spiritually and actually, and families have been ruined for success, and there have been people who have prayed for failure because of the misery success can bring in its wake.

Genuine success cannot be measured in terms of what a person has in the bank or the size of his name in lights. It is measured by the happiness in his heart and how much of that happiness he gives to others. Success has to do with balance in all things, in a feeling for and expression of equality in the way one lives and the way he treats others. It is evident in his ability to adjust, to make the best of the worst, to change obstacles into achievements, in his ability to be satisfied and pleased with his lot in life. Then, if he experiences personal achievement, it is all to the good, and it will never even then occur to him that he is successful.

A person with a mind and a heart is concerned with neither fame nor fortune, but rather with living his life in accordance with his own ideals and ideas. The person of depth does his work because he must, because he cannot do otherwise, not because of the impression it will make on others, or the glory it will bring to him. When he works he does so because of something inside him which is crying out to be answered, not because he wants to show the world anything.

I have always believed that if you believe in what you are doing and like to do it, you cannot fail. If you do what you want to do, what every fiber of your being tells you you must do, you will do it well.

And with this well-being comes a deep satisfaction of the soul that all is right with you and with the world. It is a sensation of being needed, of belonging.

264

The person who follows a religion is fortunate because of the faith he has in that religion, for without faith there is no life. But if his religion means merely church and symbols, his faith is an inanimate one and without meaning. Religion has to come from within as well as without, for ultimately we have to live with but one person, ourselves.

The world's people need the knowledge of science and the inspiration of faith to do their work and to survive spiritually. They need to learn many things about humanity and man's inhumanity to man, about understanding, forgiveness and appreciation. They need to learn to be good to themselves and to others as well.

Edwin Markham summed up, in perhaps the best way I can think of, the relationship between psychiatry and religions as they should be practiced, but so often are not:

> He drew a circle that shut me out—
> Heretic, rebel, a thing to flout.
> But Love and I had the wit to win:
> We drew a circle that took him in!

Most individuals unable to achieve those values are led astray. This achievement of values is part of mental health because in these values are imbedded a definite aim which goes beyond everyday living. Unless a person has a goal which can carry him over the daily struggle, he will be unable to measure his daily life against an ideal one.

The question is, who is going to convey this knowledge to the children? As the school situation is now, teachers have the responsibility to impart their knowledge to their pupils in such a way that they create emotionally mature children. This is, of course, difficult because it requires a mature teacher. Teachers can help to make or break children, and more than half of the reason has to do with the feelings of children, which are very strong, yet easily bent. Criteria differ insofar as what a good child really is, and all too often pathetic specimens are taken for the epitome of perfection. This is why teachers sometimes tend to cherish and perhaps make a teacher's pet out of the boy or girl who goes to any and all lengths to please and to do the right thing. It is understandable that such children would be most appreciated by a teacher, for classroom problems are many and varied. But, whereas the boy who kicks his classmate in the shins occasionally may not be exactly appealing, he may have a more normal life ahead of him than the goody-goody. The extremely good child is that way because he dares not behave any other way; if he behaves otherwise he is afraid that he will either be punished or virtually disowned. He therefore seeks constant approval because he feels so insecure. Such a child is a sick one who will not learn from mistakes as will the normal child, because he sees to it that he attempts perfection. And while the parents and teachers of this model boy or girl are patting themselves on the back and purring to one and all about their great ability and luck, the child is in a state of unhappiness and agitation. And whereas now he may look for relaxation of his tensions with children who are younger or in daydreams, later on it may be in emotional maladjustment with or without delinquency. The child who is angelic with adults seldom gets along with those of his own age, for he is exacting, inclined to sit in judgment of them and is often bossy. These attitudes are only little signs of the discontent and rebellion the perfect child dares not show with oldsters, but they are also the beginnings of an ingrained hostility.

This is but one of the infinite examples of maladjustment in children, but it is also one of many good reasons why teachers should be well versed in child psychology, and why they should have a working relationship with parents. I often think it a pity that children cannot start school during their first year rather than their fifth, particularly with the general lack of co-ordination that exists between parent and teacher today. By the very fact of the children's school age, it is necessary to have more teamwork insofar as upbringing is concerned. It is therefore necessary that the nursery school become a part of the school system in the whole country.

As things stand today, it is not uncommon for something resembling competition to exist between teacher and parent, with resentment if one criticizes the other. In other words, each adult in such an instance is thinking of his or her own pride and fixed opinions while the child, the important mainspring, is essentially neglected both from the standpoint of his feelings now and his possible behavior later. It is all very well to take a seemingly deep interest in any child, but when selfish motives exist under the guise of altruism, this is perhaps a little worse than utter negligence. At least the latter is honest.

The school system suffers from too many inequities. Requirements for teachers differ from state to state. When children all over are essentially the same, the standards for teacher's training and ability should by and large be the same. This ideal requirement cannot yet be met. In some communities the teachers' salaries are deplorably low. Our teachers are expected to inflame the imaginations of children with the romance and adventure in the various aspects of education. How can they be expected to do this without the incentive of a decent salary; how can they be expected to help mold future giants of destiny if by the very evidence of our appreciation of them, they themselves are looked upon as mere mechanical tools? The world screams for lower taxation, which would suggest a continuation of the low rate of pay for teachers. But would you not prefer to pay them more in order that you may pay less to maintain the emotionally maladjusted persons or delinquents they will otherwise in time help to create? In illustration of the present state of affairs, during the past year we spent more money on capturing and maintaining offenders than we did on our entire educational system. Just as the parents' job overlaps the field of learning and culture for their children, so must the teacher be able to recognize emotional difficulties and help straighten them out if development is to continue. It is for this reason that teachers should know, as well as they know the subjects they teach, *all* of the little signs that something is wrong in a child's outlook.

Important as it may be to learn about the three R's, it is now time to start learning the fourth R, relationship—that is, emotional relationship. The way the child behaves toward his teacher or toward other children reflects his own feelings, and it is necessary for the teacher to know about that child's emotional attitudes.

In 1950 I started trying to find out what psychiatric facilities there were in the primary and secondary schools of the country and to what extent these schools utilize the principles of mental hygiene. I was surprised that there was no source of information about these problems. We, therefore, found it necessary at Columbia University to make a survey to try to determine the emotional status of children in grammar and high schools, the amount and degree of their emotional disturbances and available psychiatric services and counseling in these schools.

By way of questionnaires sent to private boarding and day schools and to public schools in various parts of the country, we are trying to obtain a survey of conditions pertaining to mental health in the classroom, the use of textbooks on the subject of mental hygiene, the teacher's awareness of children's problems, how the school authorities handle the need for psychiatric help, etc.

It would be a complicated task for the teacher to assume new duties in addition to the ones he already has. Not only must the teacher know about the physical status of the child, but he must see to it that he attends classes, he must talk to parents once in a while and attend faculty meetings regularly. His task thus includes many and varied assignments for which there is too little time even if the teacher has a well-rounded personality and knows intimately the working of the human mind.

What it adds up to is: How efficient are teachers in their jobs? Complaints are heard that they fall down on their jobs, but it seems rather that the job is too much for the teacher, and therefore overwhelms him. At the present time we do not have any yardstick for measuring teachers' efficiency, that is, how well they impart their knowledge to their pupils. It is interesting in this respect that research indicates that a teacher, rated as to his ability to impart knowledge, may be considered a bad one by the principal but be considered by many children the best teacher they have, and vice-versa. It is often astounding that a teacher, who according to the theory should be considered good, does not perform as well as expected.

Intangible factors should go into the rating by a teacher's efficiency, among which the most prominent would be understanding the child and himself and his own resourcefulness. That is, factors belonging to the realm of mental hygiene. One particular aspect

268

of the emotional attitude of the child is that there are no male teachers in the nursery grades or in the first grades of the primary school. The children in those grades are taught only by female teachers. A child who has a domineering mother and a weak father will be quite impressed when he goes to school and find a woman teacher in authority, leading him to believe that people in authority are women and that men are weaklings. This should be no reflection upon female teachers because there are many good ones. Sometimes many of them are better than their male colleagues, but it can give a child a distorted viewpoint to be surrounded only by women until he is seven or eight years old.

This situation is to some extent counteracted in that some of the school supervisors are men, or that the male principal is a warm person.

One could make a conscious effort to engage male teachers for nursery and the early grades of primary schools if it were only possible to increase salaries.

One way of testing teachers' efficiency would be to have them take a written examination on how they would act in the face of various simple and complicated forms of student behavior. Moreover, if teachers in every state would undergo some type of psychological examination, the findings of which should be explained to him, he might better understand his own hostilities and repressions and therefore protect the children from them. Those who are shown by such tests to be highly neurotic or psychotic should be prevented from teaching the future citizens of the world. If some tests of a projective technique could be worked out suitable for testing teacher's ability, this would be an advanced step.

Although classes in child psychology are a good addition to training courses for teachers, still there are not enough. There must be a revamping of the duties of teachers; such an alteration could partly be accomplished by adding counseling teachers or school counselors or guidance counselors to the present staff.

What I have said here sounds like a large order, yet we will have to apply the principles of such a plan to some kind of working system if we believe in the betterment of man.

From my own experiences I remember many cases where some

269

guidance was of great help to teachers. Whenever I talked with them in our research, I tried to impart to them the principles of mental hygiene and to indicate their application to the children in their classes. If a child had been a truant chiefly because of his family setting, I advised the teacher that he had to talk with the parent about how important it was that the boy attend school. The teacher was advised to discuss this in such a way that it would not create in the child's mind a sense of conflict between the school and the parents.

If a child was inadequately dressed, which gave him a feeling of being different from his classmates, the teacher had to know that clothes would have to be secured for him so he would have more feeling of belonging to the class. If parents were unable to clothe the child adequately, the case should be transferred to a social agency for immediate attention. If a child had been sick for some time, we asked the teacher to find out whether the sickness was real or imagined and used merely as a means of attracting attention. If the sickness proved to have no real foundation, then the teacher should pay attention to the child's complaints and later try to gain his attention in a constructive and healthy manner.

If a child had failed in class or had a too low intelligence, we suggested that he may need another teacher or a special school. If that was not feasible, it was suggested that he be given working papers. If we dealt with a gang leader who had been truant, we first examined the boy to make sure that he was in the proper grade. If this were the case, he was given an assignment of a project together with other pupils in the classroom. We advised the teacher that he should always try to emphasize the boy's ability when he did some work on the project instead of talking so much about his failure. Such an attitude would relieve the boy's fear of punishment and the disapproval of the class.

If a boy had misbehaved in class, we advised the teacher first to try to establish a harmonious relationship with him. This was important because then the child would be sure of receiving sympathy and understanding, all of which would make it easier for him to talk over his misbehavior. The teacher was advised never to use any force: that would lead the boy to attempt to lie himself out of his predicament, or to refuse to talk with the teacher or to feel he had been unfairly treated. I stressed that force might make the boy repeat his misbehavior because too much fuss had been made over it.

It was important that in my discussions with the teacher I let him find out for himself as much as possible the answers to his problems about the children. This gave him confidence, enabling him later to handle similar situations himself.

There are, of course, problems other than emotional ones among school children. There are the physically handicapped and the mentally retarded, as well as the mentally defective and the quiz kid. And just as each emotional problem is a special one, so must each of those be treated individually.

First of all, the apparently physically handicapped and mentally retarded children may not actually be what they appear. These may be emotional manifestations which a psychologically oriented teacher could easily recognize.

The genuinely physically handicapped are more of an emotional problem than anything else, for if they are not continually reassured that they are accepted, they are apt to turn in upon themselves and in the process develop a hostile attitude toward the world. Teachers, with the help of parents, can do much to make the physically handicapped feel as important and worth-while as any other child. As we know, children can be very cruel under such circumstances, but they too can, and should, be taught otherwise.

One way around this whole last problem has been worked out in some places by way of a special school for those who have been afflicted with poliomyelitis and the like. Thus by the time such youngsters are of an age to go out into the world, they feel little or no self-consciousness about their physical affliction. In time, of course, through knowledge of nutrition and generally better living, we hope there will be less and less of such difficulty. Through experimental investigations, it has recently been discovered that children stricken with infantile paralysis had been fed on a high sugar-starch diet, thereby decreasing their physical resistance and paving the way for the disease.

271

Mental defectives present a special problem of their own. From past experience it would seem that the most satisfactory way of dealing with them, and in the long run the least expensive, is within a special school or institution. These children can learn certain things with the proper supervision: if they are treated with patience and kindness, they can learn to care for themselves and to make certain salable articles.

The overly bright youngster also constitutes a definite problem, both for others and for himself. The usual process of skipping such children to higher grades is generally unfortunate because they end up too young for their classmates and yet above those in the preceding class which tends to increase any anxieties they may have had. Through such active segregation many an emotionally disturbed boy has become worse. Therefore, skipping a child should be carefully worked out, taking into consideration his emotional make-up as well as his intellectual endowment. Frequently these children are emotionally immature, and therefore have a tendency to lag emotionally behind those of their own chronological age at the same time they are mentally superior. Yet, if they are not skipped, they become a problem for themselves, for the teachers and other children and for their parents. The exceptionally bright child should therefore be encouraged more than the average one to participate in play and sports in order to channelize his energies so he can also develop his social interests and leadership. It should be added though, that a good teacher can do this differentiated teaching.

I have had many cases in psychiatric treatment through which I have seen some of the effects of teachers' actions on people's lives. My experience is that teachers often have it within their power to make or break their pupils. This is all the more reason why preparation for the field of teaching should be an extremely careful and systematic one.

I remember a young girl in the fifth grade who learned to love the most formidable teacher in the school. Nora had been kept after school because she had been writing her English composition in geography class. During her late-hour studies in the lonely and deserted room with the aging woman of severe face, long black dress and gunboat shoes, Nora suddenly became aware that Miss Wright was staring at her hands. Soon Miss Wright went over to Nora's desk, picked up one of Nora's hands and looked at the large wart that the girl had spent so much of her life trying to hide. Nora felt herself turn red with anger and tears came to her eyes when Miss Wright said, "How long have you had this wart?" Nora told her brokenly that she had had it as long as she could remember. Miss Wright thereupon told Nora in unaccustomed sweet and mellow tones to go buy a caustic pencil at the drugstore and apply it night and morning to the ugly thing. In time it went away, but Miss Wright remained in Nora's heart forever.

There are numerous cases on record wherein teachers have recognized a spark within a child and encouraged him to make the most of it. Many teachers devote their lives to searching and seeking for a sign, a flair, and bringing it to the surface in all its richness and fullness. There was a case of a young lad who drew comic cartoons all over his history, English, and mathematics papers to the great despair of his teachers. His French teacher called him to her desk one day and talked to him about this habit of his. She asked him about his drawings, told him how good she thought they were and suggested that he draw a caricature of her for the school paper. The boy was so pleased that he drew a very flattering one of her which was run shortly thereafter. That gave him his start. His cartoons appeared regularly in the school paper from then on. They are now appearing in magazines throughout the country.

A young woman who was a patient of mine of several years ago had had a very hard time in her youth. She wanted to write, but she was afraid to, afraid of recalling the dead past, of suffering it all over again. What she didn't know was that she was reliving it all the time anyway, in her conditioned behavior, her reactions, her outlook. During one session she recalled that a teacher in grammar school had told her she had a spark, an unusual ability to write. Receiving little response to what she had said, the teacher shook the girl and told her she must write, that nothing must stop her, that she must not let her talent die. Well, she's writing now and getting her unhappiness out of her system in the way that nature provided for her. She has told me that when she is inclined

273

to sink into inertia for very long, to get lazy, to let the whole thing go, she has a vision of a middle-aged sweet-faced woman looking at her as if to say, "Don't let me down, or yourself either."

Teachers can be a great inspiration to children and a boon to the world if they will learn to do more than their job, more than is actually required of them, if they will take a personal interest in their brood. We get out of things what we put into them, and no teacher who has ever pushed a child along to his own personal goal has ever been forgotten.

Likewise, no child who has ever been ridiculed by a teacher has ever forgotten that teacher, for there can be no greater or more devastating weapon than this, none more wounding to the soul. Ridicule in anyone is a form of sadism, and sadism in a teacher of the future adults of the world is just about the last word in all that can be wrong and ghastly in any school system. . . . We must know ourselves before we can deal with others.

A young boy, Ralph, was referred to me for treatment. He was either a little monster or "unsound" according to his mother. Suppose you judge for yourself from a part of the story what his dreams and free associations disclosed to me:

Ralph was not very good in school, but the girls liked him. Anyone could see that he was handsome, and he had a sweet tenderness about him. One day in class Ralph was gazing out of the window with a faraway look in his eyes. His teacher interrupted his thoughts with the cutting remark, "Ralph, what do you expect to get by on later, your looks?" The class snickered, and Ralph put on a brave smirk, but her remark, besides hurting, also fitted right in with his thoughts at that moment. For Ralph had been wondering what it was all for anyway. When the day was over and the little girls went to their homes, he would go to his. There he wouldn't receive any sweet looks. There he would see his father, drunk as usual and his mother either pleading with him or yelling at him, depending upon what stage she had reached at the moment, which never seemed to be one of acceptance. So it went on, day by day, night by night, so why study, and what, indeed, was he going to get by with in life, and why bother anyway?

Had his teacher had any real concept of what can go on in a child's mind, she would have worked her way into his confidence, learned the situation and then through some organization within the town sought either to relieve conditions within the child's home or take him out of it. If the boy were so withdrawn that he would not confide in her, she could have made a visit now and then to his home, which she would automatically have recognized to be the basis of his trouble. She would under no circumstances have ridiculed him, nor would she suggest that he was stupid or lazy. She would have known that when you are emotionally weary, it is difficult to apply yourself intellectually.

But Ralph's teacher put more weight upon his already heavy heart. And therefore I say she should rightly have taken some of the blame when Ralph was found not long afterward beating his sick and miserable father almost to death with a fire iron, and thinking not at all about his good looks.

A girl named June, another product of unhappy home life, found more emotional security with boys than with girls, for their interests seemed more wholesome to her. Things were very abnormal at home, and June found release in ice skating, bike riding and swimming. When she sat quietly with the girls, she found her mind wandering back to her family and their fights. Then a group of boys permitted June to join them, to be one of them, to go everywhere with them. She was so grateful that she never turned "sissy" or in any way caused them to regret making her a member of the gang. The boys treated June like a sister, and she loved every single one of them.

June could see no sense to geometry and managed to fail it regularly. She received good marks in her other subjects, even though she spent less time on them altogether than she did on geometry alone. One day when June made one of her usual errors in class, her geometry teacher said to her, "All you seem to care about is having a bunch of boys run after you." June said nothing, but a big lump formed in her throat, and for the first time she felt shame for the most wonderful relationship she had ever known. She was humiliated in front of the entire class and made to feel cheap to

275

herself. Her relationship with the boys was never quite the same after that. In time she broke away from them, and shortly afterward ran away from home as well.

It was not until June undertook psychiatric treatment some time later that she learned why it was she had been feeling so embarrassed in the presence of men. One point is that a teacher had made her so. When her novel appeared, there was much therein about the mystery of things mathematical and geometrical. She tells me she will always treasure a letter she received shortly after the publication of her book. It was from a great novelist who maintained he carried a pocket adding machine with him everywhere he went, because in school he had failed everything from arithmetic to trigonometry.

This brings up a particular condition within the schools: the supposition that we can all go through the same grind and all come out in a state of preparation for life.

We do not know just why it is that some of us become lawyers, some artists and some doctors. Nevertheless, we do, and it is a good thing the field is not this limited, either, else we would not eat. The point is that, beyond the everyday necessities of knowledge, we should not all have to go through involved requirements for learning, much of which we never even remember, let alone use. If one is going to be an all-round teacher, it might make some sense. If one really wishes it, it perhaps makes more sense. But how many of us do? And how many of us essentially dislike school and take years finding ourselves because of all the extraneous material we have constantly to absorb.

If we are to have mental as well as emotional adjustment, then it is time we laid less emphasis upon all-inclusive intelligence tests and began periodically to test children for their emotional interests and aptitudes. Once these interests and capabilities have been established, the schooling should be built around them with the other subjects being treated as a side issue. In other words, it is a question of whether majoring in a particular course of study shouldn't start in grade school, rather than in college which many people cannot afford to attend anyway.

I do not mean to suggest that the student should be encouraged in one field to the exclusion of all others. Such a practice would obviously create a strange society in which the members would be well informed on one subject and virtual morons in others. Thus they would not even be able to talk, let alone live, together. No, but learning in general should be alive, colorful and flexible. It should be planned so as to give the student a maximum amount of responsibility, which will both help him in becoming an adult and encourage him to learn all he can. Then, if it becomes apparent that he has a particular fondness for and ability in one line, he should be permitted to express himself therein to his heart's content, without guilt feelings because he cannot measure up as well in something else.

It is interesting in this respect what a report, *Vitalizing Secondary Education*, issued by the Office of Education, Washington, D. C., in 1951, has to say: "High schools still lag far behind in making programs attractive enough to keep youth in school. The typical high school curriculum falls far short of preparing those not going to college for a well-rounded life and useful citizenship.

"High school programs and operations are critically in need of further changes. The rate of social change in this country is rapid and it tends to outrun the capacity of the schools for making needed adaptations. A narrow academic education far from helping all youth form desirable patterns of behavior, often caused them to develop social maladjustments, thwarted normal learning impulses, and created habits of failure which had wide and lasting implications both for youth and for society."

There are three forces at work here, all of which are perhaps equally important. One, it is good for a child's Ego and stability to feel that he can do one thing and do it well. Two, it is necessary for a child to have a good understanding of and working relationship with other people, both of his own age and position as well as otherwise, if he is going to be a fit citizen. And three, he must have a good all-round knowledge of the world, its history and its present situation if he is going to help keep it going and perhaps improve it. This would seem to require a great deal; actually all it requires is a little common sense.

Those of us who are parents know that the desire for knowledge is as natural to a child as is eating and sleeping. Children drive us nearly to distraction with their unending stream of why's. We would not, however, kill this enthusiasm for anything in the world, because it is normal and because it represents growth. Yet by our very reluctance to do something constructive about the present school system, we ourselves often kill a child's natural desire to learn by the very method in which we present education.

Do you suppose that if you were to take a child who is continually pressing for information and give him to understand that he would receive one answer at three o'clock and another at five, provided he memorized all the facts you wanted him to know between times, that his enthusiasm would not die? If you do, you suppose wrong. Human beings are not so constructed that they want their lives chopped up in little pieces for them. When they live that way as adults, they do so by rote and with an imbedded resentment against whatever made that procedure into a habit.

There have come into being schools which have been called modern and which try to combine individual and group studies, try to utilize the child's own initiative, thereby making him feel like a person rather than one of a flock. The teachers watch over the children from the standpoint of their emotional state of mind and how much they seem to enjoy or dislike their work. They then guide them from there. This is a good plan, ideally speaking, and has been carried out mostly by private schools; and that is unfortunate from two standpoints. It requires high individual tuition, and if improperly handled it tends to create a feeling of segregation among the children. One of the things for which we are striving in this world is a feeling of all being free and equal. Until we attain such a condition there will always be insufficient understanding and co-operation.

The emotional pattern we establish within children will stay with them all their lives. So it is with their educational pattern. If we make early learning a chore rather than the privilege it really is, consciously or unconsciously it will always remain that way. In illustration of this, witness the large number of people who run to the movies in search of entertainment, and look upon the library and all things educational, even the newspapers and the newsreels, as a social duty rather than pleasure.

This brings up the question of establishing useful activities for the children in school outside the classroom. Such a program has first of all to be accepted completely by the teachers and has to be supervised jointly by them and by the pupils. These activities should also recognize the pupil's rights, duties and privileges, not only as a pupil of the school but also as its citizen. When such a school program grows out of the activities taking place in the school, it would naturally fit into the pupil's life, instead of being imposed upon him. In this program should be included discussions, club activities, assembly programs and the like.

In many places throughout the country such a program has been at work for some time. The unfortunate thing is that the pupils do not get enough time to participate, according to a pamphlet issued by the Office of Education, Washington, D. C., "The Activity Period," which has based its findings upon questionnaires sent to 13,740 schools. If the extra-class activities are going to be constructive and provide for activities which could be tied more to life in general, the pupils must be given more time than heretofore. Youngsters and adolescents like to be active; they have a great deal of energy which has to be channelized in constructive ways. A youth likes to feel that he is helpful, he does not like to be idle. If he does not have a proper outlet, he may resort to undesirable activities in order to satisfy his ambitions or his fantasies.

Saying this does not mean that if a youngster has not enough activities for his surplus energy, he will then become emotionally maladjusted or delinquent. As I have stated before, delinquency comes about through interplay of various factors, of which the emotional climate in the home is the most important one. Comic books do not lead into crime, although they have been widely blamed for it. I find comic books, and so does Dr. Lauretta Bender and many others, many times helpful for children in that through them they can get rid of many of their aggressions and harmful fantasies. If a child constantly reads comic books, it means that he clings unduly to his childhood, which reflects a personality disturbance. But such a child was disturbed before he read comic books. In my experience as a psychiatrist, I cannot remember having seen one boy or girl who has committed a crime or who became neurotic, psychotic or showed a psychosomatic disturbance because he read comic books. If any of these conditions arose, it was because of the personality make-up of the individual and not because of the comic book. A child who becomes delinquent has so much of an antisocial pattern in him that any external stimulus would affect him. Therefore, it should not be necessary to forbid comics provided they were kept within certain boundaries.

Drug addiction has been in part blamed on lack of activities for boys. We have of late seen a great increase in drug addiction among youths, although we do not know for sure how large the numbers are. Edward J. Mowery, staff writer on The New York *World Telegram and Sun*, who is a close observer of dope addiction, reports that New York City is estimated to have 90,000 addicts, of whom 15,000 are under 21 years of age. Although these numbers are high, the schools can hardly be blamed for it since the parents have most of the responsibility. When a boy or girl resorts to a drug, be it marihuana, heroin, or morphine it is because the drug serves as a release from tension which indicates that the adolescent is in an emotional conflict. If drug addiction lasts for some time, it reflects a definite disturbance of the character in the person indicating the presence of a character disorder.

The high numbers given here are debatable. No doubt there has been an increase of drug addicts, but school authorities, for instance, in New York City, have found, to the contrary, very few teen-age addicts, according to a statement given by Dr. William Jansen, Superintendent of Schools, in a public hearing about drug addiction, in New York City in 1951.

A few words may be said here about treatment of addicts. Firstly, the dope peddler who, himself, most frequently is a drug addict and who usually suffers from a deep-seated character disorder has to be put out of circulation for a long time in order to protect children and juveniles against becoming drug addicts. Treatment of the drug addict is symptomatic as long as one tries only to withdraw the drug. What he needs is psychotherapy of a deep nature and that is difficult because he has an intense resistance against treatment since he has such an oral longing for the drug. For that reason treatment is a prolonged procedure and relapse is frequent. The drug

280

addict himself is a rather passive person who is closely tied to his mother. His Ego is weak, he is emotionally immature and likes to develop a feeling of omnipotence, a state which he reaches when he is under the influence of the drug. ("Heroin Addiction in Adolescent Boys," Paul Zimmering, M.D., James Toolan, M.D., Renate Safrin, M.S., and S. Bernard Wortis, M.D., *Journal of Nervous and Mental Disease*, 114: 19-34, July, 1951.)

Where there is a preponderance of drug addicts, every great city should establish a reception center for diagnostic purpose where they could be given treatment. Furthermore, when they are discharged from the hospital, they have to be given aftercare treatment on an out-patient basis. In addition to this follow-up treatment, it is necessary to interview the family since a great deal of drug addiction, as any other expression of delinquency, is very much a problem of emotional tension within the family. Furthermore, schools, as we have seen in New York City, have to take an active part in curbing this along with other manifestations which arise as a result of emotional disturbances. In a sound report of the Assistant Superintendents of the Board of Education of the City of New York about *Juvenile Delinquency in the Schools* it is stated (p. 53): "It is our considered opinion that the time for a direct educational assault on this problem [drug addiction] has come."

Teachers have to be aware of the emotional difficulties in children because only then can they prevent them developing further. Great troubles arise from small ones, and the earlier mental difficulties or antisocial symptoms can be discovered, the better is our possibility for counteracting them. One reason why I have gone into so much detail is to give teachers and parents factual knowledge which can be used as preventative means rather than rehabilitating or reformative ones. With such a preventative program which takes into consideration broad educational measures, we would be able to detect at an early stage the individual who later on becomes a robber, a rapist or a murderer.

Difficult as it is to detect the potential offender, it is also difficult for us to predict future behavior of juvenile or adult delinquents. Some attempts have been made to find criteria for the way a juvenile delinquent will behave in the future. Sheldon and Eleanor Glueck

(*Unravelling Juvenile Delinquency,* The Commonwealth Fund, 1950) have tried to establish prediction tables about criminal behavior, but these have met with criticism. Before we can arrive definitely at valid conclusions, we first have to know in detail the reason why an individual behaves as he does. Unless we know this fact unequivocally, we will not acquire any real basis for predicting future conduct of any delinquent or for that matter of any man at all.

In our own research we have learned a great deal of the psychodynamics and motivations of human behavior, and as part of our investigations we have through various tests been able to detect different degrees of an individual's aggressiveness or shyness, his cruelty or submissiveness, etc., all of which has helped us very much in prognosticating his future behavior. One complicating factor in all predictions of this type, as we have been able to show, is that so often a quantitative replacement occurs between psychological manifestations, psychosomatic symptoms and antisocial behavior. Last but not least, a moment of uncertainty is always present in any prediction of human conduct; a man might behave in a certain way, but it is not inevitable that he will behave that way.

In order to detect potential delinquents, we will need a number of mental hygiene clinics where parents, children and adolescents can receive advice and help for their troubles. Many, of course, cannot be detected. But if adequate handling of potential offenders were applied at once, the majority could be rehabilitated so that they would not become emotionally ill or delinquent.

In addition to being aware of emotional problems in childhood, attention must be called to the difficulties arising in the adolescents who can be helped a great deal if we approach their situation from an understanding point of view. Beside remedying emotional disturbances in childhood, I cannot think of any more important span of life where help is needed.

The college student from the age of about eighteen to twenty-two lives through a time where a constructive program of mental hygiene can be carried out. While a boy or a girl between the ages of fourteen to eighteen often may not be accessible to a psychiatric approach, the college years may prove to be more suitable. A fourteen-year-old boy, for instance, usually participates in a great many activities; his conscience not being completely developed, he is on the surface generous and liberal while deeper down he is apprehensive and uncertain. When he later enters college, however, he is apt to acknowledge that he may be upset or disturbed and often welcomes the idea of talking out his problems with a psychiatrist. The latter can impart to the boy a more constructive conscience, all of which makes it possible for him to identify himself with the psychiatrist. This new identification, which is the basis for a new relationship, makes it more possible for an adolescent to deal with his feelings and his conflict in a realistic and constructive way. He tries to deal with his emotions in such a way that he has not so many abnormal guilt feelings. These feelings arise particularly in connection with masturbation, an occurrence which may not be so prominent today as it was twenty or thirty years ago. Yet it still is serious for the boy. The psychiatrist is able to relieve the boy's intense guilt feelings by trying to enlighten him about the ideas which brought about these feelings in the first place. Such a change of orientation also brings about in the boy the understanding that he is able to control his instinctual drive and to deal with his compulsive masturbation constructively. As a result of letting him know that sexual life is part of a healthy life, he will, unless he suffers from deep-seated emotional problems, be able to face these experiences.

The actual handling of such a case is most difficult; it must be stressed that it is not so important what the psychiatrist says as how he explains things to the patient. A casual but at the same time constructive approach is the best. When the boy sees that the doctor takes all things in a casual way it will help to allay his guilt feelings and his fears. It would be desirable if a teacher could be so well equipped that he could take over the role of the psychiatrist in such an instance. For that purpose there should be established among teachers study groups from which they could acquire knowledge of the basic concepts of psychiatry, which they could in turn impart to their pupils. A prerequisite for such a procedure is that the teacher should be able to apply these principles upon himself.

It is unfortunate that many teachers have personality make-ups which cannot be modified sufficiently to benefit the mental health of their pupils. If a teacher is to be useful to his pupils and school, to parents and community, he must be flexible, must understand the principles underlying mental growth of children and must be tolerant of their emotional attitude and deviated behavior. Furthermore—and this is one of the most important factors—the teacher has to make himself a part of his pupils in such a way that he indirectly becomes responsible for their mental health. Instead of asking absolute conformity to conduct in classroom, he should guide his pupils to proper behavior. A classroom where the child is permitted to express himself within reason is the happiest one for him; it gives him a sense of freedom and may help him to get rid of the frustrations and anxieties he has experienced in his home. Although the child must be able to accept the code of social conduct, he should not become a slave to it. In other words, the teacher has to have the capacity to learn, even from children. The teacher, therefore, has to know himself in order to know his children. Only then can he act as a free human being for the good of his pupils. As Epictetus put it: "No man is free who is not a master of himself."

Essential as it is to have education in mental health, it is also necessary to have mental health in education. As a proponent of mental hygiene, I believe that our educational method must be directed toward teaching our children to think logically for themselves and at the same time teaching them to tolerate frustrations within certain limits. Most of our educational system crams the minds of our children with sometimes very superficial and piecemeal information. We train them to memorize certain things but not the meanings of things; therefore, we do not teach them to think logically without being biased.

It is important for the child that the teacher point out to him that he should try to achieve realistic goals within his reach, and that simultaneously he should be told indirectly or directly that he will have to postpone the achievement of some of these goals, else he will feel dissatisfied and frustrated. The pupil should be given to understand that all people have limitations, and that accepting them does not mean that they have failed. Only by learning to accept his own limitations and those of his environment will the child be able to adjust to the order of the classroom. It is in general believed that any person's ability to adjust depends upon how able he is to endure frustrations. Each person has a certain level of frustration which by and large is determined by his experiences in his home. When an easily frustrated child is put under too much pressure in the classroom, he will react in a negative way in contrast to that pupil with a high frustration level who will gain by being urged. It is therefore necessary for the teacher to find out what kind of pressure the individual child can stand and from which he can profit the most. Too many teachers are apt to instruct children in a negative or threatening way. The good teacher knows that he can get the best achievement from the pupil when he directs him in an accepting way and thereby gives him a feeling of belonging so he feels secure. Through this means the child is given to understand that he is a member of the class, that he has a task there and a contribution to give.

This sense of belonging is extremely important for every child because it has a bearing upon his mental health. Teachers are too often concerned with the unruly, talkative and active child because he is frequently so difficult to handle. At the same time the teacher forgets about the quiet or shy pupil who very often may be withdrawn or depressed and about whom in general he should be much more concerned. Because he is not noticed, the quiet one may lack any sense of belonging, and that may bring about a lack of identification in him which may give rise to emotional difficulties or delinquencies.

When the teacher tries to get the pupil to become aware of his own limitations, the child will be able to adapt himself to his own problems and to the limitations of others, including society. Thus we see that the fundamentals of mental hygiene have to be translated by the teachers into practical purposes which will make children stronger in a psychological way and so make them more effective as adults. Consequently, our philosophy of education will have to stress the mental health and growth of the child so it can make him more adaptable when he leaves school. Mental health and education are both a process of learning which has to take into consideration the psychological needs of children.

"But for learning, Heaven and Earth would not endure," one of our old wise men once said. True, but learning is not only out of books. It is from life and from the minds of the people who make it.

12

Education Is Prevention

EACH society has the number of criminals it deserves. We must carefully examine whether or not people are interested in helping or curing offenders even if they are in a position to do so. The average man has always had a need for a scapegoat because he has always needed to blame someone for misfortune. If he did not find a scapegoat, he would create him. In our case this has not been necessary because we have always had delinquents as an easy target for the law-abiding citizen who could let out his aggressions by having them punished.

We now understand that this is partly because the ordinary man does not dare to carry out criminal acts. Filled with his own pent-up resentments and hostilities, which might be transformed into antisocial actions, he instead lets off steam in other directions, and often it is directed against the offender. What the citizen really does is to punish the delinquents for the evil he himself feels and thinks.

Technically speaking, the world is full of criminals, and yet we lock up only a few of them. Or, to put it another way, at least half of the world is sick, but we punish only those who overtly display their illness. Stated still a third way, psychiatrists who specialize in the field of delinquency recognize that when men break the law, they are giving expression to their mental illness. The public in general has the outlook that criminals are basically different from other people, that they are evil and that they must "pay" for their crimes if they are ever to straighten out.

In the first place, it is illogical to work on the assumption that

287

anyone can pay for a crime. Once a crime has been committed, it has been committed for all time, and nothing can make up for it. We cannot really "pay" for a misdeed, even with our lives. What is more, to foment the idea that crime can be paid for is in itself another crime, for the very theory tends to promote rather than prevent crime.

More important, when society and the law created by society continues with the ancient idea that offenders are a special brand of people who must suffer for their evil, who must give "an eye for an eye and a tooth for a tooth," they are not only being barbaric, they are being superficial, inhuman, and, in fact, evil themselves.

In every one of us there are feelings of hostility, resentment and other ignoble emotions. The difference is a matter of degree and of the method of expression. Since we ourselves are emotionally involved with the offender, we who make up the bulk of society must change our attitude in order to create a better understanding of the delinquent person. I have tried to show what we know today of the working of his mind. We have seen that it is irrational for the offender to behave as he does, but for the same reason it is also irrational for us to continue to take a condemning and destructive view of him. When he is wrong, it does not help matters for us to be wrong too. Betterment and improvement, wherever it takes place, requires a positive and constructive attitude by every one of us. If every one carefully thought over his own feelings toward the delinquent, he might then understand his own punishing attitude toward him. This is difficult because we would have to think very deeply and for a long time about ourselves since so much of our thinking is mixed up with our feelings.

We are often proud of the fact that we have justice, and there is reason for us to be proud of it, but only to a certain extent. There is as yet too little of humanity in justice just as there is a great lag between science and law. Oliver Wendell Holmes said once that "the life of the law, has not been logic; it has been experience." What is this experience?

Firstly, we must approach the problem of the delinquent with an open mind. This does not mean, I repeat, that we shall have to free all criminals. There are those who are dangerous and therefore have to be kept out of circulation as long as they are that way; there are also those who are psychotic and therefore have to stay in a hospital until cured.

Secondly, as we have seen, the problem of the offender himself is only part of the whole problem of eradicating crime. Eliminating criminal activities goes beyond the criminal; it includes the whole area of social behavior covering social, ethical and cultural standards, all governed by our motivations. Certain principles and ideals must be laid'down for conduct of men.

Thirdly, we have seen that psychological processes responsible for antisocial acts start to work in the person a long time before he actually commits the crime. We have seen how crime is created and how it grows.

Fourthly, we know too that criminal behavior is far indeed from being merely something evil, developing from an intrinsically evil heart. Delinquent inclinations are symptoms of a deep and often devasting distortion or sickness of the mind, one which requires as a remedy understanding, skill and patience, without which recovery is impossible.

Lastly, we have seen that there are multiple causes for criminal behavior; the same is also true for mental illness. In criminal behavior we have stressed that the causes are relative, and that the earmark of the delinquent individual is his antisocial character. The tendency to commit a crime is present all the time because of the personality make-up together with the destructive influences that took place in childhood. Loss of love, loss of prestige, a rise of anxiety, or a sudden temptation which is directly related to a previous but now unconscious emotion may bring about an actual crime, or, by causing an actual break from reality, bring about a severe mental illness.

In view of all our scientific findings about human behavior, it is now time to apply our knowledge to future prevention of delinquent behavior and also to mental illness since those two manifestations are so interrelated. But in doing so we must try to use methods which can meet the demands of society and which can be understood by everyone.

This means that we must first develop a new general and mandatory treatment for the delinquent. We will have to find the emotional problems which have made him turn to crime. We will then discover the basic causes within the home, which do not exclude precipitating causes to criminal behavior outside the family. We will then have to treat the delinquent himself, but in addition look into the emotional relationship with his parents, or foster parents, or close relatives, or with the wife or husband of the offender. In other words, we have to take into treatment or give guidance to those who have been or will be close to the delinquent.

When we have a method of treatment accepted as fundamental by workers in the field of delinquency and by the general public, then we will be able to have a comprehensive understanding of the offender as a human being and as a transgressor. Only then will we be able to replace the delinquent's basic hostility, resentment, and fear with constructive traits so that a character can be built which in time can bring about real social behavior.

We have pointed out that we have been able to link together social and psychobiological functions. Bridging these two has a direct bearing upon the problem concerned. What can the average man do about preventing criminal behavior in his home or in his community?

As mentioned before, emotional tension exists in every family. If we are not aware of it, that is only because our attention is not directed at discerning it. It is not only a question of, for instance, a rejecting mother or a stern father, but of the whole family setup. It is the tension among family members which is mainly the driving power behind any maladjustment, be it physical or mental.

Such an idea is not theoretical, it is based on experience with research of families both here and abroad. Thus, every mother and father has an important task, and that is to establish a well-integrated and harmonious home for their children.

This is a large order—as we know too large for many parents. There are too many of them who, because of their own emotional shortcomings, never should have had children. It is also certain that if their children have been in trouble, that trouble did not start

290

with them but with their grandparents or great grandparents or even further back.

We cannot remake society in a minute nor undo the ills and guarantee that we will build and not destroy. This will take years and generations. It will take faith and belief and a universal desire for a better world of happier people. But we can start now: if we lay only the thinnest foundation, it will be a starting point.

Also, since the main spring of criminal activity is imbedded in human beings, I have to mention some significant points in the relationship between parents and children, which have a bearing upon antisocial behavior.

The most common error that parents make in the beginning is of wanting perfect children in order that the children may be a reflection of themselves. When the children do not live up to expectations, the parents usually reject them in one way or another. Then, in order to compensate for the rejection and get even with the parents, the children frequently resort to crime and/or become ill. This makes the children that much less perfect, and therefore less acceptable.

This diabolical pattern can grow to such proportions that the children of such parents will eventually expect rejection everywhere, and therefore receive it. In time they are wanted by no one —and all because they were wanted for the wrong reasons before they were ever born.

Disharmony, like the difference between offenders and other people, is a matter of degree, and whether the degree is small or great the effect can still be disastrous upon the mind of a child.

Parents who never quarrel but who irritate each other, who take no more than perfunctory interest in each other's activities, who are polite yet basically indifferent, will create insecurity, restlessness and a feeling of not belonging in their children which will tend to stay with them always.

When parents swear at each other and at their children, when they constantly threaten to kill each other and resort to physical abuse, they cannot possibly expect anything from their children but exactly the same mode of behavior. Children are tiny beings whose first form of learning is through imitation. They do what they see others do and, inasmuch as they see their parents first and most of the time, they naturally imitate them to the greatest degree.

It is for these reasons primarily, plus the fact that children are emotionally dependent upon others, that bringing children up to be people is perhaps the greatest, most demanding and most worthwhile task on earth. Because it naturally follows that we cannot build in others that which we do not have, or are not willing to give ourselves, we must constantly try to behave if we want our children to be as good citizens as possible.

There are people all over the country, all over the world, who consider themselves ideal parents but who are in reality day by day creating illness, future unhappiness and the beginnings of crime in their children. For although steady financial security is of great importance, genuine emotional warmth, love and cheer are infinitely more important. Such a love as is required must be as selfless as possible, and it must carry with it the capacity for feeling the way the child might feel were the circumstances reversed, were the parent the child and the child the parent.

A mother who bestows all consideration and gifts upon her child, yet inwardly resents the child because of her own diminishing youth, will communicate that resentment. A father who wishes to build his own self-esteem by encouraging his son to be interested in his business despite his son's obvious interest in something else will create hostility in the boy.

Unfortunately, however, and perhaps obviously too, it is not enough to tell a woman to forget her age and think only of her child; to remind a father that his son's life is now of the greater importance and should not be denied self-expression. For these things go deep, originating as they do in the emotions and not in the intellect. They were created either in ignorance or insecurity and they bring more of the same in their wake.

There is many a parent who indulges his children in every whim and protects them from every disappointment. He does so in order that their individuality will not be interfered with and they will know no unhappiness. Such a parent builds a false concept of the world for his children which he usually discovers with much bitterness later on. He also establishes within them an idea that they are specially privileged. When the children grow up, they will simply take what they want if they cannot get it by accepted methods.

Parents who go to the other extreme of breaking the child's will often find that he conforms to the will of anyone else who wants to take him in hand. In striking a happy medium, the child should be taught firmly but lovingly, in which process he also learns about his parents and about himself. Above all, the child needs always to feel that his parents believe in him. A child, by the simple virtue of being a child, is an emotionally dependent creature who requires guidance. Lacking both guile and tension himself, he learns best by the direct and simple method wherein the parent gives facts as though to another adult but in language the child may understand.

Once a pattern of this kind is established, and a child misbehaves, that child requires punishment. It is natural for a child to misbehave; to do so fits in with its boundless energy and natural instinct for new adventure. When the child behaves badly and is permitted to get away with it, feelings of guilt arise, which are in turn dealt with by more misbehavior in an unconscious striving for punishment. If the parents ignore the second action, the child will be well on the road to maladjustment and toward being a spoiled child, or a little brat, as well.

Thus, the parent should not have to check himself at every turn; he cannot and should not be perfect. He should be permitted to get angry when it is called for. It has to be emphasized that just as it is essential for the child to express himself, so is it also for the parents. The simple question is only: When is a parent permitted to be angry at his child and what kind of measures shall he take? The parent will first have to know what kind of child he has, whether his boy or girl demands or needs discipline or whether he is so independent that he can learn from his own painful or pleasurable experiences. There are those children who frequently know one way or another what to do, and there are those who have to learn the hard way; it is this fact parents have to know. They can learn it by trying to evaluate their child in terms of his personality.

Children are egocentric and will demand every single bit of attention they can possibly manage to get. On the other hand, if they receive an overabundance of it, they resent it, because they also desire freedom and will go to great lengths to seek it. But if they should attain this much-sought freedom, they would feel guilty because their friends are without it. They would, therefore, punish their parents by constant misbehavior in order that they in turn might be punished for their unconscious guilt feelings.

Thus we see that children are a combination of extremes which must be dealt with by the opposite, by moderation, in order that they may learn. Because the child is in a state of imbalance between the constructive, destructive, social and antisocial traits within himself, he requires first of all harmony within the home in which he grows up.

I know perfectly well this is all very easy to say and not too easy to accomplish, but no one, particularly the child, expects perfection. There will always be times when disagreements, irritability and tiredness take over in the mother or father, or perhaps in both. When this is the case, the child should not be fooled about it. He senses more quickly than we when something is wrong. When lies are given as an explanation, confusion and distrust set in, along with which naturally comes a feeling of insecurity.

Probably the greatest evil that can grow out of family tension is that of the guilt which comes from unexpressed hostility and sugar-coated lies to save face. There is no reason why people cannot talk out sensibly among themselves their anger and resentments, thus getting rid of them rather than letting them grow and fester. For we all feel anger; it is inherent in us. We all feel put upon at times. And, rather than its being a mistake for children to hear these issues, it is good for them as an example in later life. When people try to give the impression to their children and outsiders that they have no important disagreements, they are being dishonest with themselves and everyone else. They are also building a flimsy and artificial foundation for their lives which will topple when the first great difficulty arises.

It is not trouble within the homes that creates tension; it is the way in which that trouble is met, the attitude couples have toward each other and toward their children, and the courage with which they have faced situations, intelligently rather than with blinding emotion, and calmly rather than in rage. Tension and disharmony in the home, moreover, do not encourage obedience in children; when they do not respect the source, they cannot respect the suggestion, advice or the law laid down by that source.

Troubles, faced sensibly, are one of the balancing agents that children need in growing up. Unfaced troubles or those that are met with by pre-fixed attitudes of fear, envy or hatred are one of the disturbing agents, one of the creators of instability in youth.

In order to accomplish all this, I repeat, the parent has to know himself, and that is the largest order. Yet it is only through an understanding of what is wrong and what is right with our children that we can have a fighting chance. When the majority of people reach this adult state of mind, we will see a definite decrease of crime and mental illness.

The comment is all too often made that childhood and youth is the happiest time of all, for it carries with it no worries or responsibilities. It is easy for us to say this as we grow older because we tend to forget old problems as we find ourselves with new ones. It may be generally true that youth is without responsibilities, but it has plenty of conflicts and anxieties. And even if it is not the most difficult time of our lives, it is certainly the most important. For our early years, those from one to fifteen, determine the kind of adults we will be and the kind of lives we will lead in the future.

I said up to fifteen years of age although it has been stated that the early years up to five are the most important. As mentioned previously, we do not know too much about what happens with the child's emotional growth between six and thirteen or fifteen years. During this period though, many experiences occur particularly related to his sexual life and to feelings arising from his emotional state of mind. Remember that when puberty begins, the boy is bursting with emotional intensity and increases his activities immensely. He becomes aggressive or bold, and it is only with great difficulty that he is able to behave in a socially acceptable way. Even if he can check these impulses, he still may show signs of his inner turmoil. He may be sleepless or develop difficulties in his schoolwork so he looks depressed or worried. Those symptoms may reveal a sense of guilt stemming from masturbation sometimes connected with feelings of loss of masculinity or impotence.

Criminal behavior then is a problem of childhood and adolescent maladjustment. If juvenile delinquency could be eradicated, there would be no crime, for young delinquents grow up to be hardened criminals or gangsters, sick, twisted individuals who are driven into all kinds of desperate situations by unconscious drives they do not understand.

In principle, I do not consider a delinquent improved or cured unless he has achieved a positive attitude toward his family and society and the emotional attitude of the family environment has been changed so as to make the home a breeding place for constructive social tendencies.

The child who shows neurotic traits and is highly conflicted and confused (sometimes to the point of becoming a schizophrenic, often with a pseudo-neurotic condition) is usually the result of disagreement in parental handling. Neurotic traits, invariably connected with the oedipal conflict when the child was three or four years of age, constitute a main point in the delinquent that is familiar to all who work in the field.

When the parent has to deal with an adolescent of fifteen, the situation is much more difficult than with the younger truant. He has been truant for some time and may often have been involved in thefts or similar crimes which reveal on the whole a persistent antisocial pattern. The reasons for his criminal behavior all reflect his childish attitude. To be able to handle the situation, the parents must realize that adolescents who rebel or show truancy or criminal activity of any sort need more attention and care than a nondelinquent brother or sister. Because they are that way, they have more need to satisfy their wishes and desires than the nondelinquent ones.

In all these undertakings parents should play the principal part. Psychiatrists, legal authorities or any other agency should appear only as consultants. The natural question is this: Are the parents capable? I have already touched upon that problem, although I am aware of the fact that a whole book could be written on that subject alone. What we have to stress here is that without changing the parent's attitude and the family situation, it is impossible to change the attitude of the delinquent child, adolescent or adult.

I want here to mention the great help I have had from psychiatric social workers as participants in our team of psychiatrist and psychologist. The psychiatric social workers have been able to explore family situations further, make initial contacts with family membe.s and act as go-betweens. Often some members of the family find it easier in the beginning to speak to a psychiatric social worker than to an authority such as a psychiatrist, although I have also seen the reverse happen. Furthermore, where supportive relationship is indicated, the patient is at times more co-operative when he talks with the psychiatric social worker. Also the worker is helpful in preparing the delinquent for a more intensive therapy by working with him for a preliminary period. This is particularly valuable when there is a great deal of resistance to treatment as we see when there is a pronounced development of an antisocial character. The difficult point in the treatment is always the transference situation since several psychotherapists are involved here. A delinquent of such a type tries to utilize this to his own immediate and narrow advantage, and to the detriment of the treatment, a matter of which the psychotherapist must be aware.

Through experience we have learned that returning a delinquent to his family or neighborhood most often gives rise to new delinquency. Therefore, it is mandatory not only to treat the delinquents, but also the members of their families, fathers, mothers, brothers and sisters, a matter we have carried out for many years in our research work. Such an emotional change throughout the entire family setup has brought about the necessary change in the offender's environment with ultimately rewarding results.

An interesting case is that of fourteen-year-old Barry, who had been a truant and was apprehended for stealing. His home life was turbulent since his parents had been divorced when he was eight, and he was forced to live with his mother and a much-disliked stepfather. His stepfather was a punishing, rigorous, moralistic man who had given little affection and love to the boy, and it was decided that the boy's real father should try to give him protection and indulgence, a principle contrary to any conventional treatment. Through the affection of the father and through a changed attitude of the mother, the boy changed so much that he was able to continue his schooling. At the same time he stopped his thefts, a modified behavior that on the whole indicated that Barry had overcome his hostilities.

A situation may arise when the parent is helpless and has to consult a psychiatrist or an agency equipped to handle such a case. The youngster or the adolescent may be so emotionally displaced that he has to be sent to a foster home or an institution for help. Or if the law has been transgressed several times, he may be sent to a reformatory. In all our dealing with delinquents, we must take into consideration human welfare, that is, both the individual and the community. However, we do not do that often enough. Usually when we deal with human beings we are more concerned with the law and order than with individuals. The delinquent person being emotionally displaced is constantly seeking his emotional place, most often without finding it because he cannot recognize his own emotions. We have of late heard much about displaced persons. We forget the emotionally displaced ones, those who are maladjusted psychologically or socially or both. It is time that they be taken into consideration by our laws.

This is tragic, for it speaks of so much waste. But so it is with many of our laws and habits which have become old established and worn-out customs and which essentially ignore the human side of the story. This is true in so many phases of our everyday life that for the better part of the time we are not even aware of what is being done to us. We accept what is given us because it is law, and we overlook the fact that those who are shaping our lives, dealing out our justice or injustice are human beings the same as we are, some better, some worse, but human beings nonetheless.

Therefore also, we have many obvious discrepancies between the law and humanity; I can only give a few instances here.

In some states it is unlawful for an unmarried man to have sexual intercourse. The punishment for such an act is three years' imprisonment. In another state for the same crime the punishment is one thousand dollars fine and/or twelve months' imprisonment.

In one state if any sleeping-car passenger remains in a compartment other than the one he is assigned to, he is subject to a fine of one thousand dollars and/or twelve months in jail. In one state the use of any contraceptive is punishable by a fine and imprisonment up to one year. If a married couple practice cunnilingus or fellatio, even if only as a prelude to normal sexual intercourse, it is just as illegal as for unmarried persons; and the penalty in two states is life imprisonment, while others have maximum prison sentences of two to sixty years. There is a more severe punishment for female prostitutes than for male ones, and the patron of prostitution is treated more severely than either if discovered. In accordance with the law, a man of twenty-one can be sent to prison for having relations with a girl one day short of eighteen because she is one day too young for such things. A man guilty of indecent exposure may get more time than one who has committed second-degree rape. A person with a solitary criminal offense can be sent to prison, the same as one who has many or even thousands to his credit.

There is on record the case of a man in one state who served fourteen years for incest, and of another in a different state who under practically identical circumstances involving the same crime received a sentence of three months. In the State of Indiana a school teacher can be convicted, if the judge so desires, of sodomy for telling a student that masturbation does not harm him.

In the State of Missouri one who practices sodomy is liable to execution. Even masturbation is against the law in a few states. Though homosexuality is forbidden, more than one third of our male population has at one time indulged in homosexual activities. Mouth to genital relations, a common practice among animals and therefore obviously quite instinctive, are illegal—and 30 to 40 per cent of the people perform it.

These are only small examples of the kind of laws we have. Who made those laws, heaven only knows, but apparently they were made for the purpose of protecting society. The laws forgot about the individual.

This world of ours is filled with people of high principles and strong moral concepts who through unconscious motivations are

299

quite capable of murder, rape and theft. Many of those that we in psychiatry question after they have committed a crime tell us in all honesty and sincerity that to tell a lie or do an evil thing of any kind goes against what they have learned. And it is this learning that they demonstrate in court. It is this learning that so often decides their fate, for they are no more aware of unconscious motivation than are those who sentence and punish them.

John Galsworthy in his touching story of justice, which he called just that, told of the slow death that came to a man who was a first offender and who was given no consideration for the circumstances involved. Galsworthy indicated that the man was maladjusted, by the continual reference to his nervousness; but the court decided he knew right from wrong. So he was not insane; therefore he was guilty. While in prison, he lost no weight, so of course he was healthy enough in the eyes of the law. Once he had served his sentence, however, and was a human wreck because of it, no one wanted to employ him. His girl, through poverty, had turned to prostitution to live and support the children given her by a brutal and insane husband. Finally the young man, then a common criminal in the eyes of many, killed himself.

The world needs education, but of the heart, feelings and instincts as well as of the intellect, which in insanity is disconnected from all of these and is therefore no criterion for anything whatsoever. This lack of connection is sometimes obvious to one and all, the deviation from the normal being so great as to leave no question of the existing psychosis. There are many other cases, however, in which the thinking process has for certain periods of time remained relatively unimpaired, so that the person in question, though basically distorted, may give the impression of being mentally well.

In order to determine whether or not a person is in possession of his mental faculties, the court uses in many states a Right and Wrong Test, or as it is called, the McNaghten Rule, which says that a knowledge of right and wrong is all that is needed to determine the sanity or the insanity of an accused person (see *Crime and the Human Mind*, pp. 177 etc.) This law has, since 1843, shown so many disheartening aspects that all psychiatrists and many lawyers who know more about psychological mechanism than

300

the average citizen have tried to modify or change it, but to no avail. In some instances the court heeds what the psychiatrist has to say about the case. The courts do not employ any tests of the emotions, such as we in psychiatry use constantly in the diagnosis and throughout the treatment of different cases. I refer for example to the Rorschach Test or other psychological tests. The object of this test is to determine what the person, be he patient or a delinquent, sees in these ten ink blots that differs from the normal. This is the kind of test upon which it is impossible to cheat for there are no expected or correct answers. Whatever is seen is both an illustration of what the individual sees in everyday life and a projection of his own emotions. Thus a person who sees many threatening or fighting figures is merely demonstrating his own internal conflict, the very conflict which indicates his emotional sickness and which can drive him to commit crime and yet know the difference between right and wrong.

Even though it sounds simple in the cursory explanation above, this test is a very involved one. People give themselves away even when they are trying not to do so. Only a trained psychologist can determine, through scoring of human and animal movements and the like, what is going on within the person.

Each one of the ten ink blots represents a colored large chart in which it is possible to see a great number of things. The movements, the lack thereof, the type of figures seen, the reaction to color, all of these things go toward determining the person's emotional life. Thus it happens daily that we discover people to be neurotic, psychotic or suffering from a character disorder although in their jobs and homes they are considered as normal as thee and me, however normal that might be.

Important as it is to determine the presence of a psychosis in criminal trials, it is also essential to decide at which time the delinquent became insane. This is a point about which the psychiatrist has to be careful; then too, he has to be aware of the legal aspects of insanity since it is used as a defense under the law. The psychiatrist should also realize his own responsibility here because he serves a double purpose: protecting society and the individual at the same time.

There are other cases too, not recognized by the courts, of mental abnormalcy which is not insanity but which nevertheless constitutes a condition for which the offender can hardly be held responsible. These are the neuroses which can drive a person to commit crime in order that he may receive the punishment he unconsciously feels he deserves. These are the neuroses that can cause a man to use a gun because he was made to feel inadequate and insufficient as a growing youth. These are the neuroses that can make a person steal to obtain the affection and attention that was denied him in his home.

These are the persons who are mentally abnormal without being legally insane. The most adequate way to deal with an illegal offender would be to have him examined by two psychiatrists, appointed by the court, who utilize psychological tests. Their findings should then be permitted to be introduced into the court so that the judge or the jurors could take cognizance of them. It is time now that the law take into consideration the irrational emotions in human and antisocial behavior. We, the psychiatrists, on the other hand, need the ever-watchful eye of criminal law to safeguard and protect society from those dangerous individuals who should never go out into society until or unless there has been a thoroughgoing change in their personalities. It is time for psychiatry and criminal law to work together in such a way that they will no longer conflict but will coincide.

To this end psychopathology of delinquent persons should be taught to students of law. In the course of their study, particularly those interested in criminal law should visit psychiatric institutions, reformatories and prisons and be given instruction as to mental pathology in individual cases. Such instruction would also be helpful to judges of criminal courts. It is gratifying to mention that through co-operation with Professor George Dession of Yale Law School, I outlined a few years ago a course in psychiatry for the law students which is being given each year.

It should now be recognized and established how criminals become what they are and what can be done about them. We do not claim that we can cure them all, even if it were feasible for us to reach them all, which it is not. Yet, we know we can cure many of them. Treatable offenders need substitute parents in the form of specially trained personnel to point out to them the causes for their behavior, to indicate the right road, to act as props for them until they can act in a mature manner rather than like narcissistic spoiled children.

Psychiatric treatment of parolees should be made a condition of parole if such treatment is considered necessary by the examining psychiatrist. To parole an offender from prison, after his having served a long sentence, without some psychiatric help is in many ways equal to insisting that a baby walk when it can hardly raise its head.

In this connection, it is necessary to mention our juvenile courts which handle children's cases in the states of the union and in the territories and the District of Columbia. About 275,000 children come every year to the attention of juvenile courts as delinquents. In addition, 100,000 children are handled by the courts because of neglect, dependency or custody hearings. It is estimated that almost 300,000 children or about 12 in every 1,000 children between the ages of seven and seventeen came to the attention of juvenile courts in 1949 because of delinquency. (Juvenile Court Statistics, 1946–1949, Children's Bureau, Statistical Series m.8.) Although we have provisions to prohibit or control the jailing of children, a study made by the National Probation and Parole Association shows that about 50,000 children are detained in jail every year. Austin H. MacCormick, who is well known in the field of prevention of crime, has stated *(Federal Probation,* p. 41, September, 1949) "If we accept the more realistic estimates of 50,000 to 100,000—and we seem safe in doing so—it means we jail annually the equivalent of the entire ten-to-seventeen-year-old population of a city the size of Pittsburgh, San Francisco, Denver, Atlanta, or Cincinnati." (See also *Report on Juvenile Detention,* National Conference on Prevention and Control of Juvenile Delinquency, Washington, D.C., November, 1946.)

A great deal of discussion has been going on as to whether or not the juvenile courts have outlived themselves, the reason being that apparently there is little evidence that the rate of delinquency has decreased since they were established in 1899. One reason for

303

the court's inability to cope with the complex situation of delinquency is that it has not had enough resources. Its scope has been
too narrow because it has not been able to take into complete
consideration the family setup of the individual delinquent, a matter
to which attention must be paid if we expect durable results. A
further step in development of juvenile courts is the family court
(Home Term) for which Judge Anna Kross of New York City has
been such an able spokesman.

It is necessary that we try to alter our life according to scientific
findings. If it is true that the delinquent can be changed into a lawful citizen by remaking him and his home atmosphere, such a point
must be taken into consideration when it comes to changing our
court system. Furthermore, if it is also true that a man very often
is led by his unconscious forces when he acts antisocially, then our
attitude in dealing with an offender must also be changed.

To my mind comes the term "criminal," which implies not only
that a person is responsible to the law and may be imprisoned if
found guilty, but also connotes a moral judgment. The word
"criminal" reflects a punitive and legal aspect and unfortunately
when we transfer this term to the field of psychiatry it brings here
the same impression. The word "criminal," which is a self-righteous
and opinionated word, should be abolished. Difficult though it may
be to find another term, I would suggest that we use the term
"delinquent." All human beings err, and delinquent behavior covers
all wrong doings including the criminal ones. It is now time for us
to create more humanity in our concept of the person who is
called a criminal. It is interesting to see that when we deal with
antisocial children or adolescents we use the term "delinquent" but
when they become older we call them criminals. In denoting
people who have transgressed the law as delinquents, we connote
that they have done so because of a human error and we do not
put a moral opinion on their action, thereby condemning them; that
would be the same as condemning people who become sick. We
usually try to help sick people and not condemn them. So it should
be with persons who commit antisocial acts.

It must be kept in mind that one aspect of criminal law is a
moral behavior. Lord Macmillan said ". . . The conception of

crime which the ordinary citizen entertains involves the commission of some act which transgresses not merely the law but morality . . ." (Foreword to Radzinowicz, *A History of English Criminal Law* [1948] vii.)

We have come to look upon law and order with such reverence and respect that we have forgotten the essential issue. We are the law, or should be. As Charles W. Ferguson says in his fine little book, *A Little Democracy Is a Dangerous Thing,* we have a limited democracy in this country. We appoint others to make up our rules and then we are content to live by them, whatever they may be. We have become so soft that we make no solid attempt to hold enough citizens' meetings even to interfere when we are incensed by injustice, let alone to decide the law ourselves, as we should in a true democracy.

There are times when I wonder why these admirable writers make such worthy but apparently vain attempts. Others read their works and say fine, beautiful, bravo. Then they put the books back on the shelf and forget about them. What's the good if those at whom such heart- and back-breaking words are directed are impregnable? This means you, and it means me. It's got to start somewhere, and if we keep waiting for the fellow beside us to come through, as many of us did in school, there will be no progress, and we will all rot in the ruts of our own making.

It is most unfortunate that we do not have any research institute where delinquents can be studied and treated. Yet for many years we have had research institutions for conditions, such as cancer and tuberculosis and others. That we still are without delinquency research institutes reflects the public's reaction to offenders. And so the same public complains that we know so little about them and we cannot do anything with them anyway. Both statements are fallacies. Only by knowing the delinquent's condition as well as possible can we diagnose him and start treatment. But the public is not even interested in letting the scientist come to the first base, that is, to studying the delinquent, because it is against establishing research facilities for that purpose. Remember how many millions of dollars this country spends every year trying to discover the cause or causes of cancer or infantile paralysis. The New York State Depart-

305

ment of Correction spends $25,000,000 a year for the custody of prisons. "This figure does not include the cost of local jails and penitentiaries, of criminal courts and prosecutors and of the police, which amount to many millions more. Nor does it include the cost of crime to its victims in money and suffering, or the cost in mental suffering to those who become offenders, or alcoholics, or subjects of multiple divorce, whose personality problems are all closely related. In view of all this it is both remarkable and regrettable that human intelligence, which has plumbed so many mysteries of physical science, which has created such superhuman miracles of destruction, has made so little progress in understanding and bettering its own misdirected inadequacies and aggressions."

When we multiply this figure by the number of prisoners throughout the country we come to an unbelievably high figure. Yet the taxpayer gladly continues to pay that amount of money because that is the way it has always been. This same taxpayer apparently does not know that every gadget or invention he uses every day in his home or factory came through long and tedious research made in laboratories in which a good deal of money was spent. But when it comes to studying or treating a problem which is a nightmare for this country, he still goes on with the same means his grandfather and greatgrandfather used. This is the same as if he would use a kerosene lamp instead of a flashlight when he went down to the basement, or use a horse and buggy instead of a car when he takes a ride.

There is still much unknown about the delinquent and we have to continue research with the small means which are for our disposition. But research takes a long time, and costs very much money. Yes, it costs money, but only for the moment compared with the long-lasting effects of present-day ill handling of the criminals. In the long run, we could save a great deal more, not only in money but also in human happiness.

Unfortunately, there is no institute, other than closed ones, where potential or actual offenders can be diagnosed and treated. The public, and for that matter many psychiatrists, lawyers, probation officers and judges should always remember that treatment of offenders requires *specialized* methods, which call for thoroughly trained specialists. Psychiatric treatment is much more than a diagnosis; it is the first step toward a cure, as had been evidenced so many times.

One main reason that our countermeasures against crime have been so unrewarded is that so far we have had no scientific medium in which planned research of the mind of the criminal and his actions could be undertaken.

Most emphatically I advocate the establishment of a National Research Institute for delinquents for treatment of offenders and their family members. The Institute would serve as an observation center for the study and diagnosis of delinquents and the recommendation of special types of treatment and handling to the courts —under whose jurisdiction the offenders would remain. This Institute would also provide expert training and instruction, not only for physicians and lay psychotherapists, but also for law students, teachers, psychologists, sociologists, probation officers and prison personnel.

We must do further research, the results of which must be applied to the practical aspects of counteracting criminal behavior. We do not as yet have any clear understanding of the mechanisms by which our minds and bodies can withstand exposure to criminal inclinations or mental disease. Neither do we have any way of measuring inborn resistance toward criminalistic tendencies or acquired resistance or "immunity." It is questionable whether delinquency can be overcome by conventional thinking. What we need is an educational process in which the public has to take a part. And this educational process will also have to cover those responsible for administering scientific research. I very much doubt whether research in the field of delinquency or, for that matter also in mental illness, should be concerned only with working out further details about principles which we have already established. Will not advance in research here and in other fields come from investigators who do not keep to previously trodden paths but who are bold enough and who have sufficient vision and imagination to dare searching into areas heretofore unexplored? What we need more than conventional workers are trail blazers who can turn the light on where there previously was darkness.

In this research there has also to be included application of our findings upon social regulations as a means of preventing mental maladjustment and delinquent behavior. Through research we have been able to find new ways and means of preventing and curing many diseases and have thereby enabled ourselves to control them. Through research we may be able to find new means for social control through our laws.

But such research will mean that charitable foundations and agencies have to co-operate in encouraging investigators in the field of delinquency. Although the scientist and the public will have to collaborate, the final solution of this problem is up to the people. It is obvious that improved housing, community facilities and more playgrounds are of importance here because a child must have activities and an outlet for his aggressions. At best, however, they are inadequate substitutes for better relations in the home. We need to educate or train people who can cope professionally with the problem. I mean not only psychiatrists, psychologists or psychiatric social workers, but also educators, clergymen, school teachers, sociologists, anthropologists, child-guidance workers and social workers in the community. We will need a broad basic program of mental hygiene and of general enlightenment in which the whole community can be mobilized, extending from churches to Boy Scout groups and parent-teacher organizations.

Parents here have an important task to fulfill. They must remember that they must not try to shape their children in their own images, that one of the most significant things they must teach their children is the reasonable proportion between their ambitions and their abilities. Parents will have to be aware of the fact that when they do not show their children genuine love or affection, it affects the child not only in regard to his own emotional response but also to his whole body. It will, for instance, affect the way he eats and how much, the way he reacts to music or language, the way he responds to vitamins or to feelings or ideas expressed around him. In short, it will influence the rest of his life.

Furthermore, every parent must keep in mind that it is often painful for a child to grow up, that it takes a great deal out of him to become independent and that therefore the parent should help, not only physically but also emotionally, in his growth, a matter parents often know little about because they themselves frequently are not emotionally grown up. Sigmund Freud once said, "In our innermost soul we are children and remain so throughout our lives." Parents, like their children, would like to be children but since the former have to be guides, they have to grow up. Their own mental growth will reflect upon their children's future conduct. Today we may not blame parents for being largely instrumental in getting their boys or girls into trouble, be it a mental condition, a psychosomatic disease or delinquency. But twenty or thirty years from now, we will have to point our finger against those parents who because of neglect or ignorance, wittingly or unwittingly bring out the worst in their children.

People in general will have to help the scientist who, for his part, always has to remember to be modest in his claims. When the scientist and public work hand in hand and both give their best to the cause of eradicating delinquency, we will not fail.

But people will not be able to eliminate delinquency unless they recognize their own feelings and the feelings of others. To conquer crime, we have to show courage and wisdom, and at the same time humility. If we can eliminate or reduce those factors eliciting hate and fear in the family, the home will then become, instead of the incubator of crime, the cradle of emotional happiness.

Appendix
GLOSSARY OF PRISON JARGON

(The following excerpts are from a slang dictionary compiled by Joliet prisoners)

ALLIGATOR BAIT–poor food
ALLEY APPLE–brick used in street fighting
ALTAR–a toilet

BALDY–an old man
BALE OF HAY–blonde woman
BANDHOUSE–jail
BANJO–a shovel
BATTER THE DRAG–beg on the street
BEAGLES–sausages
BENNY–an overcoat
BINDLE STIFF–a tramp carrying his bedding
BISCUIT–pistol
BLINKY–one with poor eyes
BOB–shoplifter
BOILER–car; camp cook
BRACE–to ask for money
BRASS–fake jewelry
BRODIE–a leap; failure
BULL BUSTER–one with passion to assault police
BULLETS–beans
BUM DOGS–sore feet
BUM FLIPPER–a sore hand
BUNDLE–loot or plunder
BURY–to get a long sentence

BUSH PAROLE–escape
BUTCHER–prison physician
BUTTONS–a messenger

"C"–cocaine; a one-hundred-dollar bill
CANARY–an informer
CARRYING A FLAG–traveling under assumed name
CAT HEADS–biscuits
CHIV–a knife
CIRCUS BEES–body lice
COLD SLOUGH PROWLER–a robber of empty houses
CRACKED ICE–unset diamonds
CREEPERS–felt shoes
CUSH–money
CUTIES–body lice
CZAR–warden of a prison

DAMPER–a cash register
DAUBER–forger
DINERO–money
DIP–pickpocket
DIRTY TOWEL–barbershop
DOG EYE–to scan minutely
DONNEKER–wash room
DOUBLE "O"–to spy
DROPPER–a paid killer

311

Dugout–a heavy eater
Dutch Act–suicide
Duster–freight-car thief

Fall Togs–good clothing for a trial
Fan a Sucker–search victim's clothing for loot
Fink–an informer
Fish–new prisoners
Flat Dog–bologna sausage
Flip–board a moving train
Fly a Kite–to send underground letter from prison
Fly Cop–a detective

Gapper–a mirror
Glass Jaw–a coward
Gold Dust–cocaine
Gopher–a gangster
Gospel Fowl–chicken
Gull–a thief's victim

Happy Dust–cocaine
Harness Bull–uniformed cop
Harp–challenge, complain
Hay Burner–a horse
Heavy Man–armed watcher in gambling house
Heifer–a young woman
Hole–solitary punishment
Hoop–a ring; auto tire
Hot Short–stolen car
Hump–half a prison term
Hunky–a common laborer

Irish Turkey–corned beef

Jit–five cents
Jive–small talk

Johnson–coffee
Joy Powder–morphine

Keister–a suitcase
Kelly–a hat
Kuter–twenty-five cents

Lettuce–paper money
Loser–an ex-convict
Louse Cage–a hat

M & C–morphine and cocaine
Mell Moll–a woman cook
Moll Buzzer–a pickpocket preying on women
Mop Mary–a scrubwoman
Moss–hair
Mud–opium

Nail a Rattle–to board a fast moving train
Necktie–hangman's noose
Nip–to steal jewelry

Office–a warning
On the Boost–shoplifting

Pad–a bed
Paper–a railroad ticket; bad checks
Pearl Diver–a dishwasher
Pedigree–criminal record
Pen–a forger
Peter Man–safeblower
Pill–a cigarette
Pinhead–a drug addict; a clerk; a fool
Pork–a corpse
Poultice–bread and gravy
Prop–diamond pin or stud

Puff–powder to blow safe
Punk and Gut–bread and cheese
Push–a gang or clique

Quail–an old maid

Rank–to inform on a pal
Rat Crusher–boxcar thug
Raw Hide–a hard worker; a severe task master
Red Eye–liquor; fried egg
Red Lead–catsup
Rhino–money; cash
Ringtail–grouchy person
Rumble–to recognize
Rum Dum–intoxicated

Sand–sugar
Sap–policeman's club
Saw Buck–ten-year sentence
Scissor Bill–an outsider
Scoff–to eat
Scratch House–a cheap lodging
Scratch Man–a forger
Settled–sentenced
Sewer Hogs–ditch diggers
Shag–organized pursuit
Sheepskin–a pardon
Shill–a decoy
Shiv–a razor, knife
Shroud–a suit of clothes
Skins–paper money
Sleigh Ride–drug debauch
Slop Up–get intoxicated
Slough–to assault
Slum–cheap jewelry

Smoke–cheap liquor
Snark–an informer
Snipe Shooting–picking cigarettes off the street
South Gate Discharge–death in jail
Spoiled Water–soft drink
Stash–to hide
Stilts–crutches
Stinger–an onion
Stir Bug–one who is simple from long imprisonment
Stone John–jail
Stretchers–shoe laces
Strides–trousers
Sugar–money
Scallion Skinners–prisoners in vegetable room

Tamp Up–assault
Third Rail–cheap liquor
Tin Ear–to eavesdrop
Tongue–attorney
Torpedo–bodyguard
Typewriter–a machine gun

Wake-up–day of release
Wingy–a man with one arm
Wire–a pickpocket
Wren–a young girl

Yap–a farmer; newcomer
Yen Shee–opium

Zoo–a prison

Bibliography

PSYCHIATRY, PSYCHOANALYSIS, PSYCHIATRIC CRIMINOLOGY AND PSYCHOLOGY

ABRAHAM, KARL, *Selected Papers*, London, 1927.

ABRAHAMSEN, DAVID, *Crime and the Human Mind*, New York, Columbia University Press, 1944; 3rd ed., 1945.

———— "Evaluation of the Treatment of Criminals," *Failures in Psychiatric Treatment*, Grune & Stratton, 1948.

———— "Family Tension, Basic Cause of Criminal Behavior," *Journal of Criminal Law and Criminology*, Sept.-Oct. 1949, Vol. 40, No. 3.

———— *Mind and Death of a Genius*, New York, Columbia University Press, 1946.

———— "Mass Psychosis and Its Effects," *Journal of Nervous and Mental Disease*, Jan. 1941, XCIII, No. 1, pp. 63–72.

———— "Motivation of Crime," *Journal of Nervous and Mental Disease*, 103, No. 6, June, 1946.

———— "Personality Reaction to Crime and Disease," *New York Academy of Medicine*, 21:435, 1945. *Journal of Nervous and Mental Disease*, 104: 1, 1946.

———— "Psychiatric Aspects of Delinquency," *Journal of Educational Sociology*, Vol. 24, No. 1, Sept. 1950, pp. 40–44.

———— "Psychodynamics in Criminal Behavior," Speech for Psychoanalytic and Psychosomatic Medicine, New York City, June 6, 1944. *Journal of Nervous and Mental Disease*, Vol. 102, No. 1, July, 1945.

———— "Psychosomatic Disorders and Their Significance in Antisocial Behavior," *Journal of Nervous and Mental Disease*, Vol. 107, No. 1, Jan. 1948.

———— *Report on Study of 102 Sex Offenders as submitted to Governor Thomas E. Dewey*, New York, March, 1950.

———— & PALM, ROSE, "Family Role in Diagnosis and Treatment of

Offenders," *Journal of Nervous and Mental Disease*, Vol. 112, No. 4, Oct. 1950.

ACKERMAN, NATHAN, "Psychoanalysis and Group Therapy," *Group Psychotherapy*, 3:204–215, 1950.

"A Critical Survey of the Existing Concepts of Psychopathic Behavior in Infants and Children," *American Journal of Orthopsychiatry*, 21: 223, 1951.

ADLER, ALFRED, *Social Interests: A Challenge to Mankind*, New York, Putnam, 1939.

ADLERBLUM, EVELYN D., "Beginning School Guidance Early," *Mental Hygiene*, Vol. 34, No. 4, Oct. 1950, pp. 600–610.

AICHORN, AUGUST, *Wayward Youth*, New York, Viking Press, 1944.

ALEXANDER, FRANZ AND HEALY, WILLIAM, *Roots of Crime*, New York, Alfred A. Knopf, 1935.

ALEXANDER, FRANZ AND STAUB, HUGO, *The Criminal, the Judge and the Public*, New York, Macmillan Co., 1931.

ALLEN, FREDERICK H., "Evolution of Our Treatment Philosophy in Child Guidance," *Mental Hygiene*, 14: 1, Jan. 1930.

ASCHAFFENBURG, GUSTAV, *Beiträge zur Kriminalpsychologie und Strafrechtsreform*, Heidelberg, 1926.

Association for Supervision and Curriculum Development, National Education Association, *Fostering Mental Health in Our Schools*, Yearbook, 1950.

BAKWIN, HARRY, "Emotional Deprivation in Infants," *Journal of Pediatrics*, St. Louis, Vol. 35, No. 4, Oct. 1949, pp. 512–521.

BARKER, ROGER ET AL., EDS., *Child Behavior and Development*, New York, McGraw-Hill, 1943.

BATES, JEROME E., "Abrahamsen's Theory of the Etiology of Criminal Acts," *Journal of Criminal Law and Criminology*, Vol. 40, No. 4, 1949, pp. 471–475.

BECK, BERTRAM, *Youth Within Walls*, Community Service Society of New York, June, 1950.

BENDER, L., "Behavior Problems in the Children of Psychotic and Criminal Parents," *Genetic Psychology Monographs*, XIX, 1937, pp. 229–338.

—— "Child Psychiatric Techniques: A Diagnostic and Therapeutic Approach to Normal and Abnormal Development Through Patterned Expressive and Group Behavior," Springfield, Ill., Charles C. Thomas, 1950.

—— "Genesis of Hostility in Children," *American Journal of Psychiatry*, 105:241–245, 1948.

—— "Organic Brain Conditions Producing Behavior Disturbances," *Modern Trends in Child Psychiatry*, Ed. N.D.C. Lewis & B. Pacella, New York, Grune & Stratton, 1945, pp. 360–377.

—— & ABRAM, BLAU, "The Reaction of Children to Sexual Relations with Adults," *American Journal of Orthopsychiatry*, 7:500–518, 1937.

BENNET, J., *Federal Probation Quarterly*, March, 1949, p. 19.

BERGLER, E., "Supposition about the Mechanism of Criminosis," *Journal of Criminal Psychopathology*, 5:481, 1944.

—— *The Basic Neurosis; Oral Aggression and Psychic Masochism*, New York, Grune and Stratton, 1949.

BETTELHEIM, B., *Love Is Not Enough*, Glencoe, Ill., The Free Press, 1950.

BRENMAN, M. AND GILL, M. M., *Hypnotherapy. A Survey of the Literature*, Publication of the Josiah Macy Jr. Foundation Review Series, Vol. II, No. 3, New York, International Universities Press, Inc., 1944.

BREUER, F. AND FREUD, SIGMUND, *Psychic Mechanism of Hysteric Phenomena*, Vienna, 1893.

BRUCH, HILDE AND TOURAINE, GRACE, "Obesity in Childhood: The Family Frame of Obese Children," *Psychosomatic Medicine*, 2:141, April, 1940.

BULLIS, H. EDMOND AND O'MALLEY, E. E., *Human Relations in the Classroom*, Delaware State Society for Mental Hygiene, Hambleton, 1947 and 1948.

CANNON, W. B., *Wisdom of the Body*, Rev. ed., New York, Norton, 1939.

Children Absent from School, Citizen's Committee on Children of New York City Inc., 1949.

CLECKLY, H., *The Mask of Sanity*, St. Louis, C. V. Mosby Co., 1941.

COLEMAN, JULES V., "The Child Guidance Clinic and Community Mental Health Program," *Mental Hygiene*, Vol. 32, No. 4, Oct. 1948, pp. 539–548.

CONN, JACOB H., "The Aggressive Female Psychopathic Personality," *Journal of Nervous and Mental Disease*, XCV, March, 1942, No. 3, pp. 316–334.

CURRAN, FRANK J., "Psychotherapeutic Problems of Puberty," *American Journal of Orthopsychiatry*, 10:510–521, 1940.

CURRAN, FRANK AND SCHILDER, PAUL, "A Constructive Approach to the Problems of Childhood and Adolescence," *Journal of Clini-*

cal Psychopathology, 2:125–142, Pt. I (1940); 2:305–320, Pt. II (1941).

Department of Child Guidance, Newark, N. J. *Mental Hygiene in the Classroom*, New York National Committee for Mental Hygiene Inc., 1949.

DESSION, GEORGE H., "Psychiatry and the Conditioning of Criminal Justice," *Yale Law Journal*, Vol. 47, No. 3, Jan. 1938.

DEUTSCH, HELENE, *The Psychology of Women*, Vols. I & II, New York, Grune & Stratton, 1944, 1945.

DOSTOEVSKI, F. M., *Stavrogin's Confession with Psychoanalytic Study of the Author by Sigmund Freud*, New York, Lear Publishers, 1947.

DUNBAR, THOMAS, *Emotions and Bodily Changes. A Survey of Literature on Psychosomatic Interrelationship 1910–1945*, New York, Columbia University Press, 1945.

EISSLER, KURT R., ED., *Searchlights on Delinquency—New Psychoanalytic Studies*, New York, International Universities Press, 1948.

ERIKSON, ERIK, *Childhood and Society*, New York, W. W. Norton, 1950.

FEDERN, PAUL, "Mental Hygiene of the Psychotic Ego," *American Journal of Psychotherapy*, 3:356–371, 1947.

FENICHEL, OTTO, *The Psychoanalytic Theory of Neurosis*, New York, W. W. Norton & Co., 1945.

FOULKES, S. H., *Introduction to Group Analytic Psychotherapy Studies in Social Integration of Individuals and Groups*, New York, Grune & Stratton, 1949.

FOXE, ARTHUR N., *Studies in Criminology*, New York, Nervous and Mental Disease Publishing Co., 1950.

FRANK, JAN, "Lobotomy under Psychoanalytic Scrutiny," *Psychiatry*, 13:35–42, 1950.

FREMONT-SMITH, FRANK, "Mental Health, Education and International Cooperation," *Pastoral Psychology*, Dec. 1950, Vol. 1, No. 9.

FREUD, ANNA, *Introduction to Technic of Child Analysis*, New York, Nervous and Mental Disease Publishing Co., 1928.

——— *Psychoanalysis for Teachers and Parents*, Emerson, 1935.

FREUD, ANNA AND BURLINGAME, DOROTHY, *Report on Hampstead*, London, April, 1942.

FREUD, SIGMUND, *An Outline of Psychoanalysis*, New York, W. W. Norton & Co., 1949.

——— *Beyond the Pleasure Principle*, London, International Psychoanalytic Press, 1922.

——— *Civilization and Its Discontents*, New York, Jonathan Cape & Harrison Smith, 1930.

——— *Collected Papers*, Vols. 1–4, London, International Psychoanalytic Press and Hogarth Press, 1924, 1925; Vol. 5, 1950.

——— *The Ego and the Id*, Authorized Translation by Joan Riviere, London, 1927.

FRIEDLANDER, KATE, "The Antisocial Character Formation," *A Psychoanalytic Study of a Child*, New York, 1945.

——— *The Psychoanalytic Approach to Juvenile Delinquency*, London, 1947.

FROMM, ERICH, *Escape from Freedom*, New York, Farrar & Rinehart, Inc., 1941.

FROMM-REICHMANN, FRIEDA, "Recent Advances in Psychoanalytic Therapy," & "Remarks on Philosophy of Mental Disorder," *A Study of Inter-Personal Relations*, ed. by Patrick Mullahy, New York, Hermitage Press, Inc., 1949.

FROSCH, JACK AND BROMBERG, WALTER, "The Sex Offender—A Psychiatric Study," *American Journal of Orthopsychiatry*, IX, Oct. 1939, No. 4, pp. 761–776.

GARDNER, GEORGE E., "The Criminal Within Us," *The Future in Medicine*, New York Academy of Medicine Lectures to the Laity, No. XIV, New York, Columbia University Press, 1950.

GESELL, ARNOLD AND AMATRUDA, C. S., *Developmental Diagnosis, Normal and Abnormal Child Development*, New York, Paul B. Hoeber, Inc., 1947.

GITELSON, MAXWELL, "The Role of Anxiety in Somatic Disease," *Annals of International Medicine*, 28:289–297, Feb. 1948.

GLOVER, EDWARD, *Mental Abnormality and Crime*, London, Macmillan, 1944.

——— "The Diagnosis of Delinquency, being a clinical report of the Institute during the Five Years 1934 to 1941," *I.S.T.O. Pamphlet*, No. 1, London, 1944.

GLUECK, SHELDON AND ELEANOR, *Unravelling Juvenile Delinquency*, The Commonwealth Fund, 1950.

GUTHEIL, EMIL, *The Language of the Dream*, New York, Macmillan Co., 1939.

HALL, JEROME, "Mental Disease and Criminal Responsibility," *Columbia Law Review*, 45:677, 1945.

HEALY, WILLIAM, *Twenty-five Years of Child Guidance*, Springfield, Ill., State Dep't of Public Welfare, 1935.

HEALY, WILLIAM AND ALPER, BENEDICT S., *Criminal Youth and the Borstal System*, New York, The Commonwealth Fund, 1941.

HEALY, WILLIAM AND BRONNER, AUGUSTA, *Delinquents and Criminals, Their Making and Unmaking*, New York, Macmillan Co., 1926.

—— *New Light on Delinquency and Its Treatment*, New Haven, Yale University Press, 1936.

—— *Treatment and What Happened Afterward: A Study from the Judge Baker Guidance Center*, Boston, Judge Baker Guidance Center, 1939.

HOCH, PAUL H., *Failures in Psychiatric Treatment*, New York, Grune & Stratton, 1948.

HOLMER, PAUL, "The Use of the Play Situation as an Aid to Diagnosis," *American Journal of Orthopsychiatry*, 7:523, Oct. 1937.

ISAACS, S. S., *Social Development in Young Children*, New York, Harcourt, Brace & Co., 1933.

Joint Committee on Health Problems in America, *Mental Hygiene in the Classroom: How Would You Help a Child Like This?* National Association for Mental Health.

JONES, ERNEST, *Anal Erotic Character Traits*, New York, Wm. Wood & Co.

JOSIAH MACY JR. Foundation, *Transactions of the Conferences on Ministry and Medicine in Human Relationships*, New York, 1950.

—— *Twentieth Anniversary Review*, New York, 1950.

Juvenile Court Statistics, 1946–1949, *Children's Bureau Statistical Series*, No. 8.

KALLMAN, FRANZ JOSEF AND BARRERA, EUGENE, "The Heredoconstitutional Mechanisms of Predisposition and Resistance to Schizophrenia," *American Journal of Psychiatry*, XCVIII, Jan. 1942, No. 4, pp. 544–550.

KANNER, LEO, *Child Psychiatry*, 2nd ed., Springfield, Ill., Charles Thomas & Co., 1948.

KARPMAN, B. (chairman), "The Psychopathic Delinquent Child," *American Journal of Orthopsychiatry*, 20:223–265.

KINSEY, ALFRED C., POMEROY, W. B., & MARTIN, C. E., *Sexual Behavior in the Human Male*, Philadelphia, W. B. Saunders, 1948.

KLEIN, MELANIE, *Psychoanalysis of Children*, authorized translation by Alix Strachey, New York, W. W. Norton & Co., 1932.

KNIGHT, R. P., *The Dynamics and Treatment of Chronic Alcoholic Addiction*, Bulletin of Menninger Clinic, No. 1, 1937, pp. 233–250.

LAMBERT, ALEXANDER, "Therapeutics of Drug Habits," *New England Journal of Medicine*, Vol. 215, No. 2, July, 1936, pp. 72–82.

LEONARD, SHIRLEY, "Psychiatric Social Work in a Public School System," *News Letter of the American Association of Psychiatric Social Workers*, Vol. 5, No. 3, Jan. 1937, p. 12.

LEVINE, JULIUS AND ALBERT, HAROLD, *Journal of Nervous and Mental Disease*, April, 1951, Vol. 113, pp. 332–341.

LEVY, DAVID M., "Attitude Therapy," *American Journal of Orthopsychiatry*, 7:103, Jan. 1937.

———— "Critical Evaluation of the Present State of Child Psychiatry," *American Journal of Psychiatry*, Vol. 108, No. 7, Jan. 1952.

———— *Maternal Over-Protection*, New York, Columbia University Press, 1943.

———— "Use of Play Technique as Experimental Procedure," *American Journal of Orthopsychiatry*, 3:266, 1933.

LEVY, JOHN, "Relationship Therapy," *American Journal of Orthopsychiatry*, 8:64, Jan. 1938.

LEVY, JOHN AND MONROE, RUTH, *The Happy Family*, New York, Alfred A. Knopf, 1946.

LEWIS, NOLAN D. C., *A Short History of Psychiatric Achievement*, New York, W. W. Norton & Co., 1941.

LINBERG, B. J., *Psycho-Infantilism*, Copenhagen, Munksgaard, 1950.

LOMBROSO, CESARE, *Crime, Its Causes and Remedies*, translated by H. Horton, Boston, Little Brown & Co., 1918.

———— *L'Uomo Delinquente (Criminal Man)*, Torino, Fratelli Bocca, 1896.

LOWREY, LAWSON G., *Psychiatry for Social Workers*, 2nd ed. New York, Columbia University Press, 1950.

MACLOED, ROBERT B., *Religious Perspectives of College Teaching in Experimental Psychology*, New Haven, The Edward W. Hazen Foundation.

MENG, H., *Die Prophylaxe Des Verbrechens*, Basel, Switzerland, Benno Schwabe & Co. Verlag, 1948.

MENNINGER, KARL A., *The Human Mind*, New York, Alfred A. Knopf, 1945.

Midcentury White House Conference on Children and Youth, *Children and Youth at the Midcentury*.

MORENO, J. L., *Psychodrama*, New York, Beacon House, 1946.

MORSE, WARREN W. AND LIMBURG, CHARLES C., "Availability and Use of Psychiatric Clinics," *Mental Health Statistics,* National Institute of Mental Health, Maryland, March, 1950.

MÜHL, ANITA, "Report of Research Studies of Emotional Factors in Three Types of Psychically Handicapped Children," *Medical Women's Journal,* Sept., 1949.

NEWBURGER, MAURICE, "The School and the Maladjusted Child," *Understanding the Child,* Vol. XVII, No. 1, Jan. 1948.

OBENDORF, C. P., GREENACRE, P., & KUBIE, L., "Symposium on the Evaluation of Therapeutic Results," *International Journal of Psychoanalysis,* 29:1–27, 1948.

OVERHOLSER, WINFRED AND RICHMOND, WINIFRED, *Handbook of Psychiatry,* Philadelphia, J. B. Lippincott Co., 1947.

PEARSE, INNES AND WILLIAMSON, G. SCOTT, *The Case for Action,* London, Faber and Faber, 1931.

PELLER, LILI E., *Significant Symptoms in the Behavior of Young Children: A Checklist for Teachers,* National Association for Mental Health.

PIOTROWSKI, ZYGMUNT A., PH.D., "A Rorschach Compendium—Revised and Enlarged," *Psychiatric Quarterly,* Vol. 24, pages 543–596, July 1950.

——— AND LEWIS, NOLAN D.C., M.D., "A Case of Stationary Schizophrenia Beginning in Early Childhood with Remarks on Certain Aspects of Children's Rorschach Records," *The Quarterly Journal of Child Behavior,* Vol. II, No. 2, April, 1950.

——— "An Experimental Rorschach Diagnostic Aid for Some Forms of Schizophrenia," *The American Journal of Psychiatry,* Vol. 107, No. 5, November, 1950.

RANK, OTTO, *The Trauma of Birth,* New York, Harcourt, Brace & Co., 1929.

RAY, ISAAC, *A Treatise on the Medical Jurisprudence on Insanity,* Boston, Little Brown & Co., 1838.

REICH, WILHELM, *Der triebhafte Character,* Vienna, Internationaler Psychoanalytischer Verlag, 1925.

REIWALD, PAUL, *Society and Its Criminal,* New York, International Universities Press, Inc., 1950.

RENNIE, THOMAS A., *Mental Health in Modern Society,* New York, Commonwealth Fund, 1948.

Report on Conference on Mental Health in Schools and Teacher Education Institutions, Federal Security Agency, 1949.

Report of the Harlem Project, *The Role of the School in Preventing and Correcting Maladjustment and Delinquency—A Study in Three Schools*, sponsored jointly by The New York Foundation, The Hofheimer Foundation and The Board of Education of The City New York, Sept. 1943–June 1945. 1947.

RICHARDSON, HENRY, *Patients Have Families*, New York, The Commonwealth Fund, 1945.

ROBINSON, G. CANBY, *The Patient as a Person; A Study of the Social Aspects of Illness*, New York, The Commonwealth Fund, 1939.

SAUL, LEON J., *Emotional Maturity*, Philadelphia, Lippincott, 1948.

SCHILDER, PAUL, *Goals and Desires of Man, A Psychological Survey of Life*, New York, Columbia University Press, 1942.

——— *Meaning of Neurosis and Psychosis in Psychoanalysis Today*, ed. by S. Corard, New York, International Universities Press, 1944.

——— *Psychotherapy*, ed. by Lauretta Bender, New York, W. W. Norton & Co., 1951.

——— "The Child and the Symbol," *Scientia*, July 1938, pp. 21–26.

——— & WECHSLER, DAVID, "The Attitudes of Children Toward Death," *Journal Genetic Psychology*, 45:406–451, 1934.

SENN, MILTON J. E. (ed.) *Symposium on the Healthy Personality*, New York, Josiah Macy Jr. Foundation, 1950.

SLAUSON, S. R., *Introduction to Group Therapy*, New York, Commonwealth Fund, 1943.

——— *The Practice of Group Therapy*, New York, International Universities Press, Inc., 1947.

STEVENSON, GEORGE S. AND SMITH, GEDDES, *Child Guidance Clinics: A Quarter Century of Development*, New York, Commonwealth Fund, 1934.

THOMPSON, CLARA, *Psychoanalysis, Evolution and Development*, New York, Hermitage House, Inc., 1950.

WECHSLER, DAVID, "Nonintellective Factors in General Intelligence," *Journal of Abnormal & Social Psychology*, Jan. 1943, No. 1, 101–103.

——— *The Measurement of Adult Intelligence*, 3rd ed., New York, Williams & Wilkins Co., 1944.

WEST, RANYARD, *Conscience & Society (A Study of the Psychological Prerequisites of Law & Order)*, New York, Emerson Books, Inc., 1945.

WIKLER, ABRAHAM, M.D., "Clinical Aspects of Diagnosis and Treatment of Addictions," *Bulletin of the Menninger Clinic*, Vol. 15, No. 5, Sept. 1951, Topeka, Kans.

WITTELS, FRITZ, *Freud and His Time*, New York, Liveright, 1931.

WITMER, HELEN L., *Psychiatric Clinics for Children with Special Reference to State Programs*, New York & London, Oxford University Press, 1940.

WOLBERG, LEWIS R., *Medical Hypnosis*, New York, Grune & Stratton, 1948.

ZACHRY, C. B., *Emotion and Conduct in Adolescence*, New York, Appleton-Century, 1940.

ZILBOORG, GREGORY, "Clinical Variants of Moral Values," *American Journal of Psychiatry*, Vol. 106, No. 10, April 1950.

—— *Mind, Medicine, & Man*, New York, Harcourt, Brace & Co., 1943.

ZIMMERING, PAUL, M.D., TOOLAN, JAMES, M.D., SAFRIN, RENATE, M.S., and WORTIS, S. BERNARD, M.D., "Heroin Addiction in Adolescent Boys," *Journal of Nervous and Mental Disease*, 114:19–34, July 1951.

CRIMINOLOGY, LAW, ANTHROPOLOGY & SOCIOLOGY

ABRAHAMSEN, DAVID, *Crime and the Human Mind*, New York, Columbia University Press, 1944, 3rd ed., 1945.

—— *Men, Mind and Power*, New York, Columbia University Press, 1945.

—— "Family Tension, Basic Cause of Criminal Behavior," *Journal of Criminal Law and Criminology*, 1950.

—— "Psychiatric Aspects of Delinquency," *Journal of Educational Sociology*, pp. 40–44, Vol. 24, No. 1, Sept. 1950.

—— *Report on Study of 102 Sex Offenders as submitted to Governor Thomas E. Dewey*, New York, March 1950.

—— "The Dynamic Connection Between Crime & Personality," *Journal of Criminal Psychopathology*, V, Jan. 1944, No. 3, 481–488.

AICHORN, AUGUST, *Wayward Youth*, New York, Viking Press, 1944.

Alcoholics Anonymous, *The Story of How One Hundred Men Have Recovered from Alcoholism*, New York, Works Publishing Co., 1937.

ALEXANDER, FRANZ, AND HEALY, WILLIAM, *Roots of Crime*, New York, Alfred A. Knopf, 1935.

BATES, JEROME, "Abrahamsen's Theory of the Etiology of Criminal Acts," *Journal of Criminal Law and Criminology*, Vol. 40, No. 4, Nov.–Dec. 1949.

BECK, BERTRAM, *Youth Within Walls*, Community Service Society of New York, June, 1950.

Children Absent from School, Citizen's Committee on Children in New York City, Inc., 1949.

Criminal Statistics, England & Wales, 1949, Table E, p. 17, Courtesy of Dr. Gruenhut, Oxford, England.

Department of Institutions & Agencies, Trenton, New Jersey, *Offenses of Adult Males Committed by the Courts to State Penal and Correctional Institutions, 1945–1950*, 1951.

Department of Institutions & Agencies, Trenton, New Jersey, *Sex Offenders in State Penal and Correctional Institutions of New Jersey—A Statistical Analysis*, 1950.

DESSION, GEORGE H., "Psychiatry & the Conditioning of Criminal Justice," *Yale Law Journal*, Vol. 47, No. 3, Jan. 1938.

Det Statistiske Centralbyrå, *Statistisk Årbok for Norge 1938*, Oslo, 1938.

ERIKSON, ERIK H., *Childhood & Society*, W. W. Norton, 1950.

Federal Bureau of Investigation, Report of 1941; Report of 1946; Report of 1949; Report of 1950.

FRIEDLANDER, KATE, *The Psychoanalytical Approach to Juvenile Delinquency*, London, 1947.

GAULT, ROBERT H., *Criminology*, New York, D. C. Heath & Co., 1932.

GLUECK, SHELDON AND ELEANOR, *Unravelling Juvenile Delinquency*, The Commonwealth Fund, 1950.

GORING, CHARLES, *The English Convict*, London, 1913

GRUENHUT, M., "Statistics in Criminology," *Journal of the Royal Statistical Society*, Series A, Vol. 64, Part II, 1951.

HOOTON, E. A., *Crime and The Man*, Cambridge, Harvard University Press, 1939.

HOOVER, J. EDGAR, Statement Before Special Committee to Investigate Organized Crime in Interstate Commerce, March 26, 1951.

JUNG, CARL G., *Modern Man in Search of a Soul*, translated by W. S. Dill & H. G. Baynes, New York, Harcourt, Brace & Co., 1933.

———— *Psychology and Religion*, New Haven, Yale University Press, 1938.

Juvenile Court Statistics, 1946–1949, Children's Bureau, Statistical Series No. 8.

KEFAUVER, ESTES, *Crime in America*, edited by Sidney Shalett, Garden City, New York, Doubleday & Co., 1951.

KINSEY, ALFRED C., POMEROY, W. B., & MARTIN, C. E., *Sexual Be-*

havior in the Human Male, Philadelphia, W. B. Saunders, 1948.

LEVY, SHELDON, "Interaction of Institutions and Policy Groups: The Origin of Sex Crime Legislation," *The Lawyer and Law Notes*, Vol. 5, No. 1, Spring 1951.

LISZT, FRANZ VON, *Strafrechtliche Aufsätze und Vorträge*, 2 vols., Berlin, 1905.

LOMBROSO, CESARE, *L'Uomo Delinquente*, Torina, Fratelli Bocca, 1896.

MALINOWSKI, B., *Crime and Custom in Savage Society*, New York, Harcourt, Brace & Co., 1926.

MENG, H., *Die Prophylaxe Des Verbrechens*, Switzerland, Benno Schwabe & Co. Verlag, 1948.

MICHAEL, JEROME, AND WECHSLER, HERBERT, *Criminal Law and Its Administration*, Chicago, The Foundation Press, 1940.

OVERHOLSER, WINFRED, "Psychiatry and the Law—Cooperators or Antagonists?", *Psychiatric Quarterly*, XIII, Oct. 1939, pp. 622–638.

PLOSCOWE, MORRIS, *Sex and the Law*, New York, Prentice Hall, 1951.

RADZINOWICZ, Foreword to *A History of English Criminal Law*, 1948.

RECKLESS, C. W., "The Etiology of Delinquent & Criminal Behavior," Bulletin 507 of the Social Science Research Council, New York, 1943.

REICH, WILHELM, *Der triebhafte Character*, Vienna, 1925.

REIWALD, PAUL, *Society and Its Criminal*, New York, International Universities Press, Inc., 1950.

Report of the Harlem Project, *The Role of the School in Preventing and Correcting Maladjustment and Delinquency—A Study in Three Schools*, Sponsored jointly by The New York Foundation, The Hofheimer Foundation and The Board of Education of the City of New York, Sept. 1943–June 1945.

Report on Juvenile Detention, National Conference on Prevention and Control of Juvenile Delinquency, Washington D.C., Nov. 1946.

SELLIN, THORSTEN, *The Criminality of Youth*, Philadelphia, The American Law Institute, 1940.

SHAW, GEORGE BERNARD, *The Crime of Imprisonment*, New York Philosophical Library, 1946.

SHELDON, W. H., *Varieties of Delinquent Youth*, 1949.

Statistick Centralbyrån, *Brottslighetens Utveckling Åren*, 1913–1917, Stockholm, 1949.

SUTHERLAND, EDWIN H., *Principles of Criminology*, Philadelphia, J. B. Lippincott Co., 1934.

WECHSLER, HERBERT AND JEROME, MICHAEL, "A Rationale of the Law of Homicide," *Columbia Law Review*, Vol. XXXVII, Nos. 5 & 8, May & Dec. 1937.

WEST, RANYARD, *Conscience & Society (A Study of the Psychological Prerequisites of Law and Order)*, New York, Emerson Books, Inc., 1945.

WESTERMARCK, EDVARD, *Origin and Development of the Moral Ideas*, 2 vols., London, 1906–8.

EDUCATION

ABRAHAMSEN, DAVID, *Crime and the Human Mind*, New York, Columbia University Press, 1944; 3rd ed., 1945.

—— *Men, Mind and Power*, New York, Columbia University Press, 1945.

—— *Mind and Death of a Genius*, New York, Columbia University Press, 1946.

—— "Family Tension, Basic Cause of Criminal Behavior," *Journal of Criminal Law and Criminology*, 1950.

—— "Psychiatric Aspects of Delinquency," *The Journal of Educational Sociology*, pp. 40–44, Vol. 24, No. 1, Sept. 1950.

—— "Psychosomatic Disturbances and Their Significance in Antisocial Behavior," *Journal of Nervous and Mental Disease*, Vol. 107, No. 1, Jan. 1948.

—— "Relationship Between Children and Parents," Lecture given at the faculty at Dalton School, New York City, 1948.

—— *Report on Study of 102 Sex Offenders as submitted to Governor Thomas E. Dewey*, New York, March, 1950.

—— "Teacher and Child in the School," Lecture given for the Faculty at Putney School, Putney, Vermont, 1950.

—— "The Function of Language and Its Development in Early Childhood," *Acta Psychiatrica et Neurologica*, Copenhagen, XIII, Jan. 1938, 1–9.

ADLERBLUM, EVELYN D., "Beginning School Guidance Early," *Mental Hygiene*, Vol. 34, No. 4, Oct. 1950, pp. 600–610.

AICHORN, AUGUST, *Wayward Youth*, Viking Press, New York, 1944.

ALLEN, WINIFREDY AND CAMPBELL, DORIS, "The Creative Nursery Center," *Family Service Association of America, 1948*.

American Association of Better School Administration, "The Nation's Schools," Sept. 1951.

American Council on Education, *Helping Teachers Understand Children, 1945.*

Association for Supervision and Curriculum Development, National Education Association, *Fostering Mental Health in Our Schools,* 1950 year book, Washington, D.C.

BARKER, ROGER, G., ET AL., EDS. *Child Behavior and Development,* McGraw-Hill, 1943.

BATES, JEROME E., "Abrahamsen's Theory of the Etiology of Criminal Acts," *Journal of Criminal Law and Criminology*, pp. 471–475, Vol. 40, No. 4, 1949.

BETTELHEIM, B., *Love Is Not Enough,* The Free Press, Glencoe Illinois, 1950.

BULLIS, H. EDMOND AND O'MALLEY, E. E., *Human Relations in the Classroom,* Delaware State Society for Mental Hygiene, Hambleton, 1947–1951. Courses I, II & III.

CHASSEL, CLARA F., *The Relation between Morality and Intellect,* New York Teachers College, Columbia University, 1935.

Children Absent from School, Citizen's Committee on Children of New York City, Inc., 1949.

COLEMAN, JULES, V., "The Child Guidance Clinic and Community Mental-Health Programs," *Mental Hygiene,* Vol. 32, No. 4, Oct. 1948, pp. 539–548.

Department of Child Guidance, New Jersey, *Mental Hygiene in the Classroom,* New York National Committee for Mental Hygiene Inc., 1949.

FREMONT-SMITH, FRANK, "Mental Health, Education and International Cooperation," *Pastoral Psychology,* Dec. 1950, Vol. 1, No. 9.

FREUD, ANNA, *Psychoanalysis for Teachers and Parents,* Emerson, 1935.

HAMMETT, FREDERIK S., "Integration in Science Teaching," *The Scientific Monthly,* May 1946, published by The American Association for the Advancement of Science, Washington, D.C.

HARTWELL, SAMUEL W., *A Citizen's Handbook of Sexual Abnormalities and the Mental Hygiene Approach to Their Prevention,* A Report to the Committee on Education of the Governor's Study Commission on the Deviated Criminal Sex Offender, Michigan, 1950.

HEALY, WILLIAM AND BRONNER, AUGUSTA F., *New Light on Delinquency and Its Treatment,* New Haven, Yale University Press, 1936.

HINTZ, HOWARD, "Philosophy and the Liberal Arts College," *Bulletin of the American Association of University Professors*, Vol. 33, No. 1, Spring, 1947.

Joint Committee on Health Problems in Education, *Mental Hygiene in the Classroom: How Would You Help a Child Like This?* The National Association for Mental Health.

KANNER, LEO, *Child Psychiatry*, 2nd ed., Springfield, Ill., Charles G. Thomas & Co., 1948.

KARLSEN, FRANK E. JR., "A Layman Looks at Academic Freedom," *School and Society*, Vol. 69, No. 1789, pp. 241–244, April 2, 1949.

KEMPFER, HOMER, "Identifying Educational Needs of Adults," Federal Security Agency Office of Education, Circular No. 330, 1951.

KILPATRICK, WILLIAM H. AND VAN TIL, WILLIAM, EDS. *Intercultural Attitudes in the Making*, Harper, 1947.

KINSEY, ALFRED C., POMEROY, W. B. AND MARTIN, C. E., *Sexual Behavior in the Human Male*, Philadelphia, W. B. Saunders, 1948.

LEVY, JOHN AND MONROE, RUTH, *The Happy Family*, New York, Alfred A. Knopf, 1946.

LIBERMAN, SALLY, *A Child's Guide to a Parent's Mind*, New York, Henry Schuman, 1951.

Midcentury White House Conference on Children and Youth, *Children and Youth at the Midcentury*. 1950.

MORSE, WARREN W. AND LIMBURG, CHARLES C., "Availability and Use of Psychiatric Clinics," *Mental Health Statistics*, National Institute of Mental Health, Maryland, 1950.

National Council of Independent Schools, "The Function of Independent Secondary Education in the United States," *School and Society*, Vol. 74, No. 1916, Sept. 1951, pp. 145–150.

NEWBURGER, MAURICE, "The School and the Maladjusted Child," *Understanding the Child*, Vol. XVII, No. 1, Jan. 1948.

Office of Education, Washington, D.C. "The Activity Period," 1951.

——— "Vitalizing Secondary Education."

PEARSE, INNES H. AND WILLIAMSON, G. SCOTT, *The Case for Action*, London, Faber & Faber, 1931.

PELLER, LILI, E. *Significant Symptoms in the Behavior of Young Children: A Checklist for Teachers*, National Association for Mental Health.

PRESCOTT, DANIEL A., *Emotion and Educative Process*, Amer. Council on Education, Washington, D.C., 1938.

329

REDL, FRITZ AND WATTENBERG, WILLIAM, *Mental Hygiene in Teaching*, New York, Harcourt, Brace & Co., 1951.

RENNIE, THOMAS A., *Mental Health in Modern Society*, New York, Commonwealth Fund, 1948.

Report of Conference of Mental Health in Schools and Teacher Education Institution, Federal Security Agency Office of Education. Public Health Service, April, 1949.

Report of the Harlem Project, *The Role of the School in Preventing and Correcting Maladjustment and Delinquency—A Study in Three Schools*, Sponsored Jointly by The New York Foundation, The Hofheimer Foundation and The Board of Education of the City of New York, Sept. 1943, June 1945, 1947.

RIDENOUR, NINA, "Community Education Through Press, Radio, Films and Drama," *Mental Hygiene*, Vol. 33, No. 1, Jan. 1949, pp. 71–77

SENN, MILTON J. E., ED., *Symposium of the Healthy Personality*, New York, Josiah Macy Jr. Foundation, 1950.

SHACTER, HELEN; JENKINS, GLADYS GARDNER AND BAUER, W. W., *Into Your Teens*, New York, Scott Foresman & Co., 1951.

SHAW, GEORGE BERNARD, *The Crime of Imprisonment*, New York, Philosophical Library, 1946.

STEINBERG, MILTON, *The Common Sense of Religious Faith*, New York, The Jewish Reconstruction Foundation, 1947.

STEVENSON, GEORGE AND SMITH, GEDDES, *Child Guidance Clinics: A Quarter Century of Development*, New York, Commonwealth Fund, 1934.

TRAGER, HELEN, *The Primary Teacher*, The National Committee for Mental Hygiene, 1949.

Papers from the 2nd Conference on the Scientific Spirit and Democratic Faith, "The Authoritarian Attempt to Capture Education," King's Crown Press, New York, 1945.

WICKMAN, E. K., *Teachers and Behavior Problems*, National Association for Mental Health.

WITTY, PAUL, (ED.) *The Gifted Child*, Boston, D. C. Heath, 1950.

ZACHRY, C. B., *Emotion and Conduct in Adolescence*, New York, Appleton-Century, 1940.

ZILBOORG, GREGORY, "Clinical Variants of Moral Values," *American Journal of Psychiatry*, Vol. 106, No. 10, April 1950.

INDEX

abnormality of the delinquent, 122–42
abortion, 93
Abrahamsen, Dr. David, *Crime and the Human Mind*, 17, 144, 153, 300
  Mind and Death of a Genius, 93
  paper on family tension, 127
Abrams, Dr. Arnold, 240
accidents, proneness to, 99, 112
Ackerman, Dr. Nathan W., 240
"acting out," 154–55, 240
action, and inclinations, 65
  and personalities, 21
  and reaction, 97
  and thought, 80
  bases of, 20
  compulsive, 45
  determination of, 73
  doubt, and inability to act, 69
  dynamic, 65
  future, forecasting of, 282
adaptation, attempts at, 88
  inner, 61
  lack of. *See* maladaptation
  of personality, 21
  personal and group, 13
adjustment. *See* adaptation
adolescence, 282, 295, 296
Adonis, Joe, 6
aggrandizement, self, 66
aggressiveness, 65, 93, 109, 114, 135, 136, 148, 164, 176, 242
  and passivity, 71
  direct and indirect, 70
  localization of, 240
  oral, 71
  self-defense against, 69
  varieties of, 71
Aichorn, Dr. August, *Wayward Youth*, 114, 127
aims in life, 55
Al, case of, 144
alarm (panic) reaction, 46, 70
Albert, Dr. Harold, 251
Alcoholics Anonymous, 239
alcoholism, 160, 208, 247
  and rape, 89
Alex, case of, 28, 32, 34, 35, 41, 42, 43, 44, 46, 64, 185
Alexander, Franz, 155
Alexander and Healy, *Roots of Crime*, 127, 232
Alexander and Staub, *The Criminal and the Public*, 146
Alice, case of, 18
ambition, 7
American Criminal, by Hooton, 17
American Journal of Orthopsychiatry, 243
anal-sadism, 41, 148, 183
anamnesis, associative, 101, 123
Angelo, case of, 195
Ann, case of, 182
anthropometry, 55

anxiety, 41, 59, 106, 147, 160
arson, 150, 151, 152

B. R. I. Sorting Test, 123
"Ballad of Reading Gaol, The," by Wilde, 213
Barry, case of, 297
bedwetting (enuresis). *See* children
Beethoven, Ludwig van, 122
behavior. *See* action
Bellevue-Wechsler Test, 123
"belonging," need for, 14, 285
Bender, Dr. Lauretta, 279
Bennett, James V., 210
Bergler, E., 71
betting. *See* gambling
Binet-Simon Test, 123
Bob, case of, 40, 43
Bobby, case of, 166
body and mind, 55, 97–119
Bowman, Dr. Karl, 254
brain, the, 60
  damage, due to disease, 45
Briggs Law, Massachusetts, 124
bullying, 103
Bureau of Child Guidance, New York City, 260

capital punishment, 212–13
Capone, Al, 4
castration. *See* sexuality
character, deformation of, 114, 115, 116, 132, 138, 140, 147, 154, 156
  development of, 116, 130
  distinguished from personality, 116
Charlie, case of, 139
child and family. *See* home; tension, family
child-guidance clinics, 259
Child Guidance Clinics, by Stevenson and Smith, 260
child-parent-guidance clinics, 259
childbirth, pain in, 191
Childhood and Society, by Erikson, 262
children, 25–47
  and parents, 290–95
  antisocial, 31
  bedwetting (enuresis), 26, 28, 29, 41, 152, 245
  "belonging," sense of, 285
  bright, 272
  center of attention, 35
  comic books, 279
  Conference, White House, 261
  conflict with parents, 62
  corporal punishment, 28
  courts for, 303
  death wishes against parents, 43
  defecation, 42
  defectives, mental, 272
  delinquency. *See* delinquency
  desires, and social demands, 61

331

339